SHIPWRECKS
OF THE
STRAITS OF MACKINAC

By

Dr. Charles E. Feltner
and Jeri Baron Feltner

December 1991

Reprints: January 1996; September 1997

SEAJAY
PUBLICATIONS
P. O. BOX 2176
DEARBORN MI 48123

DEDICATION

*To the People who
shared Mackinac with us*

Cover Illustration: *What a Way to Go* by Ed Pusick, Wyoming, Michigan, 1991

Library of Congress Catalog Card Number: 91-62285

Published by Seajay Publications, P. O. Box 2176, Dearborn MI 48123

Printed in the United States of America

First Printing 1991, Second Printing 1996, Third Printing 1997

10 9 8 7 6 5 4

ISBN 0-9609014-1-8 (Softcover)
ISBN 0-9609014-2-6 (Hardcover)

THEY THAT GO
DOWN TO THE SEA
IN SHIPS
1623 — 1923

"They that go down to the sea in ships,
that do business in great waters;
these see the works of the Lord,
and His wonders in the deep."

— Psalm 107

Memorial in Gloucester, Massachusetts, by sculptor Leonard Craske, 1925
(Photo by Mark Feltner, 1985)

Jeri Feltner and the figurehead of the brig *Sandusky*
(Photo by Chuck Feltner, 1981)

CONTENTS

PART IV — UNDISCOVERED WRECKS

FOREWORD

Divers descend to the depths of the seas to increase man's knowledge and understanding of the mysteries of his past. One little-explored primary source of this past is the Straits of Mackinac.

The mystique of the Mackinac region has drawn explorers and exploiters to it ever since the glaciers retreated northward 10,000 years ago. This unique strait that joins two Great Lakes has been geographically important in historical times for more than three centuries.

Beginning with the first sailing vessel on the upper Lakes — the *Griffin* — men and women have used these freshwater seas and the Straits as highways of commerce. However, a price for this use has been extracted by the manitous of the Lakes in terms of the loss of ships and the people who sailed them. Because only basic navigational instruments were used over poorly charted waters having few lights and markers, the risks of stranding, collision, and foundering were great. The Mackinac Straits, with its dangerous shoals, violent storms, and treacherous icing conditions, made for an even more hazardous passage. Many ships had a very short lifespan.

Since the early 1800s, some 100 shipwrecks have occurred in the Straits from the Beaver Island archipelago in the west to the Les Cheneaux Islands and Spectacle Reef in the east. Each is a snapshot of history at the time of its loss — forever frozen in time patiently waiting for the day of discovery. As recently as the mid-1950s, the Straits was virgin territory to scuba divers. While a few nineteenth century wrecks were found and salvaged by hard-hat divers, the vast majority were unlocated and untouched. Moreover, the history of these wrecks had been sparsely researched and insufficiently recounted.

I first met Chuck and Jeri Feltner in the late 1970s after my several years of underwater exploration had ended. They had come to

Mackinac to dive on and document the shipwrecks in the Straits. I marveled at their energy and intensity. Through countless hours of meticulous historical research in the libraries of the Great Lakes region, this couple prepared for the hunt of the shipwrecks as painstakingly as research scientists. Then with the same passion and thoroughness, they diligently searched the Straits from the spring ice break-up until the snows came. Their devotion to this cause was tested on more than one occasion. I recall a spring day in April 1980 when their search boat, the *Gemini II*, was dodging ice floes off the Mackinaw City Harbor.

Each discovery was precisely located, carefully surveyed and documented, and accurately identified. Articles were written and published in historical journals. Still and motion pictures were taken. Some of the finest footage I have seen of the intriguing underwater world is contained in their film of the brig *Sandusky* that sank in the Straits in September 1856.

The engineering background of Dr. Feltner has prepared him well for his avocation. The support of his equally talented wife and diving buddy, Jeri, combined with their ability to communicate the fascinating biographies of the many wrecks described herein, make this an exciting book. In my judgment, their book will stand for time as the definitive literary work on the shipwrecks of the Straits of Mackinac. As additional underwater historical treasures are discovered, future explorers and writers will have a benchmark by which to chart their course.

As Justice Benjamin Cardoza noted, "Life in all its fullness must supply the answer to the riddle." So, too, does this continuing underwater archaeology and historical chronicling of shipwrecks help us understand the mysteries of our past.

Kenneth Teysen

Mackinac Island State Park Commission
Mackinaw City, Michigan
December 1991

PREFACE

By the time we arrived in the Straits of Mackinac on Memorial Day weekend in 1977 to make our first Great Lakes shipwreck dive, we had experienced the undersea wonders of numerous coral reefs in the warm, crystal clear waters of the scuba diving centers of the Caribbean and Gulf of Mexico. In our more sardonic moments, it seemed to us that diving in cold water with poor visibility and limited marine life to look at a piece of underwater junk was a ridiculous waste of time. However, after much persuasion by our friend Dave Trotter, we agreed to bring our boat to Mackinaw City and dive with him on the wreck of the *Cedarville* — a 589-foot long ore carrier resting in 105 feet of water. Circumstances were such that we didn't reach the wreck site until late afternoon and the brilliant May sun was fast disappearing. The whole thing still seemed a bit absurd.

Cruising to the wreck location, Dave filled our ears with the details of the *Cedarville* tragedy. Several sailors had lost their lives and there was a heroic rescue of the survivors by crewmen in a lifeboat from a nearby German ship. All of this history sounded interesting but not sufficiently so to merit jumping into frigid water with darkness fast approaching. But we did — and when the giant steel wreck loomed out of the greenish, murky depths, what history we had absorbed suddenly came to life. Our imaginations ran wild with the intoxication of the moment. On surfacing, the fireball sun was dropping below the far off Lake Michigan horizon. Only our hooded heads bobbed above the still water. The exhilaration was incredible. We looked at each other and realized that we were forever hooked on Great Lakes shipwreck diving.

Wreck diving became our relentless pursuit. Over the winter of 1977-78, we bought a spanking new boat and equipped it with lots of electronic wreck searching gizmos including one of the first

LORAN C units sold on the Great Lakes. On a cold, overcast day in October 1978, we discovered our first virgin shipwreck — the schooner *Northwest* — sunk in the Straits in 1898. But, at the time, the wreck could not be identified. Thus began our assiduous research of vessels sunk in the Straits. The emotional high of finding a virgin shipwreck drove us to search for others. In April 1980, we found the remains of the propeller *Eber Ward* — a wreck that had been long sought by several zealous wreck hunters. The key to this discovery had been historical research. Next came the finding in May 1981 of the brig *Sandusky*, an absolutely magnificent shipwreck. Later came the finding of *Chuck's Barge* and the propellers *Uganda* and *Canisteo*.

During this period we spent an enormous amount of time researching shipwrecks lost in the Straits of Mackinac. The experience gained in wreck research was shared with other divers through weekend courses we conducted on how to research Great Lakes shipwrecks. Former students found three of the wrecks described in this book. These courses resulted in the development and publication in December 1982 of our first book *Great Lakes Maritime History: Bibliography and Sources of Information*. Additionally, we learned underwater archaeology methods. This, combined with historical research, led to the identification of 17 previously unidentified wrecks in the Straits region. Underwater films were made of the wrecks of the *Eber Ward* and *Sandusky* and numerous presentations were given around the Great Lakes region. Since that first dive on the *Cedarville* in 1977, we have made well over 1,000 dives on the 41 discovered shipwrecks in the Straits. This book is the culmination of all these efforts.

The book was written for three audiences — the shipwreck divers, the maritime historians and those people with a general interest in shipwreck stories and regional history. For the divers, we have included information on the condition and features of the wrecks, their location and, where applicable, information on unusual diving conditions. Our stories offer the diver the opportunity to commune with the shipwrecks. For the maritime historians, we have paid particular attention to the fidelity of the vessel histories through careful research. Primary sources, such as Certificates of Enrollment, vessel registers and newspapers of the day, were extensively used. Source material for each vessel is meticulously documented.

Good shipwreck stories impart suspense to foregone conclusions. They override the knowledge of how things turned out by recapturing the anxieties and uncertainties displayed by the participants while the outcome is still in doubt. For the entertainment of our general interest readers, we hope we have accomplished this. Many of the shipwreck stories have a historical theme that is related to some particular aspect of the vessel. These themes were woven into the stories to provide the context for the shipwrecks.

Many events described in this book took place before the existence of a myriad of modern-day devices. Over half the shipwrecks described herein occurred before the telegraph or railroad reached the Straits of Mackinac. Imagine yourself in a Mackinac world where the electric light, telephone and automobile had not even been invented. This book aims to engender a willful suspension of present-day reality such that you, our reader, may experience the shipwrecks of the Straits of Mackinac in the same way as did the mariners who sailed them. We hope you enjoy this experience as much as we have in bringing it to you.

Chuck & Jeri Feltner

Dearborn, Michigan
December 17, 1991

ACKNOWLEDGEMENT

For kind assistance in the preparation of this book we are indebted to many people. The late *Professor Walter Hirthe* of Marquette University in Milwaukee taught us how to do maritime historical research and was our mentor. We received valuable help from C. *Patrick Labadie*, Director of the Canal Park Museum in Duluth, Minnesota. He also reviewed the manuscript. The late *Dr. Richard J. Wright*, former Director of the Institute for Great Lakes Research in Perrysburg, Ohio, helped substantially with vessel research. *John Steele* of Waukegan, Illinois, and *Dick Campbell* and *Ken Teysen* of Mackinaw City, Michigan, provided much information on discovered shipwrecks in the Straits of Mackinac. *Bill Duman* of Cheboygan, Michigan, helped identify several of the shipwrecks in the Cheboygan area. Additionally, he unraveled for us the mystery surrounding the old docks at Cheboygan. *Paul Horn* and *Ben Cline* of Westland, Michigan, personally worked with us on vessel research. *Chris Rottiers* of Birch Run, Michigan, made a major contribution through his research work on vessel documentation. *Ralph Roberts* of Saginaw, Michigan, provided several photographs, helped with vessel research and reviewed the manuscript.

Several people, other than those already mentioned, reviewed the manuscript and gave us useful input. They include *Dr. John R. Halsey*, State Archeologist for Michigan, *Dr. David A. Armour*, Deputy Director of Mackinac State Historic Parks, *Rev. Edward J. Dowling*, Professor Emeritus, University of Detroit, and *Mike Kohut*, President of Recreational Diving Systems in Royal Oak, Michigan. *Larry Baron* of Dearborn, Michigan, did the wreck maps and the drawing of the *Maitland* wreck. *Dave Donovan* of Chelsea, Michigan, did the drawings of the *Cayuga, Cedarville, Eber Ward* and *Sandusky* wrecks.

Substantial cooperation and help was received from many of the major libraries and maritime organizations around the Great Lakes. Both present and former staff members of these institutions who contributed significantly over the past 12 years include: *Alice Dalligan* and *Michael Knes*, Detroit Public Library; *O. O. Stretch Liljequist, Gregory Gregory, Paul Woehrmann, Suzette Lopez*, and *Sandy Broder*, Milwaukee Public Library; and *Jay Martin, Bob Graham*, and *Stuart Givens*, Institute for Great Lakes Research, Bowling Green State University, Perrysburg, Ohio. Special thanks to the staffs of the public libraries in Buffalo, Chicago, Cleveland, Dearborn, and the University of Michigan. Additionally, we appreciate the help of the staffs of the Dossin Great Lakes Museum, the Michigan Maritime Museum, the Great Lakes Historical Society, the Buffalo and Erie County Historical Society, the Chicago Historical Society, and the National Archives and Records Service in Washington D.C.

We were ably assisted in our on-water search activities and diving operations by *Paul Horn, Ben Cline, Stan Stock, Tony Gramer* and *Ted Sledz*. Several other individuals have helped us in a variety of ways. Some of them, but certainly not all, are *Brownie Brown, Nancy Campbell, Dick Charboneau, Edna Coffman* (deceased), *Larry Coplin, John Dulzo, George Dunkelberg, Roy Golsch, Jerri Hayden, Marty Jahn, Mike Kohut, John Polascek, Dick Race, Jim Ryerse, Mary Belle Shurtleff* (deceased), and *Dave Trotter*. To all of these and a host of others too numerous to mention, we owe a warm thank you.

Last, but not least, both of us would like to express our deep sense of gratitude and appreciation to our *families* and our *friends* who enthusiastically supported us throughout this project — and to *Seajay* — who kept it all together.

Chuck & Jeri Feltner

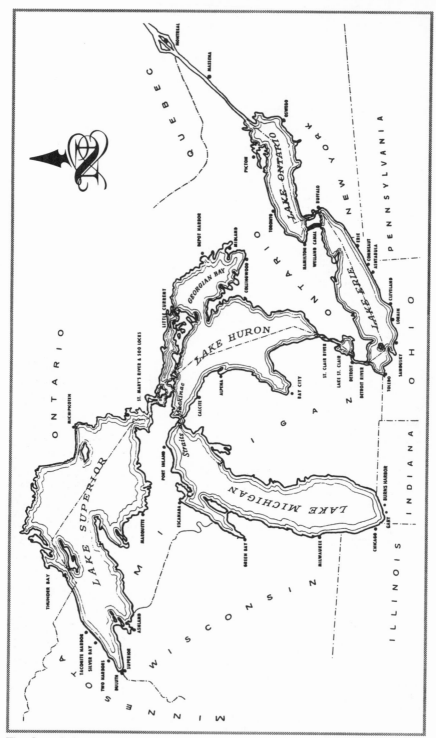

The Great Lakes (Courtesy Lake Carriers' Association)

SHIPWRECKS OF THE STRAITS OF MACKINAC

INTRODUCTION

To the amazement of many people, there are over 5,000 shipwrecks lying on the bottomlands of the Great Lakes. Michigan alone has about 1,500 such wrecks. Not surprisingly, they cluster in regions where the ship traffic was high and the navigational hazards were most treacherous. The Straits of Mackinac match these conditions perfectly.

Separating the Upper and Lower Peninsulas of the State of Michigan, the Straits of Mackinac connect Lake Huron to the east

Satellite photo of the Straits of Mackinac, 1976
(Courtesy Earth Resources Observation Systems Data Center, U. S. Department of the Interior)

1

with Lake Michigan to the west. At their narrowest point, they are only 3.6 miles wide. Although the boundaries of such a body of water are debatable, common usage has resolved this issue. Sailing westward on Lake Huron from Rogers City, Michigan, you are "approaching" the eastern end of the Straits when you are abreast of Spectacle Reef Light and "entering" them when you pass by Poe Reef Light. Conversely, the western approach from southern Lake Michigan is Ile Aux Galets or "Skillagalee" Light with the entrance being marked by Grays Reef Light. The western approach from northern Lake Michigan is a point about halfway between Lansing Shoal Light and Simmons Reef, the entrance being abreast of White Shoals Light. From approach-to-approach are roughly 400 square miles of water which, from a sailor's perspective, are both dangerous and deceptive. Several thousand vessels failed to make this passage without involvement in some form of wreck incident. Over 75 vessels never made it at all, having found a permanent resting place on the bottomland of the Straits of Mackinac.

In July 1634, the intrepid French explorer Jean Nicolet and his seven Huron Indian paddlers pushed off in a bark canoe from the shores of Georgian Bay in Lake Huron. Beyond lay the mysterious west — the unknown realm that he was to explore. By late summer,

Voyageurs at camp, painting by Frances Hopkins
(Courtesy Public Archives of Canada)

after circumnavigating the entire northern shore of Lake Huron, he would be the first white man to pass through the Straits of Mackinac.[1]

After Nicolet came more explorers, followed by voyageurs and fur trappers. Next came the soldiers of three nations — France, Great Britain and the United States. Close behind were the first settlers. In their footsteps were the waves of immigrants from Europe. To support this great human march westward in the 1800s, required thousands of wooden sailing and steam vessels. From the eastern port cities on Lake Erie and Lake Ontario they brought coal, lumber, foodstuffs, hardware and general merchandise to the developing cities along the shores of Lake Michigan. On their return trip they carried iron ore from the mines of the Upper Peninsula of Michigan and grain from the rich farmlands of new States such as Illinois, Wisconsin and Minnesota. Passenger traffic boomed. By the turn of the last century, there were more than 4,500 registered American and Canadian vessels operating on the Great Lakes.[2] In the halcyon days, the Marine Reporter stationed at Mackinaw City reported over 10,000 vessel passages a year. The Straits of Mackinac was surely the *crossroads of the Great Lakes.* For many years the Mackinaw City water tower bore that nickname. With such heavy traffic, collision was an ever-present danger.

Water tower at Mackinaw City in 1982
(Authors)

Before Government improvements began, the perils to navigation on the Great Lakes were many. Harbors were almost non-existent and sand bars blocked the mouths of most rivers. Channels and reefs were unmarked. Weather forecasting was something akin to witchcraft. As a result, few vessels retired because of old age. Shipwreck was the common fate. Matters were made worse by the crankiness and lack of maneuverability of early vessels compared with today. Cold weather froze the rigging solid on many a vessel making it impossible to handle the hemp lines. Frozen water-spray sheathed ships in heavy coats of ice making them more unmanageable. In the early spring, ice floes were a constant danger. Maneuvering an early sailing vessel through the confined Straits in storm, darkness, ice or fog with heavy traffic was a sailor's nightmare.

The combination of ship traffic, poor navigational aids, immature vessel technology, inadequate weather forecasting and the narrow confines of the Straits, made for a dangerous passage. Since the time of Nicolet, thousands of ships passed safely. This book is about those that didn't make it. They are the *Shipwrecks of the Straits of Mackinac.*

Modern-day freighter under the Mackinac Bridge
(Photo by Anne O'Connell, 1991)

ABOUT THIS BOOK

Stories about 78 individual shipwrecks are divided into two major parts: *Part III – Discovered Wrecks*, and *Part IV – Undiscovered Wrecks*. Within each part, a consistent format for each wreck story has been maintained, particularly as it relates to factual information. For example, each wreck story includes a module entitled *Vessel Facts* that contains 15 basic historical facts characterizing the vessel. A detailed explanation of the meaning of these facts is contained in *Appendix A*.

In-depth stories on ten of the discovered shipwrecks have been published previously by the authors. These stories contain much more detail than that given in this book. Included in this group are the *Cayuga, Cedarville, Colonel Ellsworth, Eber Ward, Maitland, Minneapolis, Northwest, Richard Winslow, Sandusky*, and *William H. Barnum*. References to these published stories are contained in the *Bibliography*.

Two sections precede the stories on individual shipwrecks. *Part I – Sketches of the Straits* is a series of historical vignettes that provide a context for the shipwrecks in the Straits. *Part II – Overview of the Shipwrecks* renders a panorama of the most noteworthy aspects of the wrecks, and it bounds the conditions for choosing the wrecks to be included. Also in this section is a set of wreck statistics that describe the technical characteristics of the wrecks as a group.

Footnotes have been placed at the end of the book. Sources used in the research process are listed in the *Bibliography*. Maritime terminology used herein is defined in the *Glossary*. The State of Michigan has passed laws for the protection of shipwrecks and the establishment of underwater preserves. *Appendix B* contains a brief description of the *Straits of Mackinac Bottomland Preserve* and how it came about.

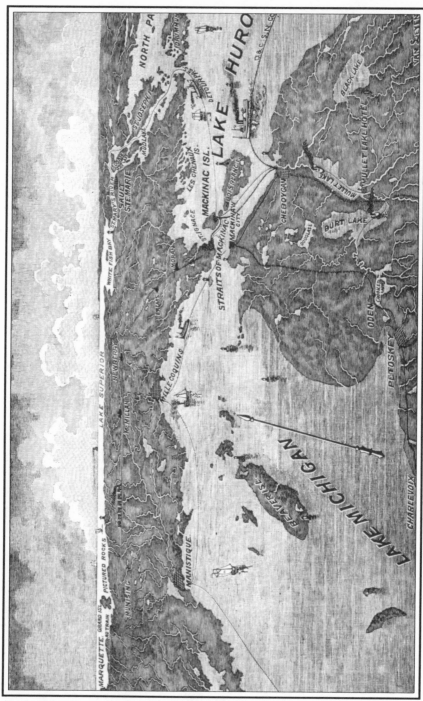

Straits of Mackinac map from Polk's Marine Directory, 1888
(Courtesy Great Lakes Marine Collection, Milwaukee Public Library)

SHIPWRECKS OF THE STRAITS OF MACKINAC

PART I

SKETCHES
OF THE
STRAITS

INTRODUCTION TO
SKETCHES OF THE STRAITS

Long before any of the towns and cities of the Great Lakes came into existence, Michilimackinac was a center of power and influence. As a wilderness headquarters, it played a significant role in the history of three nations — France, England and the United States. What follows are short sketches of various aspects of the history of the region. They are intended to give the reader a mere taste of what could be consumed and provide context for the shipwrecks.

Indeed a very large body of literature exists on Michilimackinac country. One of the best descriptions of the extant literature is contained in an essay entitled "The Literature of the Mackinac Country" by Larry Massie. This essay appears at the beginning of the recently reprinted book *Early Mackinac* by Meade C. Williams.[1] In our view, one of the better histories of the region is that published by Wood.[2] Throughout the remainder of this book, the Authors recommend specific publications that are most noteworthy with respect to the subject under discussion.

The name Michilimackinac (land of the great turtle) is often misspelled and mispronounced. There is argument to this day over its meaning and the shortened version, Mackinac, is used in a variety of ways. Originally there was Michilimackinac country and the Straits of Mackinac. In time there was Mackinac Island out in the Straits and Mackinac County on the north shore of the Straits. On the south shore, spelling the name the way it is pronounced, there is Mackinaw City. Connecting the two shorelines is the Mackinac Bridge. Finally there are Mackinaw coats and Mackinaw boats — both widely known items developed in the area. Exploring the meaning and origin of the name has become a virtual pastime for students of the region.

The following sections are sketches of the Straits of Mackinac's *Geological Formation, French Discovery and Occupation, Three Flags at the Straits, Islands of the Straits, Lighthouses in the Straits,* and *Transportation Across the Straits.*

GEOLOGICAL FORMATION

The last glacial advance of the ice age ended about 10,000 years ago. With that came the formation of the Great Lakes. This process has been effectively described by several authors.[1] Ancient river beds were covered over by the Lakes but their route can still be traced today. The accompanying map, prepared by geologist J. W. Spencer,[2] shows the original route of the Laurentian River (St. Lawrence River).

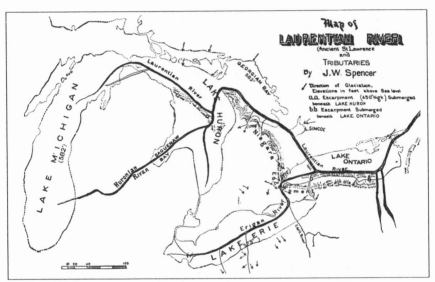

Map showing course of the ancient St. Lawrence River and its tributaries
(Reprinted from History of the Great Lakes by J. B. Mansfield, J. H. Beers & Co., 1899)

The Laurentian River bed extends across Georgian Bay and Lake Huron, passing through the Straits of Mackinac and on into Lake Michigan. Mariners who have travelled the Straits area recognize that there is a narrow channel extending to depths of 300 feet beneath the center span of the Mackinac Bridge. This channel has played a part in at least one of the shipwrecks of the Straits — the propeller *Uganda*. She sank in 1913 about 15 miles west of the Mackinac Bridge

9

after her hull was cut open by ice. Modern-day wreck hunters searched in vain to find her remains. When finally discovered in 1983, it was apparent why she was so difficult to locate — she sits hiding at the bottom (207 feet) of the narrow channel of the old Laurentian River.

The Barquentine
(Reprinted from "The Book of Old Ships," by Henry B. Culver, drawn by Gordon Grant, 1924)

FRENCH DISCOVERY AND OCCUPATION

The French dominated Michilimackinac country from the discovery of the Straits of Mackinac by Jean Nicolet in 1634 to the fall of Quebec in 1759 when General Wolfe of the English defeated Montcalm of the French in the famed battle of the Plains of Abraham. In between, the French made a lasting impression.

Exploration of the region had its beginnings with the discovery of the St. Lawrence River by Jacques Cartier in 1535. He was followed by Samuel de Champlain who founded Quebec City in 1608. All five Great Lakes were discovered by the French. The order of their discovery is as follows:[1] Huron in 1615, jointly by Father Joseph Le Caron, a Franciscan friar, and Champlain; Ontario, in the same year, by Champlain; Superior about 1629 by Etienne Brule; Michigan in 1634 by Nicolet; and Erie by Louis Joliet in 1669. Erie was the last to be discovered because its approaches were guarded by the fierce Iroquois Indians — a tribe that had quickly come to hate the French.

Samuel de Champlain

France as a nation laid claim to this vast territory in search of a route to China. Second to exploration came the exploitation for profit of natural resources, which for all practical purposes was animal furs. Thirdly, the missionary spirit was active in the Catholic Church in France during this time. Side by side with the explorer in search of fame and fortune came the priests, led by the Jesuits, who were committed to Christianizing the Indians. Both were accompanied by a peculiar class of men — wild, daring bush rangers, or *coureurs de bois* — who according to Parkman[2] were mostly lawless, half-civilized vagrants. The principal vocation of these voyageurs was to lead the canoes of explorers, government traders and missionaries on the lakes and rivers of the interior while at the same time carrying on fur trading.

11

Activities of the early Jesuit missionaries are well documented, for they were required to keep detailed diaries that were sent back to France and collated as the *Jesuit Relations*.[3] They first appeared in Michilimackinac country at Sault Ste. Marie, Michigan, in 1641 where Fathers Isaac Jogues and Charles Raymbault preached to 2,000 Ojibways,[4] and by 1668 Father Jacques Marquette had estab-

Father Jacques Marquette

lished a mission there. In 1671, with a group of Huron Indians, he established the mission at St. Ignatius (now St. Ignace) on the north shore of the Straits of Mackinac.[5] Father Phillipe Pierson replaced Marquette when he departed in 1673 with Louis Joliet on an expedition to explore the Mississippi River. On the return trip in 1675, Marquette died on the eastern shore of Lake Michigan, near Ludington, Michigan, at the mouth of a river that now bears his name. His remains were subsequently placed in a vault in the mission chapel at St. Ignace. In 1701, Antoine de la Mothe Cadillac moved the French garrison to Detroit and most of the Indians followed. By 1705, the mission was abandoned.[6]

Many famous French explorers and voyageurs spent time at the settlements in the Straits during the late 1600s. Included were Louis Joliet, Pierre Esprit Radisson, Medard Chouart Groseilliers and Antoine de la Mothe Cadillac. One of the most famous voyageurs was Daniel Greysolon Duluth (or de Lhut) for whom the city of Duluth, Minnesota, is named. He was a distinguished leader of the *coureurs de bois* and a frequent visitor at St. Ignace.[7]

On August 27, 1679, amid great fanfare, Robert Cavelier, Sieur de la Salle sailed into East Moran Bay offshore from the wilderness outpost of St. Ignace. His vessel, the small schooner *Griffin (Le Griffon)*, had been built in 1679 on the Niagara River at the east end of Lake Erie and is accorded the distinction of being the first vessel to sail on the upper Great Lakes. With La Salle came Father Louis Hennepin, a Recollect Friar, and Henry de Tonty, a competent sailor with an artificial iron hand. After a week at St. Ignace, La Salle set sail for Green Bay where he filled the *Griffin* with fur pelts. La Salle decided to remain in the Lake Michigan area and he sent the *Griffin* back to Niagara with her cargo. On September 18, 1679, with a parting salute from her cannon, the *Griffin* left Green Bay. That night a severe storm blew across Lake Michigan and the *Griffin* was never heard from again.[8] Several theories have been advanced regarding her demise,[9] but none have been proven. Perhaps she lies sunk somewhere in the Straits of Mackinac.

Building of the *Griffin* on Lake Erie in 1679 (Father Louis Hennepin, 1704)
(Reprinted from "History of the Great Lakes," by J. B. Mansfield, J. H. Beers & Co., 1899)

13

THREE FLAGS AT THE STRAITS

The title of this section is borrowed from an excellent book of the same name by Walter Havighurst in which he recounts the history of the forts of Mackinac under the flags of France, England and the United States.[1] Fort de Buade, the first fort, was built by the French at the St. Ignace settlement around 1678. Garrisoned by the *coureurs de bois*, the Fort had several commandants including M. de la Villeraye (1681-1684), Daniel Greysolon Duluth (1684), and M. de la Durantaye (1684-1690).[2] In 1690, Count de Frontenac sent Louis de La Porte, Sieur de Louvigny, with 150 regular troops, to command the fort. The troops were actually there to regulate the fur trade. However, they failed miserably, and Louvigny was replaced in 1694 by Antoine de la Mothe Cadillac, a stern disciplinarian.

Cadillac was unable to stop the unlawful trade by the *coureurs de bois* and the poaching by the English, who were sent there from the north by the Hudson Bay Company. With the fur market in France awash in pelts, the order came to close the fort at St. Ignace. Cadillac succeeded in convincing the King of France to build a fort in Detroit. In 1701, the garrison abandoned Fort de Buade, moved to Detroit, and established Fort Pontchartrain. At St. Ignace, the Indians and fur traders melted away and, in 1705, the Jesuits abandoned St. Ignace.[3]

In short order a settlement began to develop on the south shore of the Straits of Mackinac to the west of present-day Mackinaw City in an area known by the Indians as *Pequotenong (Headland)*. By 1715, a new fort had been constructed here with Constant le Marchand de Lignery as commandant.[4] Fur trading and commerce of all types was carried on for many years by the French and Indians living around the fort.

By the close of the first half of the decade, English traders had moved westward over the mountains and ingratiated themselves to the Indians throughout what is today Ohio. This threat was met by the French from Mackinac, who, in 1752, under the leadership of Charles de Langlade, attacked and defeated a major settlement named Pickawillany on the Miami River near present-day Piqua,

Ohio. This victory by the French precipitated the French and Indian War ultimately won by the English with the surrender of the French in Montreal in 1759.

Word of the French surrender didn't reach Fort Michilimackinac until 1760. In late September 1761, British Captain Henry Balfour took possession of the Fort from the French commandant, Charles de Langlade (Langlade Street in Mackinaw City is named after this French officer). The Fleur-de-Lis was lowered and the British flag now flew at the Straits.

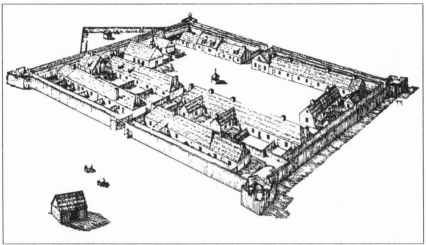

Fort Michilimackinac in 1749
(Courtesy Mackinac Island State Park Commission)

The Indians in midwestern America chafed under British rule. In 1763, Pontiac, chief of the Ottawa, led a multi-tribe uprising against the English by attacking 14 British forts, including Fort Michilimackinac. The attack on Fort Michilimackinac was particularly vicious. Under the ruse of a celebration for the birthday of the King of England, Indian tribes collected at Mackinac and staged a special game (baggatiway) played with a racquette and ball. Indian women, gathered near the Fort entrance, hid tomahawks under their blankets and when the ball was "accidentally" hit inside the Fort, the young braves dashed inside with the tomahawks and massacred the garrison before the alarm could be sounded.

Alexander Henry
(Courtesy Thunder Bay Historical Museum Society, Ontario)

One of the few survivors was an English trader named Alexander Henry. He later wrote a book describing the massacre and his miraculous escape.[5] Initially captured in the raid, Henry was ransomed from his Ottawa captors by the Chippewa chief, Wawatam, whom Henry had befriended in earlier years. Threatened again by a group of Indians from Saginaw Bay, recruiting warriors for the

Chief Wawatam enroute from St. Ignace to Mackinaw City
(Authors, 1980)

prolonged battle at Fort Detroit, Chief Wawatam spirited Alexander Henry across the waters of the Straits to St. Ignace. From here, Henry escaped to the north to Sault Ste. Marie. Almost two centuries later Chief Wawatam and Alexander Henry were remembered by modern-day mariners by having vessels named after them.

From 1911 to 1986, the ice-breaking car ferry *Chief Wawatam* retraced its namesake's route from Mackinaw City to St. Ignace hauling rail cars.[6] Sub-sequently, she was cut down to a barge and based in Sault Ste. Marie, Michigan. The Canadian ice-breaker *Alexander Henry* was stationed at Port Arthur, Ontario, on Lake Superior until 1985 when she was converted to a floating bed-and-breakfast hotel and educational facility moored next to the Marine Museum of the Great Lakes at Kingston in Kingston, Ontario, on Lake Ontario.

Major Robert Rogers

Following Pontiac's defeat in 1764, the British returned to Fort Michilimackinac. Within two years, Major Robert Rogers took command arriving in August 1766 aboard the schooner *Gladwyn*, the first sailing vessel in the Straits since the *Griffin*. The *Gladwyn*, along with the schooner *Beaver*, had been built in Detroit in 1762. Rogers was a flamboyant and audacious man who had distinguished himself in the French and Indian War and was instrumental in breaking Pontiac's siege of Fort Detroit. In 1765, he wrote a book describing his personal experiences in North America.[7] It was well received, particularly in London, where English folk marveled at his exploits in the wilderness. He put in place grandiose plans for the exploration of the territory westward from Michilimackinac. Extravagances, both in his personal and professional life, led to his downfall. In 1767, Rogers was arrested for treason but was eventually acquitted of these charges in Montreal. A broken man, he eventually died a debtor and an alcoholic in 1795 in London.

The British continued to occupy the Fort at old Mackinac up through the early part of the American Revolution. By 1780, Commandant Patrick Sinclair decided to move the Fort from old Mackinac to Mackinac Island to create a more defensible position. Here, in 1780-81, he built the Fort that still stands today. When the move to Mackinac Island was made, the name was shortened to Fort Mackinac. In 1780-81, the sloops *Welcome, Angelica* and *Archangel* and the schooner *DePeyster* wintered at Fort Mackinac.[8] In previous winters they had been laid up at the mouth of the Cheboygan River under the watchful eye of Catherine and Samuel Robertson, who lived there in a cabin.[9] Following the conclusion of the American Revolution in 1783, the Michilimackinac territory was ceded to the Americans, but it took until 1796 before the Fort was actually turned over to American troops. A third flag – the Stars and Stripes – now flew at Michilimackinac.

When the Union Jack came down at Fort Mackinac on October 2, 1796, there were 12 merchant vessels and several sloops, brigs, and schooners based at Detroit.[10] Some of these vessels were used by the British to move their garrison to a new fort in Canada on St. Joseph Island at the north end of Lake Huron — only 45 miles from Fort Mackinac. From here, they could keep a close eye on events in the Straits.

Fort St. Joseph in 1804
(Courtesy William L. Clements Library)

Major Henry Burbeck, the new American commandant, arrived at Fort Mackinac aboard the sloop *Detroit* with his supply ship, the schooner *Swan*. He took over a fort that was in need of serious repairs with the task of establishing military authority over a vast region filled with French, British and Indian peoples who were potentially hostile. During his stay, and that of succeeding commanders, civilian law and infrastructure was established by Northwest Territory officials under the Northwest Territory Act of 1787.[11] In the village around the fort, life went on as usual with the Frenchmen continuing their thriving trade with the British merchants in Montreal. This peaceful coexistence did not last, for by the fall of 1811, the winds of war were blowing across the United States.

On July 12, 1812, Captain Charles Roberts, commander of the British fort on St. Joseph Island, received word that war had been declared on the United States. He was advised to take "the most prudent means of either offense or defense." Taking the offensive, he captured Fort Mackinac in a surprise flanking action — landing on the far side of Mackinac Island (a spot now known as British Landing) and attacking the Fort from the rear. The American schooners *Salina* and *Mary* were captured by the British in this action. In the summer of 1814, an American fleet, under the command of Captain Arthur Sinclair, unsuccessfully laid siege to Fort Mackinac.[12] In Captain Sinclair's command were the brigs *Lawrence* and *Niagara*, and the schooners *Caledonia*, *Scorpion*, and *Tigris* — all having fought in Oliver Hazard Perry's victory at Put-in-Bay on Lake Erie, a year earlier.[13] This was the only significant naval engagement ever to occur in the Straits of Mackinac.

With the close of the War of 1812, Fort Mackinac once more was ceded to the U.S. by the Treaty of Ghent and reoccupied by the Americans in July 1815. The fur trade flourished with John Jacob Astor's American Fur Company, headquartered at Mackinac Island, dominating the trade. The first steamship on the upper Lakes, the side-wheeler *Walk-in-the-Water*, arrived at Mackinac Island in June 1819 amid much fanfare. Vessel traffic soared and, not unexpectedly, so did the shipwrecks. In 1875, Mackinac Island was declared a National Park and 20 years later, with transferral of ownership to the

State of Michigan, the Mackinac Island State Park was established and the last U.S. troops departed the Island.

Walk-In-The-Water 1818, drawing by Samual Ward Stanton c.1895
(Reprinted from Great Lakes Steam Vessels, 1962)

ISLANDS OF THE STRAITS

Within the arbitrary boundaries of the Straits of Mackinac set forth in the *Introduction* of this book are four islands that are a part of the maritime history of the Straits region — St. Helena, Mackinac, Round, and Bois Blanc. Shipwrecks that have accumulated on their shores or in their harbors include the schooners *Bonnie Doon* and *Flight*, and the propeller *Sea Gull*, all stranded on the shores of Bois Blanc and the propeller *Peshtigo* stranded on Mackinac Island, along with an unidentified sailing vessel sunk in that Island's harbor.

ST. HELENA ISLAND

St. Helena Island is the most westerly of the four islands being about seven miles west of the northern end of the Mackinac Bridge. It sits nearly two miles off the shores of the Upper Peninsula of Michigan, southwest of the bluff of Gros Cap. The Island is about one mile long in the northwest to southeast direction and one-half mile across at the widest point. A small but beautiful harbor on the northeast side faces toward Gros Cap. Except for an excellent chapter in the book by Marion Morse Davis,[1] there is a paucity of written material about the Island. The origin of its name is a mystery, although it first appeared on a map in 1744 by Father Pierre Francois Xavier de Charlevoix as Isle Ste. Helene.[2]

The Island was part of the land ceded to the Federal Government under an Indian Treaty of 1836 for roughly ten cents per acre,[3] making the price of the Island (approximately 250 acres) about $25. It was patented to William Belote in 1849, who subsequently sold it to Archie and Wilson Newton in 1853.[4] The Newton brothers later played a major role in the development of the city of Cheboygan. Presently, St. Helena is owned by the heirs of Prentiss Brown, a former U.S. Senator who was instrumental in the building of the Mackinac Bridge. By 1850, a small village and dock had developed on the Island, with the principal commerce being fishing and supplying steamers with wood for fuel. The harbor was a favorite roadstead for all types of vessels in gales blowing from the west and southwest. St. Helena was the last port of call for vessels headed out onto Lake Michigan.

It was from the harbor of St. Helena that the infamous attack against the Mormons on Beaver Island was launched.[5] Animosity between the gentile fishermen in the Straits and the Mormons had been growing for years, particularly over fishing rights. On June 16, 1856, King James Jesse Strang, the Mormon leader, had been mortally wounded by his own followers. In July 1856, led by Archie Newton, scores of men from around the Straits boarded the schooner *C. L. Abell* and sailed to St. James Harbor at Beaver Island.[6] Within days they had forced over 2,500 people to leave the Island. This episode was captured in verse:[7]

> *Then was the little harbor thronged*
> *With fishers and their boats*
> *Canoes and skiffs and sloops they used*
> *Most every craft that floats.*
>
> *Then was there gathering in the dusk,*
> *And hurrying in the dawn,*
> *From Epoufett, from Point aux Chenes,*
> *Where'er the news had gone.*
>
> *From Manistique to Rabbit's Back,*
> *Seule Choix and far Death's Door,*
> *The Poverty and Summer Isles,*
> *Each sent three or four.*
>
> *From Scott's Point and from Mille Coquin*
> *They came to Saint Helene,*
> *"Arch Newton now must lead us on,*
> *We'll sweep the Beavers clean."*

The Mormon kingdom of St. James had lost its King and its followers and never again would be an influence on Beaver Island.

The lighthouse on St. Helena was built in 1873 with Thomas P. Dunn appointed the first keeper.[8] Around 1922, the light was automated and it was left unattended. By 1986, the lighthouse and

St. Helena Island Lighthouse
(Photo by John L. Wagner, 1988)

associated buildings were badly deteriorated when the Great Lakes Lighthouse Keepers Association and two Michigan Boy Scout Troops took over its restoration. Even before this lighthouse was built, St. Helena contributed to the lighting of the Straits. When the Waugoshance Lighthouse was to be built in 1851, a 90 x 100 foot wooden crib for the lighthouse base was constructed at St. Helena. This crib was then towed from St. Helena to Waugoshance and set in place by filling it with stones.[9]

Today, St. Helena Island is deserted with only the foundations of the old village houses evident. The dock in the harbor has long since disappeared. Modern-day recreational boaters use the harbor as a daytime playground and an overnight anchorage.

BOIS BLANC ISLAND

The largest island in the Straits is Bois Blanc. It lies north-northwest and east-southeast with a length of 11.5 miles and a width of 4.7 miles at its southeasterly end and 1.2 miles at its northwesterly end. Located seven miles east of the northern end of the Mackinac Bridge in Lake Huron, Bois Blanc Island forms the north side of what

23

is called on navigational charts, the South Channel of the Straits of Mackinac. It was acquired by the U.S. Government from the Chippewa Indians in 1795 as part of the Treaty of Green Ville at no cost being "an extra and voluntary gift of the Chippewa nation."[10] The name, Bois Blanc, means "white wood" and has been corrupted to Bob-low. It was held by the Federal Government as a wood reserve for Mackinac Island with part of it being sold in 1884 to raise money

Bois Blanc Island Lighthouse with new Light in foreground
(Photo by John L. Wagner, 1987)

for the improvement of carriage roads and bridle paths on Mackinac Island. The remainder was given to the State of Michigan at the same time as Mackinac Island in 1895. Although a part of Mackinac County on the north shore, activities of the Island are more closely associated with Cheboygan County to the south. Presently, about one-half of the Island is privately owned.

During the 1800s, Mackinac Islanders used Bois Blanc for growing gardens and apple orchards as well as for obtaining maple syrup from sugar camps.[11] The first lighthouse was established on the north side of the Island in 1829 and was manned by Eber Ward, the namesake of one of the wrecks in the Straits. During a violent storm in 1838, the lighthouse was blown down. Frances Ward Hurlburt captured this harrowing experience in an exciting story as told by Emily Ward, the keeper's daughter.[12] Although a U.S. Coast Guard (nee U.S. Life Saving Service) Station was maintained for many years at Walker's Point on the east end of the Island, their exploits were never of such a nature as to appear in the newspapers.

The Sand Bay Sawmill operated in the early 1900s on the south side of Bois Blanc at Point Aux Pins. For many years, the lumber dock

Sand Bay Sawmill at Bois Blanc Island with the *Helen Taylor* c.1923
(Courtesy William C. Duman)

also served as a dock for the ferry boats from Cheboygan, but in recent times the ferry landing was moved 1.2 miles to the east. In most winters, a solid ice bridge forms between Point Aux Pins and Point Nipigon on the mainland allowing transportation to the Island by snowmobile. Currently, the principal function of the Island is to serve as a site for summer vacation cottages.

The southeast corner of Bois Blanc has been the sight of hundreds of vessel strandings. To our knowledge, only two became permanent

25

shipwrecks — the schooners *Flight* and *Bonnie Doon*. The tug *Sea Gull* caught fire and was run ashore on the northeast side of the Island.

ROUND ISLAND

Two thousand feet to the west, across a shallow, rocky channel from Bois Blanc, lies Round Island. This small, hilly Island is only about three miles in circumference with an abandoned lighthouse at the northwest tip, facing Fort Mackinac on Mackinac Island. The Island was used as an Indian burial ground from the earliest times. During the cholera epidemic in 1832, most boats were forbidden to land at Mackinac Island. Those who had died enroute were buried on Round Island.[13]

When the Americans laid siege to Mackinac Island during the War of 1812, they put a landing party ashore on Round Island to build a gun emplacement for bombardment of Fort Mackinac. However, after several skirmishes with Indian war parties sent across the passage by the British, they were driven off. Round Island has always been Federally-owned land with no private residences.

MACKINAC ISLAND

Mackinac Island, queen of the Islands of the Straits, has a charm and lore that has been diligently written about by so many authors that present-day writers may only hope to fill in a few gaps. This brief synopsis is provided for the purposes of completeness. For further information, we suggest that our readers consult any of the hundreds of references described by Larry Massie in the front matter of Meade C. Williams' book *Early Mackinac*.[14]

The "Island," as it is referred to, is three miles in length northwest to southeast and 1.7 miles across at its widest point. It is hilly with high limestone bluffs on the southwest side that command a view of all that sails through the Straits. The harbor, town, and fort are on the southeast side facing Round Island. Before the construction of Fort Mackinac in 1780, Mackinac Island was a summer camping spot for the many Indians who passed through the area. The profitable fur trade was the major driver in shaping the Island's history up through the 1830s. As described in previous sections, the Union Jack and the Stars and Stripes flew over Fort Mackinac from 1780 until 1895 with the British and Americans fighting for control of this strategic outpost until the conclusion of the War of 1812.

It was here on Mackinac Island that the American Fur Company made John Jacob Astor a rich man, that Henry Schoolcraft negotiated treaties with the Indians ceding vast lands to the U.S. Government, that Doctor William Beaumont significantly advanced medical knowledge by studying the digestive process through a non-healing wound in the stomach of a French trader, and today, that a vast and modern army of tourists gather each summer to consider all this history and enjoy the sights of the Island.

By the second half of the nineteenth century, Mackinac Island's climate, environment and historical sites began to attract large numbers of vacationers. First they came by water on magnificent steamships like the *City of Mackinac* of the famous D & C Line.[15] Next they

City of Mackinac c. 1890
(Courtesy Institute for Great Lakes Research, Bowling Green State University)

came by passenger train to Mackinaw City and then to the Island by ferry. In the first quarter of the twentieth century, automobiles began to replace the trains and today, Great Lakes Air provides scheduled service between St. Ignace and Mackinac Island. Wealthy lumber barons from Michigan and meat packers from Chicago built splendid Victorian cottages on the Island in the 1890s. Guest houses and hotels flourished with the stately 700-room Grand Hotel opening in 1887. Fudge has become the specialty food prepared on the Island with more than 100 tons of sugar imported each year. Today, the "magic Island" of Mackinac attracts over 800,000 visitors annually.

From a maritime perspective, the port of Mackinac Island has served the fur, fishing, military, and tourist businesses as well as being a waystation offering fuel for passing steamers and a rest stop for all kinds of travelers from Indians to immigrants. Except for downbound traffic from Lake Superior to Lake Michigan, most vessel traffic in the Straits passed by the Island about five miles offshore. Generally, it has not been a significant hazard to navigation. Consequently, few vessels have been wrecked on Mackinac Island. Shipwrecks that have accumulated there include the propeller *Peshtigo*, stranded at the east end of the harbor, and an unidentified sailing vessel sunk in the harbor.

Mackinac Island Harbor with Fort Mackinac above
(Courtesy David A. Armour, Mackinac Island State Park Commission)

LIGHTHOUSES IN THE STRAITS

There is a certain romance about lighthouses that captivates the human spirit. They evoke feelings of hope and trust, of unceasing watchfulness, of widespread helpfulness and of steadfast endurance under all conditions. They stand on the highways of the Great Lakes as eternal sentinels, the quintessence of maritime safety. In fair weather they appear picturesque. In darkness and storm they appear as the humanitarian work of a caring society. Their history parallels that of the ships they tried to save. In their honor, we choose to spend some time describing for our readers some of the lighthouses in the Straits of Mackinac.

Round Island Lighthouse
(Authors, 1980)

On the Great Lakes, approximately two-thirds of the lighthouses designate harbor entrances, with the remaining one-third marking potential hazards such as islands, shoals, points and reefs. By contrast, in the Straits of Mackinac, over 80% of the presently operating lights mark potential hazards. A summary description of both past and present lighthouses in the Straits is contained in the *Table* following this section, and their locations are shown on the shipwreck charts that follow.

Five of these 16 lighthouses are no longer in commission. *Waugoshance* is abandoned and in disrepair, while *Cheboygan Lighthouse* on Lighthouse Point has been destroyed. *Round Island Lighthouse* was transferred to the U.S. Forest Service and has been restored with help from private historical societies and government agencies. *Old Mackinac Point Lighthouse* now belongs to the Mackinac Island State Park Commission and serves as a maritime museum. *McGulpin Point Lighthouse* has been restored and is now a private residence. Likewise, the abandoned lighthouse buildings on Bois Blanc Island are a private residence, with the currently operating light a short distance away.

The first lighthouse in the Straits was *Bois Blanc Island Lighthouse* built on Bois Blanc Island in 1829, just nine years after the very first lighthouse on the Lakes was constructed

Cross section of Spectacle Reef Lighthouse
(Reprinted from "Famous Lighthouses of America," by Edward Rowe Snow, 1955)

at Fort Niagara on Lake Ontario.[1] Waugoshance Point was considered so dangerous that it received the first lightship stationed anywhere on the Lakes in 1832.[2] At that time the technology did not exist to build a lighthouse in the open water that could withstand the weather, particularly the ice, of the northern Lakes. This lightship was replaced with the now abandoned *Waugoshance Lighthouse* in 1851.[3]

As the technology developed so did the magnitude of the feats of the engineers who built the lighthouses. *Spectacle Reef Lighthouse*, at the eastern entrance to the Straits, was considered the most significant engineering accomplishment on the Lakes when it was completed in 1874. This monolithic stone structure was over ten miles from the nearest land, and when the keepers returned to the site after the winter of 1873-74, they found the ice piled against the Lighthouse to a height of 30 feet requiring them to tunnel through to the entrance.[4]

Federally-funded lightships were not placed on White Shoals and Grays Reef until 1891.[5] Private shipping interests had considered White Shoals such a serious hazard that, by 1878, they had stationed their own lightship on this reef. Maintenance on this vessel was always a problem as can be seen by the following article that appeared in the November 6, 1886, *Detroit Free Press*:[6]

White Shoals Lighthouse
(Authors, 1979)

31

"*A Heavy Gale at Mackinac.* Mackinac, November 5. — At 6 o'clock the wind went to the northwest and blew a gale nearly all day. The White Shoal lightship broke from her moorings during the night and drifted down and passed here at 9 a.m. There was only one man aboard on her and he was making frantic signals for help. The propeller *Oceanica* went to his assistance and succeeded getting a line to her and was bringing her in but the line slipped off and the sea was so heavy it was impossible to get a line to her again and she was left to the mercy of the waves. A dispatch was sent from here to Cheboygan for a tug to go to her assistance. It is probable she was picked up and taken into port."

McGulpin Point Lighthouse
(Authors, 1979)

Many dangers were associated with the job of manning lighthouses in the Straits. Eber Ward, namesake of the wreck described later, was the first keeper of *Bois Blanc Island Lighthouse*. His daughter, Emily Ward, was almost killed when a violent winter storm in January 1838, caused the main Lighthouse tower to collapse.[7] Three keepers at *Grays Reef Lighthouse*, although not injured, were badly frightened when the 504-foot steel freighter *J. E. Upson* smashed into the Lighthouse in a dense fog on May 6, 1965.[8] The vessel suffered more damage than the Lighthouse, but was able to continue on her way.

Travelling to and from waterbound lighthouses in early spring or late fall was always risky. Many lives were lost in the process, with the following article from the April 19, 1883, *Cheboygan Democrat* describing an example:[9]

"William Marshall, light keeper at *Spectacle Reef*, tried with three assistants to make that station last Sunday afternoon from St. Ignace. When about two miles west of *Bois Blanc Light*, their boat capsized and James Marshall was drowned. The survivors were in the water over three hours."

And then there were other problems mostly born in the minds of the keepers, who lived a lonely existence and had more than enough time to imagine most anything. Some committed suicide, while others were convinced that their lighthouse was inhabited by ghosts. In 1894, keeper John Herman drowned when he fell from a pier alongside *Waugoshance Lighthouse*. For years thereafter, strange incidents attributed to his ghost were documented by his successors. Shortly after *White Shoals Lighthouse* was completed in 1910, *Waugoshance Lighthouse* was shut down because it was supposedly obsolete. But everyone who was familiar with the situation knew the real reason was that the Lighthouse Service could not find a keeper who was willing to contend with the ghost of John Herman.[10]

The history of lighthouses on the northern Great Lakes, particularly those in the Straits of Mackinac, is indeed rich. The reader who wishes to explore this history further will find the book, *The Northern Lights* by Charles K. Hyde, especially interesting.[11]

LIGHTHOUSES
IN THE
STRAITS OF MACKINAC
(By Site Letter, Total 16)

MAP SITE	NAME
(See page 62)	
A	**Skillagalee (Ile Aux Galets) Light (1850, 1888)****
B	**Grays Reef Light (1936)*****
C*	**Waugoshance Light (1851)*****
D	**White Shoals Light (1910)*****
E	**St. Helena Island Light (1873)**
F*	McGulpin Point Light (1869)
G*	**Old Mackinac Point Light (1892)**
H*	**Round Island Light (1895)**
I	Round Island Passage Light (1947)
J	Bois Blanc Island Light (1829, 1868)
K	Cheboygan Crib Light (1926)
L	Fourteen Foot Shoal Light (1930)
M*	Cheboygan Light (1853)
N	Poe Reef Light (1929)***
O	Spectacle Reef Light (1874)
P	Martin Reef Light (1927)

* Decomissioned
** First date is original structure, second date is current structure
*** LIGHTSHIPS: Waugoshance, 1832-1851
White Shoals, 1891-1910
Grays Reef, 1891-1936
Poe Reef, 1893-1929
NOTE: Lighthouses shown in **boldface** are listed in the *National Register of Historic Places.*

Transportation Across the Straits

In the days of exploration and settlement, Indians and fur traders used canoes and bateaux to make their way across the Straits of Mackinac. Later, military men from three nations employed Mackinaw boats and other small sailing vessels to traverse the expanse of water separating the Upper and Lower Peninsulas of Michigan. After the War of 1812 and up to 1881, transportation across the Straits was provided by the people living in Mackinaw City and St. Ignace. Local residents ferried goods and passengers between the two cities. Sail boats were used in the summer and horse and sleigh across the ice in the winter. When the ice was thin in the late fall, people would walk or skate across the Straits often pulling a small sleigh.[1]

Railroad Car Ferries

The first railroad link to Mackinaw City was established in 1881 when the Michigan Central Railroad was extended from Saginaw to Mackinaw City. Later the same year, the Mackinac and Marquette Railroad completed its track from St. Ignace to Marquette. The

Railroad car ferry *Sainte Marie (2)* on right, with the steamer *Adventure*, at Mackinaw City c. 1915
(Reprinted from Memories of Mackinaw, courtesy Nancy Campbell)

35

following year, the Grand Rapids and Indiana Railroad arrived at Mackinaw City. The owners of these three railroads formed the Mackinac Transportation Company in 1881 with the intention of transporting goods across the Straits between the railheads at Mackinaw City and St. Ignace.[2] For this purpose, they contracted with the Detroit Dry Dock Company to build the 486-ton, 127-foot, wood hull propeller *Algomah* (described later in this book).

Sainte Marie (2) in the Straits of Mackinac c.1915
(Courtesy Institute for Great Lakes Research, Bowling Green State University)

Originally, freight carried on the *Algomah* was off-loaded from the railcars onto the vessel and then transported across the Straits. At this point it was taken from the *Algomah* and reloaded onto outbound railcars. Because this process was so time consuming, the Mackinac Transportation Company purchased the barge *Betsey* that was towed behind the *Algomah* and could hold four railcars.[3] To increase capacity, the wood hull propeller *St. Ignace,* which could carry ten railcars, was built in 1888.[4] At this time the *Algomah* was sold. Further capacity was added in 1893 with the addition of the wood hull propeller *Sainte Marie* that could carry 18 railcars. In 1911, the 26-car capacity all-steel propeller *Chief Wawatam* was added.[5]

The *St. Ignace* and the *Sainte Marie* were sold in 1913 when the new, 14-car capacity steel propeller *Sainte Marie (2)* was built.[6]

All these vessels had been designed as ice-breakers and operated year-round. However, the steel hulls proved far superior to the wood hull vessels. These vessels played an important role in Lakes navigation as they were often hired by the shipping companies to help their vessels through the ice-choked Straits. With the opening of the Mackinac Bridge in 1957, rail traffic declined, and in 1961 the *Sainte Marie (2)* was sold for scrap. In 1977, the Mackinac Transportation Company ceased operations and the State of Michigan purchased the *Chief Wawatam*. When she was retired by the State in 1986, railroad car ferry service across the Straits ended.

Besides railcars, the Mackinac Transportation Company boats also carried mail, passengers and some miscellaneous freight. The advent of automobile travel led to an increased need for transportation across the Straits. However, the Mackinac Transportation Company never fully comprehended the potential of the automobile ferry. Their boats were not equipped with the proper facilities for significant numbers of people or cars. Automobiles, for example, were drained of their gas, loaded on flatcars and charged the same rate as other freight. In 1916, this amounted to a charge of $40, a substantial sum for that time.[7] Loud protests and increased pressure from citizen groups resulted in legislation in 1923 that created the Michigan State Ferries under the jurisdiction of the Michigan State Highway Department.[8]

AUTOMOBILE FERRIES

The first automobile ferry acquired by the Michigan State Ferries was the small wooden passenger vessel *Ariel*.[9] She made her first trip on August 2, 1923, leaving St. Ignace with three cars on board.[10] By the time service was shut down on November 20, she had carried 10,351 vehicles across the Straits at a toll charge of $2.50 per car. The *Ariel* had been built as a passenger ferry running between Windsor, Ontario, and Detroit and was not designed to handle the high seas often encountered in the Straits. Consequently, rough water played havoc with her schedule. The *Ariel* lasted only three years, and was

Ariel
(Courtesy Institute for Great Lakes Research, Bowling Green State University)

sold in 1926. In 1924, two new vessels were put into service, the *Sainte Ignace* and the *Mackinaw City*.[11] Next came the *Straits of Mackinac*, which was added to the fleet in 1928.

During the summer, these ferries ran every hour on the hour from 6:00 a.m. to 9:00 p.m. with a trip at 1:30 a.m. and 4:30 a.m. In the spring and fall, except for hunting season, they made a trip every one and one-half hours. Traffic grew rapidly and during the season of 1929, 130,942 vehicles were transported across the Straits.[12] By 1933, the toll charge had dropped to $1.25 per car. Before 1936, service was suspended during the winter as none of the ferries were ice-breakers. In the fall of 1936, the railroad car ferry and ice-breaker *Sainte Marie (2)* was leased from the Mackinac Transportation Company to provide year-round auto ferry service. She remained in this role until 1952.

Demand continued to increase and larger boats were added beginning with the *City of Cheboygan* in 1937.[13] Next came the *City of Munising* in 1938 and finally the *City of Petoskey* in 1940.[14] All these vessels were converted railroad car ferries, being the *Ann Arbor IV*, the *Pere Marquette No. 20*, and the *Pere Marquette No. 17*, respectively. They had provided service across Lake Michigan, running from western Michigan ports to Wisconsin ports. Each of these vessels

Straits of Mackinac
(Courtesy Institute for Great Lakes Research, Bowling Green State University)

could carry over 100 vehicles. With the sale of the *Sainte Ignace* and the *Mackinaw City* in October 1940, the fleet consisted of the three newer vessels, the venerable *Straits of Mackinac*, and the leased *Sainte Marie (2)*. In that year, the fleet carried 296,762 vehicles.[15]

During World War II, gasoline rationing greatly reduced the vehicle traffic across the Straits. When rationing was ended traffic boomed again. In 1949, the ferries carried 605,973 vehicles and were once more pressed for capacity.[16] After much debate and opposition

Vacationland
(Courtesy Institute for Great Lakes Research, Bowling Green State University)

from supporters of the Mackinac Bridge project, funds for a $4.5 million ice-breaking ferry were approved. The new 150-car capacity vessel *Vacationland* was launched in 1951 and put into service in January 1952. Leasing of the ice-breaker *Sainte Marie (2)* from the Mackinac Transportation Company was discontinued that year. By this time the crossing time for the ferries had been cut in half to a 30-minute trip. To pay for the cost of the *Vacationland*, the toll charges were raised to $2.00 and $2.50, depending on the car size. The ferries continued to operate until the opening of the Mackinac Bridge in 1957. At that time, the boats were sold to private interests with the docks going to the city governments of St. Ignace and Mackinaw City. The *Straits of Mackinac* was sold to the Mackinac Island Transportation Company. A summary of the vessels employed in this service over the years is given in the following *Table.*

Vessels Operated by the Michigan State Ferries

Ariel	1923 – 1926
Sainte Ignace	1924 – 1940
Mackinaw City	1924 – 1940
Straits of Mackinac	1928 – 1957
*Sainte Marie (2)**	1936 – 1952
City of Cheboygan	1937 – 1957
City of Munising	1938 – 1957
City of Petoskey	1940 – 1957
Vacationland	1952 – 1957

* Leased

THE MACKINAC BRIDGE

Although the ferry service was reasonably good, there were at least 20 days a year, mostly in the months of July and August, that long lines developed with waits of several hours. At the opening of the hunting season in November, the line would extend seven or more miles along the highway with waits up to 17 hours.[17] Moreover, schedules were often disrupted by bad weather. Ice in the winter sometimes brought ferry traffic to a complete halt. These factors, along with increasing auto traffic, created a chorus of appeals for a bridge to be built across the Straits. In response to this, the Michigan State Legislature passed a bill in 1934 that established the Mackinac Bridge Authority.[18]

Considerable opposition against building a bridge developed. The chief argument was that, from an engineering perspective, such a structure could not withstand the strong currents, the heavy ice in the winter and the strong winds. However, these arguments were

Straits of Mackinac Bridge under construction in 1956
(Courtesy Mackinac Bridge Authority, Michigan Department of Transportation)

forcefully countered by Professor James Cissel, the Secretary to the Authority and head of Structural Engineering at the University of Michigan. His speeches and papers, combined with the opening of the Golden Gate Bridge, convinced most people that the bridge was technically feasible.[19] A subjective argument in favor of the ferries was their sentimental value. Many people found the ferry boat ride across the Straits enjoyable. Bridge proponents were quick to point out the cost benefits of the time saving offered by a bridge.

41

Differing proposals for bridging the Straits had been made. One alternative was a set of bridges connecting Cheboygan to St. Ignace via Bois Blanc Island, Round Island and Mackinac Island. Other proposals included a floating tunnel.[20] By 1940, the present-day route had been agreed upon. After having received Government approvals to build a toll bridge across Federally-navigable waters, a mile-long causeway was built on the north side of the Straits. The outbreak of World War II shelved the bridge program and the causeway was used as a dock for the auto ferries (which shortened the round-trip ferry distance by 45 percent).

Straits of Mackinac Bridge
(Authors, 1977)

As part of the see-saw battle between bridge proponents and opponents, the State Legislature abolished the Mackinac Bridge Authority in 1947 and then reconstituted it in 1950. Finally, on December 17, 1953, after much political intrigue and a last-ditch effort to obtain financial backing, a bid was accepted from a group of underwriters for the sale of $99,800,000 worth of Mackinac Bridge Authority bonds. Two months later, the first construction contracts were awarded and work was begun under the direction of David B. Steinman, a noted bridge engineer.[21]

The official ground-breaking for the Mackinac Bridge took place on May 7, 1954. Slightly more than three years later, this monumental construction project was completed and the Bridge was opened to traffic on November 1, 1957. In the process, the five-mile long Bridge consumed 931,000 tons of concrete, 71,300 tons of structural steel and 5,868,300 steel rivets and bolts. The 24.5-inch main suspension cables comprise 12,580 individual strands with a total length of wire of over

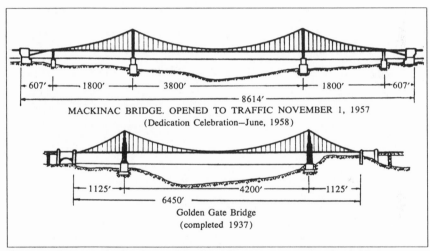

Comparative magnitude of two of the World's greatest suspension bridges
(Reprinted from "Mighty Mac: The Official Picture History of the Mackinac Bridge" by Lawrence A. Rubin, 1958)

42,000 miles. An army of 2,500 men worked at the Bridge site aided by 89,000 drawings and blueprints. The actual construction cost was $76,300,000. From anchorage to anchorage, it was 8,614 feet in length — the longest suspension bridge in the world.[22] Michigan's two peninsulas were at last linked and the State was united.

During its first full year of operation, 1,390,390 vehicles crossed the Straits bridge — 53 percent more than that carried by the ferries in their last full year of operation. By 1990, the number had increased

43

almost threefold to 3,390,203 vehicles.[23] From 1957 to 1990, the toll rate for cars had dropped from $3.25 to $1.50. Each summer, the ironworkers who toiled on the bridge hold a reunion to reminisce and partake in games of skill. Remarkably, only five men lost their lives during the construction. The Mackinac Bridge Museum in Mackinaw City contains many interesting exhibits and is dedicated to the men who designed and built the Mackinac Bridge.

GRUMMOND'S MACKINAC LINE.

Elegant Passenger Steamers
- - - FROM - - -

CLEVELAND, TOLEDO AND DETROIT
————FOR————

Mackinac, Green Bay, St. Ignace, Cheboygan, Alpena, Oscoda, Au Sable
And all Ports on
ST. CLAIR RIVER AND WEST SHORE OF LAKE HURON AND ON GREEN BAY.

DEPARTURES AS FOLLOWS:
Steamers leave for Ports on River St. Clair and Lake Huron.

CLEVELAND, Wednesdays and Fridays, at 8 P. M.
TOLEDO, Tuesdays, at 8 A. M.
DETROIT, Tuesdays, Thursdays and Saturdays, at 9 P. M.
PORT HURON, Wednesdays, Fridays and Sundays, at 7 A. M.

Steamer for GREEN BAY AND ALL LAKE HURON PORTS, will leave Cleveland, Detroit, Toledo and Port Huron every ten days during the Season of Navigation.

The only Line from CLEVELAND and TOLEDO to MACKINAC and GREEN BAY without Transfer of Freight and Passengers.

For Time Cards, Rates, etc., apply to - - -

FARASEY & MARRON, Agents, 107—112 River Street, CLEVELAND, Ohio.
F. N. QUALE, Agent, Foot of Madison Street, TOLEDO, Ohio.
ASHLEY & DUSTIN, Agents, Foot of First Street, DETROIT, Mich.
Or W. H. BEEBE, General Agent.

S. B. GRUMMOND,

General Offices, Foot of First Street., DETROIT, Mich.   Owner & Gen'l Manager.

Beeson's Marine Directory, 1890

PART II

OVERVIEW
OF THE
SHIPWRECKS

INTRODUCTION TO THE SHIPWRECKS

Shipwrecks fascinate most people. Tales of their occurrence have a universal allure. Their stories are often narratives of extraordinary courage, heroism, and fortitude. They may, on the other hand, be about ineptitude and cowardice. The universality of their intrigue seems to lie in our fascination with man's response to crisis.

The shipwrecks of the Straits of Mackinac provide abundant material to satisfy the enchantment we have with the response of sailors to crisis generated by impending disaster. Records kept by Charles T. Dagwell, Marine Reporter at Mackinaw City from 1898 to 1927, show that 8,000 to 10,000 vessels passed Old Mackinac Point annually.[1] Between the weather, the navigational hazards and the traffic, a good number were destined to be left behind — victims of shipwreck. By our count, there are over 75 shipwrecks resting on the bottomland of the Straits, a veritable underwater cemetery.

There are no shipwrecks in the Straits of Mackinac of epic proportion such as the *Edmund Fitzgerald*.[2] The one that comes closest to this description is the wreck of the *Cedarville*. Several factors about this disaster contribute to this distinction. These include her size — she was a 588-foot steel ore carrier, the loss of ten lives, the fact that the wreck occurred in 1965 making it the most recent Straits disaster, and the seemingly unbelievable bungled decision-making that led to the tragedy. Treasure ships are not among the lost as there are no wrecks that carried valuable cargo. A total of 63 lives were lost in all of the wrecks described in this book. This number is small by comparison and, for example, falls short in qualifying for the list of the ten worst single ship disasters on the Lakes as measured by loss of life.[3]

For scuba divers, the wreck with the most grandeur is that of the brig *Sandusky*. Her figurehead and bowsprit are magnificent to behold, although continued high diver traffic is beginning to deteriorate this wreck. The most foreboding wreck is that of the propeller *Eber Ward*. Several divers have been seriously injured or lost their life on this wreck. The deepest is the propeller *Uganda*. At 207 feet to the bottom, she is well beyond the accepted maximum depth of 130 feet for sport divers. The propeller *Cayuga* is the most interesting wreck. She is shrouded with the remains of equipment left behind when hard-hat divers tried to raise her.

The assemblage of wrecks in this book does not include any vessels under 50 tons in size. Consequently, craft such as early Indian canoes, voyageur bateaux, Mackinaw boats, small tugs and recreational watercraft, are not accounted. In particular, several small tugs under 50 tons are known to have been lost in the Straits but are

Reconstructed sloop *Welcome* in the Straits of Mackinac c.1982
(Courtesy David A. Armour, Mackinac Island State Park Commission)

not included in this book. The list includes the tugs *Colonial, Cygnet, G. Pershing, Lorenzo Dimick, Minnie Morton* and *Uncle Sam*. The smallest wreck listed is the propeller *J. C. Liken* at 78 tons.

If inconclusive information on shipwreck locations were used, the famous wreck of La Salle's *Griffin*, lost in September 1679, would have been included, as well as the wreck of the sloop *Welcome* from Fort Michilimackinac, lost in 1781.[4] Both are said by some to have been lost in the Straits of Mackinac.

Notwithstanding these exclusions, a few wrecks of early commercial sailing vessels may have been missed. The date of the first recorded wreck, the schooner *D. N. Barney*, is 1849. Records of marine casualties occurring in the Straits before the 1840s are extremely sparse. Other exclusions are based on our judgment whether a wreck is geographically in the Straits of Mackinac. Thus, certain known wrecks have not been listed including the schooner *Jura* at the Cross Village dock,[5] the schooner *Queen City* on Hog Island Reef,[6] the propeller *Oscoda* on Pelkie Reef,[7] the schooner *Forester* at the mouth of the Lower Millecoquins River west of Naubinway,[8] the schooner *Mary N. Bourke* in St. Martin Bay,[9] and the side-wheel steamer *Garden City* on Martin Reef.[10]

Queen City
(Courtesy Dossin Great Lakes Museum)

Inclusion of the wrecks of the schooner *Marquette* and the propellers *City of Boston, Oliver Cromwell* and *George M. Humphrey* was not forgotten. All these wrecks were raised from deep water, often years later, and put back in service.[11] Scores of other wreck incidents took place that were falsely proclaimed total losses and were subsequently recovered. In a few cases, a wreck was a total loss but all of the wreckage was removed from the Straits. To qualify for listing, the remains of the wreck must still be in the Straits of Mackinac.

Shipwreck artifacts shown in most of the photographs in this book were recovered before a law was passed in 1980 limiting their removal (see *Appendix B*). The authors strongly support a conservation ethic, however, we show these artifact photographs as a matter of history. Divers are encouraged to take only pictures and leave the artifacts on the wrecks, thus, preserving these submerged historical and recreational resources for future divers.

WRECK STATISTICS

The maritime history of any Great Lakes region is partly embodied in the shipwrecks of that region. One way to explore this history is through the analysis, interpretation and presentation of data regarding these shipwrecks. Such statistics shed light on several aspects of maritime history, including shipbuilding, navigational technology, trade routes, commerce and the shipping season. In the following pages, results of the analysis of 78 shipwrecks that occurred in the Straits of Mackinac are presented, mostly in graphical form.

In terms of type of vessel, 62% were sail powered, 36% were mechanically powered, and 2% were unpowered barges. Hulls were mostly made of wood (96%) with a few being of steel (4%). The majority of these vessels (*Graph #1*) were built before 1870 (67%) and sank before 1890 (59%).

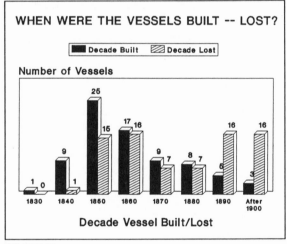

GRAPH #1

Thus, the collection of wrecks in the Straits has the essence of older, wooden sailing vessels.

The most dangerous part of the Straits is at the western entrance, which is guarded by Skillaglee Reef, Grays Reef, Waugoshance Point and White Shoals. Moreover, the narrowest section of the Straits is slightly west of the Mackinac Bridge between McGulpin Point on the south shore and Point La Barbe on the north shore, a distance of only 3.6 miles. Westward from this constriction into Lake Michigan is

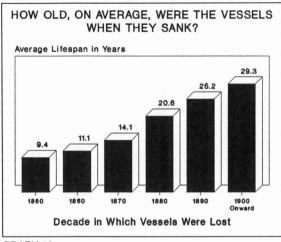

HOW OLD, ON AVERAGE, WERE THE VESSELS WHEN THEY SANK?

Average Lifespan in Years

Decade in Which Vessels Were Lost

GRAPH #2

where the ice piles up during the spring thaw. Because of these hazards, 63% of the vessels were lost in Lake Michigan with the remainder having sunk in Lake Huron (excluding abandoned vessels).

After the Civil War, the U. S. Government put in place legislation and funds that greatly improved aids to navigation and weather forecasting on the Great Lakes. Likewise, ship technology was constantly being improved. These factors had a marked effect on the lifespan of vessels travelling these waters. In the Straits, the lifespan of the wrecks in that area doubled from approximately ten years before the Civil War to more than 20 years by 1880 *(Graph #2)*.

Shipbuilding on the American Lakes began in earnest after the War of 1812 in New York on the southern shores of Lake Ontario, flourished in the ports of Lake Erie, and spread westward in step with the settlement of the Great Lakes basin. The collection of Mackinac wrecks mirrors this geographical evolution of shipbuilding *(Graph #3)*.

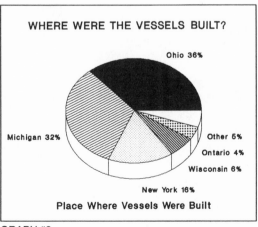

WHERE WERE THE VESSELS BUILT?

Ohio 36%

Michigan 32%

Other 5%

Ontario 4%

Wisconsin 6%

New York 16%

Place Where Vessels Were Built

GRAPH #3

51

With the many reefs, shoals, points and narrow passages in the Straits, it is not surprising that the primary cause of shipwrecks *(Graph #4)* was stranding (45%). With 10,000 vessel passages a year, collisions were common (18%). All of the wrecks that were caused by ice (9%) occurred in April.

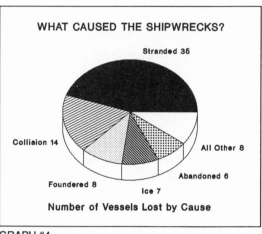

GRAPH #4

The months of July and August are the best months of the year for recreational boating in the Straits. It is warm, the weather is clear, the days are long, and the water is calm. Not unexpectedly, these

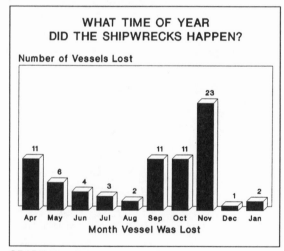

GRAPH #5

two months are the period in which the least number of wrecks have occurred *(see Graph #5).* The most wrecks have occurred during the fall stormy season (63%), with the gales of November taking the greatest toll (31%).

Interestingly, 77% of the vessels wrecked while underway were downbound (travelling west to east) with only 23% upbound. Downbound vessels, caught in storms, fog or darkness and trying to pass through the Straits, were on the open waters of Lake Michigan. There were no close by, safe anchorages and, thus, they were forced to try to get through the many reefs or ice to safer waters. Upbound vessels, on the other hand, sensing the danger in front of them, could find safe anchorage in the vicinity of Mackinaw City or Mackinac Island and wait until it passed. Even today in bad weather it is common to see large freighters moored at the edge of the channel between Mackinaw City and Mackinac Island.

During the nineteenth century, ships travelling westward carried cargos of lumber, coal and merchandise to support the growing towns along the Lake Michigan shoreline. On their return trip, the ships carried primarily grain and iron ore from the fields and mines in the vicinity of these towns. The shipwrecks of the Straits of Mackinac reflect this pattern *(Graph #6)*, with the number of grain

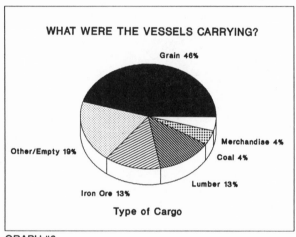

GRAPH #6

and ore wrecks (59%) being consistent with previously-noted larger number of downbound wrecks.

In *Parts III* and *IV* that follow, the vessel stories are arranged in alphabetical order using the so-called *Merchant Vessels* convention (see *Appendix A – Vessel Name*). This system alphabetizes the vessel names, first by the first initial of the name, and then by the first letter of the first name. Thus, *J. A. Smith* comes before *James R. Bentley*, both being listed under the letter "J."

Paul Horn prepares to dive off the *Gemini II*
(Authors, 1980)

PART III

DISCOVERED WRECKS

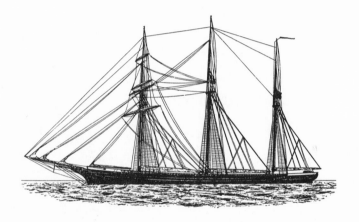

- INTRODUCTION 56
- MAP 62
- LIST BY SITE NUMBER 63
- LIST BY VESSEL NAME 64
- STORIES 65
- DISCOVERED BUT NOT IDENTIFIED 207

INTRODUCTION TO DISCOVERED WRECKS

There are a total of 78 stories about shipwrecks that have a specific name associated with them. Thirty-five of these wrecks have been *discovered* and *identified*. Additionally, there are six wrecks that have been *discovered* but *not identified*, and thus do not have a name associated with them. Consequently, there are a total of 41 *discovered* shipwrecks in the Straits of Mackinac. Data on these *discovered* wrecks is summarized in the *Table* following this section, and they have a site number that designates their position on the associated shipwreck map.

The total number of shipwreck sites shown on the shipwreck maps on pages 62 and 214, is 84, i.e., 41 *discovered* plus 43 *undiscovered*. However, some of the six *discovered-but-not-identified* wrecks may be duplicated in the set of 43 *undiscovered* wrecks. Consequently, the real number of wrecks in the Straits is some number greater than 78, but most likely less than 84.

WHAT CAUSED THE SHIPWRECKS?

Undiscovered   Discovered

Number of Vessels Lost

Cause of Vessel Loss

GRAPH #7

Although the primary cause of loss for the complete set of wrecks is stranding, most of these are among the *undiscovered* wrecks. The principal cause of loss for the *discovered* wrecks was by collision, followed by stranding *(Graph #7)*. Curiously, the majority of the *undiscovered* wrecks were lost by the end of the Civil War, while the majority of the *discovered* wrecks were lost in the period from 1890 onward *(Graph #8).* Part of the reason for this is that records and information on wrecks that are more recent is generally better and, therefore, it is more likely that research would lead to the finding of the more recent wrecks.

The location of most of the *discovered* wrecks in shallow water, near shore, has generally always been known by people living in the area. Several

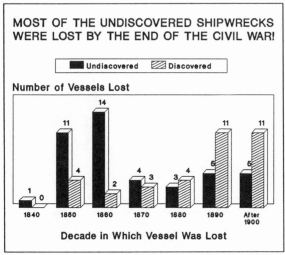

MOST OF THE UNDISCOVERED SHIPWRECKS WERE LOST BY THE END OF THE CIVIL WAR!

■ Undiscovered ▨ Discovered

Number of Vessels Lost

Decade in Which Vessel Was Lost

GRAPH #8

deeper water wrecks are known to have been dived on by hard-hat divers shortly after they sank and, therefore, their location also had been determined. These wrecks include the *Canisteo, Cayuga, Cedarville, Eber Ward, J. H. Tiffany, Milwaukee* and *William H. Barnum.* The positions of several of the wrecks that were discovered in recent times were actually shown on U.S. Lake Survey charts. These include the *Colonel Ellsworth, Henry Clay, Northwest* and *Richard Winslow.* Consequently, given all of this information, most of the *discovered* wrecks should not have been difficult to locate. Unfortunately, this was not always the case.

Anyone who has spent time searching for shipwrecks on the Great Lakes will have rediscovered an old wreck searchers axiom, i.e., "there's a lot of water out there." No matter how good your equipment, searching for and finding shipwrecks is an avocation that requires extraordinary patience. It is a process that comprises interminable hours of boredom punctuated by a few moments of exhilaration and wild excitement when the image of a shipwreck appears on the readout of the sonar. To be successful, the quest must

Wreck searchers Paul Horn and Chuck Feltner waiting for the ice to clear in the Straits of Mackinac *(Authors, 1980)*

be pursued assiduously in all types of weather and hours of the day and night. This kind of endeavor requires unusual grit.

The 41 *discovered* shipwrecks in the Straits offer some of the finest scuba diving anywhere in the world. The visibility usually ranges from 15 to 25 feet with water temperatures at depth running from 40 to 55 degrees Fahrenheit depending on the time of the year. Two-thirds of the wrecks are within ten miles of the docks at Mackinaw City, St. Ignace and Cheboygan. The geography of the area is such that it is usually possible to find a wreck that is in the lee on windy days. The wrecks lie in a range of depths suitable to the skills of most any diver

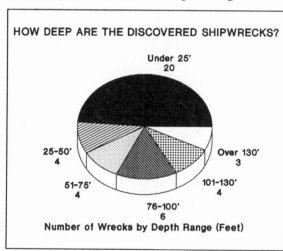

HOW DEEP ARE THE DISCOVERED SHIPWRECKS?

Under 25'
20

25-50'
4

Over 130'
3

51-75'
4

101-130'
4

76-100'
6

Number of Wrecks by Depth Range (Feet)

GRAPH #9

(Graph #9). In the following shipwreck stories, the exact location of each wreck is given in Loran C coordinates. Also included is a detailed description of the condition of the wreck as well as some interesting features of the wreck.

A significant number of the shipwrecks are intact or mostly intact *(Graph #10)*. *Appendix C* contains a set of definitions of terms for describing the wreck condition. The Straits of Mack-

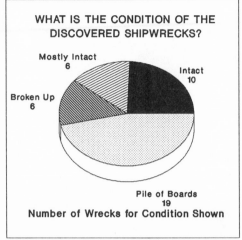

GRAPH #10

inac is a *State of Michigan Great Lakes Bottomland Preserve* — a designation that recognizes the shipwrecks as a non-renewable public resource of historical and recreational value. As such it is illegal to remove artifacts from the wrecks. *Appendix B* provides further detail on this underwater Preserve. Dive support, including air station, dive charters and equipment, is available from Straits Diving Center

Jeri Feltner with underwater camera system *(Authors, 1980)*

59

in St. Ignace. There are excellent boat launch/marina facilities at Mackinaw City, Cheboygan and St. Ignace. Divers and nondivers can also enjoy beaches, boating, fishing, hiking, touring museums and historical sites, and a host of other activities, including being a "fudgie" on famed Mackinac Island.

Straits Diving's 42-foot charter dive vessel *Rec Diver* in St. Ignace, 1991
(Courtesy Mike Kohut, Recreational Diving Systems, Royal Oak, Michigan)

Beeson's Marine Directory, 1894

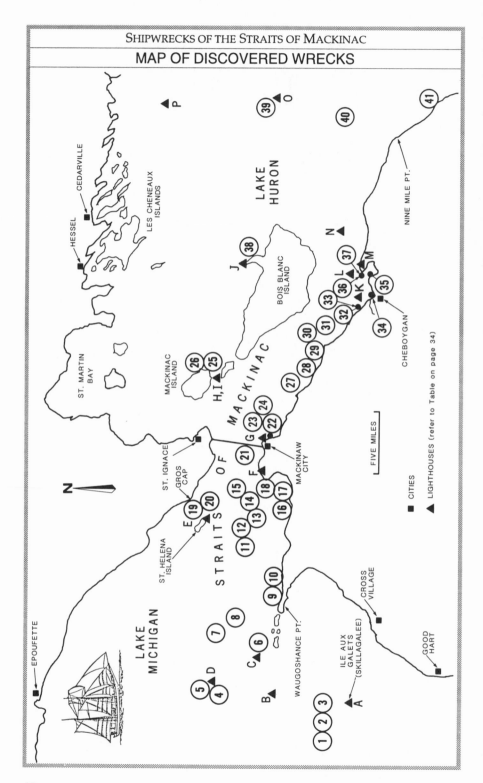

SHIPWRECKS OF THE STRAITS OF MACKINAC

MAP OF DISCOVERED WRECKS

SHIPWRECKS OF THE STRAITS OF MACKINAC

SHIPWRECKS OF THE STRAITS OF MACKINAC

DISCOVERED – BY SITE NUMBER

1	Milwaukee	22	Algomah
2	J. H. Tiffany	23	M. Stalker
3	Cayuga	24	Cedarville
4	Circassian	25	Mackinac Island Harbor Wreck
5	Richard Winslow	26	Peshtigo (propeller)
6	Canisteo	27	William H. Barnum
7	Uganda	28	Henry Clay
8	Colonel Ellsworth	29	Albemarle
9	Anglo Saxon	30	J. H. Outhwaite
10	J. A. Smith	31	St. Andrew
11	Fred McBrier	32	Myrtie M. Ross
12	Maitland	33	L. B. Coates
13	Northwest	34	Landbo
14	Sandusky	35	Islander
15	Eber Ward	36	Leviathan
16	William Stone	37	Genesee Chief
17	George's Wreck	38	Sea Gull
18	Headlands Wreck	39	Spectacle Reef Wreck
19	C. H. Johnson	40	James R. Bentley
20	Chuck's Barge	41	Hammond Bay Harbor Wreck
21	Minneapolis		

See **BY VESSEL NAME** list on following page for detailed information.

63

SHIPWRECKS OF THE STRAITS OF MACKINAC
DISCOVERED – BY VESSEL NAME
(41 Total Discovered)

DISCOVERED AND IDENTIFIED (35 Total)

NAME	SITE	RIG	LENGTH	TONS	BUILT	LOST	CAUSE	DEPTH	LORAN
Albemarle	29	sch	154	413	1867	1867	Stranded	12	31188.7/48183.1
Algomah	22	prop	127	486	1881	1942	Abandoned	NA	31228.0/48127.6
Anglo Saxon	9	sch	134	253	1864	1887	Stranded	12	31309.6/48102.8
C. H. Johnson	19	sch	137	332	1870	1895	Stranded	13	31247.0/48061.7
Canisteo	6	prop	196	856	1862	1880	Collision	15	31341.9/48070.8
Cayuga	3	prop	290	2669	1889	1895	Collision	98	31390.4/48089.8
Cedarville	24	prop	588	8575	1927	1965	Collision	105	31210.7/48130.6
Circassian	4	sch	135	366	1856	1860	Stranded	12	31356.6/48033.7
Colonel Ellsworth	8	sch	137	319	1861	1896	Collision	84	31317.2/48067.7
Eber Ward	15	prop	213	1343	1888	1909	Cut by ice	140	31253.6/48096.7
Fred McBrier	11	prop	161	442	1881	1890	Collision	104	31287.8/48085.3
Genesee Chief	37	sch	142	275	1846	1891	Abandoned	10	31156.9/48227.8
Henry Clay	28	brig	87	163	1842	1850	Stranded	10	31189.7/48183.7
Islander	35	prop	138	210	1895	1942	Abandoned	10	31158.9/48231.3
J. A. Smith	10	sch	138	255	1871	1887	Stranded	12	31309.6/48102.8
J. H. Outhwaite	30	prop	224	1304	1886	1905	Stranded	30	31187.3/48184.3
J. H. Tiffany	2	sch	137	371	1856	1859	Collision	103	31402.0/48081.7
James R. Bentley	40	sch	178	574	1867	1878	Foundered	150	31057.7/48251.1
L. B. Coates	33	sch	116	189	1874	1922	Abandoned	6	31174.2/48219.0
Landbo	34	prop	280	2292	1890	1920	Abandoned	8	31167.7/48227.8
Leviathan	36	prop	126	232	1857	1891	Burned	12	31156.5/48228.0
M. Stalker	23	sch	135	267	1863	1886	Collision	85	31213.6/48125.9
Maitland	12	bark	133	252	1861	1871	Collision	84	31273.1/48092.7
Milwaukee	1	prop	185	616	1853	1859	Collision	96	31407.2/48077.8
Minneapolis	21	prop	226	1072	1873	1894	Cut by ice	124	31226.2/48111.2
Myrtie M. Ross	32	prop	113	156	1890	1916	Abandoned	10	31174.9/48218.8
Northwest	13	sch	223	1017	1873	1898	Cut by ice	73	31270.2/48102.2
Peshtigo	26	prop	203	817	1869	1908	Stranded	10	31176.8/48108.8
Richard Winslow	5	sch	216	885	1871	1898	Foundered	32	31356.4/48026.4
St. Andrew	31	sch	135	425	1857	1878	Collision	61	31180.2/48195.1
Sandusky	14	brig	110	225	1848	1856	Foundered	83	31261.8/48100.9
Sea Gull	38	prop	160	521	1863	1893	Burned	15	31123.7/48158.4
Uganda	7	prop	291	2298	1892	1913	Cut by ice	207	31321.7/48047.2
William H. Barnum	27	prop	218	1212	1873	1894	Foundered	74	31205.5/48158.3
William Stone	16	sch	108	185	1896	1901	Stranded	10	31270.7/48128.2

DISCOVERED BUT NOT IDENTIFIED (6 Total)

NAME	SITE	RIG	LENGTH	DEPTH	LORAN
Chuck's Barge	20	barge	60	43	31255.8/48074.3
George's Wreck	17	sail	100	12	31265.2/48127.3
Hammond Bay Harbor Wreck	41	sail	90	10-12	NA
Headlands Wreck	18	prop	100	15	31252.3/48119.0
Mackinac Island Harbor Wreck	25	sail	95	52	31180.1/48110.1
Spectacle Reef Wreck	39	sail	60	45-70	31038.1/48210.5

ALBEMARLE

Immediately after the Civil War, commerce on the Great Lakes underwent enormous expansion. New sailing vessels were launched daily. The number of registered sailing vessels on the Lakes reached its greatest height in 1868 when the total was 1,855.[1] Fortunes were made in those halcyon days for, with the high freights, good and fast schooners could pay for themselves in one or two seasons.

Mast step in the keelson of the *Albemarle*
(Authors, 1979)

The Winslow brothers of Buffalo, owners of many vessels, did their best to partake of this financial feast. In July 1867, they put into service a brand new three-masted schooner, the *Albemarle*.[2] Outfitted with a scroll figurehead, she joined the great white-winged fleet and began carrying bulk cargos between the upper Lakes and ports on Lake Erie. With luck and good sailors, a vessel of this type might sail in trade for 20 years or better. The *Albemarle* was not so fortunate. Caught in one of the Lakes famous storms of November, she was driven ashore north of Point Au Sable (now Point Nipigon) on November 6, 1867.[3] She had survived less than four months.

Within days of stranding, salvors removed her masts, anchors and other equipment.[4] Attempts to save her that year failed. Salvage efforts continued throughout 1868, and most of her 900-ton cargo of iron ore was recovered.[5] Finally, in March 1869, the owners abandoned her and surrendered her enrollment papers at the Custom House in Buffalo.

Today, the wreck rests in 12 feet of water only 300 feet from the brig *Henry Clay*, and about a quarter mile from the propeller *J. H. Outhwaite*. Divers and snorkelers interested in ship construction should enjoy the broken remains of the schooner *Albemarle*.

Centerboard box on the *Albemarle*
(Authors, 1979)

VESSEL FACTS **Site #29**

NAME:	ALBEMARLE
RIG:	Schooner
OFFICIAL NO.:	1730
GROSS TONS:	413
LENGTH:	154'
HULL:	Wood
BUILT:	1867, Buffalo NY, by Charles L. Bidwell
DATE LOST:	November 6, 1867
CAUSE OF LOSS:	Stranded
LIVES LOST:	None
CARGO:	Iron ore
BOUND FROM/TO:	Escanaba/Cleveland
LAST ENROLLMENT:	July 26, 1867, Buffalo Custom House, # 263
SURRENDERED:	March 16, 1869, Buffalo, "Vessel wrecked"
CONFIGURATION:	1 Deck, 3 Masts, Square Stern, Scroll Head
DEPTH:	12'

WRECK LOCATION

Near Point Nipigon in Lake Huron, 9.4 miles, 123 degrees from Old Mackinac Point.

LORAN: 31188.7/48183.1   LAT/LON: 45 42 57/84 33 50

WRECK CONDITION AND FEATURES

The *Albemarle* is broken up. Some ribs and hull planking are standing. The centerboard box stands upright and is intact (see photo on page 66). Mast steps are visible in the keelson (see photo on page 65). Divers will find this wreck good for studying keel and keelson structure and the attachment of the centerboard box to the keelson. Some iron ore cargo is still present. Ice is gradually destroying the wreck.

ALGOMAH

Algomah as a ferry c.1885
(Courtesy Institute for Great Lakes Research, Bowling Green State University)

The *Algomah* was built by the Detroit Dry Dock Company for the Mackinac Transportation Company in 1881 specifically for transporting freight across the Straits of Mackinac.[1] She was the first vessel to offer scheduled ferry service across the Straits. Rail cars on one side of the Straits were unloaded and the freight was then loaded onto the *Algomah*. Once across the Straits, the cargo was off-loaded to rail cars on the other side. Later the *Algomah* towed a barge that

Algomah as a barge at Cheboygan in 1942
(Courtesy Institute for Great Lakes Research, Bowling Green State University)

Algomah sunk at Cheboygan c.1944
(Courtesy William C. Duman)

could carry four rail cars, thus eliminating the time-consuming process of unloading and reloading the cars.

In 1888, the *Algomah* was replaced by the propeller *St. Ignace*, which had a capacity of ten rail cars.[2] The *Algomah* then provided ferry service to Mackinac Island until 1936 when she was retired. She also provided part-time ice-breaker service in the wintertime. During most of this time, the captain of the *Algomah* was William

Algomah (top left) sunk at Mackinaw City c.1945
(Reprinted from "Memories of Mackinaw," courtesy Nancy Campbell)

Schepler of Mackinaw City.[3] Upon retirement, the *Algomah* was cut down to a barge and tied up at the Cheboygan docks.

Sometime after July 10, 1942, she sank at the dock but was raised in December 1944, and towed to Mackinaw City in an effort to clear the Cheboygan Harbor. Here, she was filled with stone and sunk to form the breakwall at the end of what is now Shepler's ferry dock. Captain William Shepler, Jr., founded the ferry service in 1947. Today, Shepler's ferry boats load and unload their passengers over the grave of the very first vessel to provide scheduled ferry service across the Straits.

SPECIAL 3 DAY

Excursion
MACKINAW CITY
—TO—
MACKINAC ISLAND
—VIA—
Steamer Algomah
Saturday, June 1

Sunday, June 2   Monday, June 3

Fare–Round Trip 75c

Children 40c

3 Day Schedule—Eastern Standard Time.
Leave Mackinaw City 9:15 a. m., 11:20 a. m.
1:45 p. m. and 6:00 p.m.
Returning, Leave Mackinac Island 10:30 a. m.
12:30 noon, 4:30 p. m. and 8:20 p. m.

TICKETS GOOD FOR ONE DAY

Island Transportation Co.

Algomah excursion ad c.1935
(Courtesy William C. Duman)

Henry Ford (age 17) as a Detroit Dry Dock Company apprentice in 1880 *(Courtesy Edison Institute)*

Interestingly, the renowned Henry Ford helped build and install the engine in the *Algomah* when he worked as an apprentice machinist at the Detroit Dry Dock Company.[4] When she was retired in 1936, he acquired the engine for the Henry Ford Museum in Dearborn, Michigan.

VESSEL FACTS	Site #22
NAME:	ALGOMAH
RIG:	Propeller
OFFICIAL NO.:	106022
GROSS TONS:	486
LENGTH:	127'
HULL:	Wood
BUILT:	1881, Detroit, Detroit Dry Dock Company
DATE LOST:	After July 10, 1942
CAUSE OF LOSS:	Abandoned
LIVES LOST:	None
CARGO:	None
BOUND FROM/TO:	At Shepler dock, Mackinaw City
LAST ENROLLMENT:	March 7, 1941, Port Huron Custom House, #21
SURRENDERED:	September 7, 1944, Pt. Huron, "Out of documenta."
CONFIGURATION:	1 Deck, 1 Mast, Plain Head, Round Stern
DEPTH:	Not applicable

WRECK LOCATION

Buried beneath the Shepler ferry dock at the foot of Central Avenue in Mackinaw City.

LORAN: 31228.0/48127.6   LAT/LON: 45 46 88/84 43 27

WRECK CONDITION AND FEATURES

Not applicable. The *Algomah* is not accessible to divers, as she is buried under the Shepler dock at Mackinaw City.

ANGLO SAXON

A long the shoreline of Lake Michigan about ten miles west of Mackinaw City, is an unique place known as *La Way Settlement*. It sits at the western edge of Big Stone Bay on Lake Michigan. Here reside the descendants and relatives of the famed Captain Edward J. LaWay. His family settled this spot in 1885 when Captain LaWay was only seven years old. He died in 1974 at the age of 96. He spent

Captain Edward J. LaWay
(Reprinted from "Memories of Mackinaw," courtesy Nancy Campbell)

his lifetime on the water and, for a while, was a hard-hat salvage diver. Captain LaWay was renowned in the Straits area for his seamanship and knowledge of local waters.[1]

As a nine-year-old boy, Captain LaWay observed the sinking of the schooners *Anglo Saxon* and *J. A. Smith*. They stranded about three miles west of his home on September 8, 1887.[2] The *Anglo Saxon* broke apart, and Captain LaWay stated that he could paddle a rowboat through the openings in the ship. In later years, he and his father salvaged iron stock from the wreck for use in making logging sleighs. They sold some of the material to a blacksmith in Harbor Springs for one-half cent a pound.[3]

The *Anglo Saxon* and *J. A. Smith* were left at anchor off Waugoshance Point while their tow ship, the propeller *Mattawan*, returned to Cheboygan for coaling up. When a storm arose, the vessels broke loose and went ashore. The *Anglo Saxon* went to pieces quickly.[4] The *J. A. Smith* (story on page 118) fared slightly better. The *Anglo Saxon* was built in 1864 at Port Dalhousie, Ontario, and was registered Canadian.[5] From 1867 through 1874, she sailed under the U. S. Flag and was then reregistered Canadian.[6]

VESSEL FACTS **Site #9**

NAME:	ANGLO SAXON
RIG:	Schooner
OFFICIAL NO.:	71213 (Canadian), 374 (U.S.)
GROSS TONS:	253
LENGTH:	134'
HULL:	Wood
BUILT:	1864, Pt. Dalhousie ON, Donaldson & Andrews
DATE LOST:	September 8, 1887
CAUSE OF LOSS:	Stranded
LIVES LOST:	None
CARGO:	Cedar Wood
BOUND FROM/TO:	Cockburn Island/Chicago
LAST ENROLLMENT:	September 22, 1880, Sarnia Custom House, #3
SURRENDERED:	December 31, 1909, Sarnia, "Out of existence"
CONFIGURATION:	1 Deck, 2 Masts, Square Stern, Plain Stem
DEPTH:	12'

WRECK LOCATION

In Lake Michigan, 12.3 miles, 260 degrees from Old Mackinac Point.
LORAN: 31309.6/48102.8   LAT/LON: 45 45 24/84 57 25

WRECK CONDITION AND FEATURES

The *Anglo Saxon* is completely broken up. Only scattered timbers remain. The wreckage is mingled with that of the schooner *J. A. Smith*. Divers will find very little of interest to see in this wreckage.

73

C. H. JOHNSON

St. Helena Island lies about ten miles west of the Mackinac Bridge near the north shore of the Upper Peninsula of Michigan. In the mid-1800s, it was inhabited by a colony of fisherman who built homes and a dock on the north side of the Island. Sailing vessels made an occasional stop to pick up fresh fish. St. Helena served another useful purpose, for it represented an excellent anchorage for vessels waiting out storms blowing from the south and southwest.[1]

Jeri Feltner measures stone block on the *C. H. Johnson*.
(Authors, 1981)

During a particularly strong southwest gale in late September of 1895, Captain Hiram Henderson of the schooner *C. H. Johnson*, decided to take advantage of the protection offered by St. Helena. He was on his way to Chicago with a load of sandstone blocks from Jacobsville in the Lake Superior redstone district on the Keweenaw

Peninsula.[2] The stones were to be used in the construction of a bank building in Chicago and, as the owner of the *Johnson*, he was eager to deliver his cargo and get back to his home port of Cleveland before winter set in. Nevertheless, the prudent action seemed to be to drop anchor and wait out the storm.

At two o'clock in the morning, the anchor chain broke and the *C. H. Johnson* was swept onto the north shore at Gros Cap. Within minutes the 35-year-old wooden schooner began to break up. Captain Henderson and his crew tried to launch their yawl boat, but it was swamped and sank. In desperation, they fired a distress gun that fortunately was heard by a local fisherman named Ambrose Corp,[3] who, with his two sons, set out in their fishing boat to rescue the crew from the rapidly deteriorating schooner. They nearly lost their lives in the attempt, but finally took them all on board and reached the shore. According to a newspaper "The woman cook was nearly dead with cold and fright and had leaped into the fishing boat half naked. The sailors lost all they possessed."[4]

Today the windlass from the *C. H. Johnson* sits on display in a small maritime park along the waterfront in St. Ignace. To our knowledge, none of the large stone blocks have been removed from the wreck. They are about eight feet long, four feet wide and two feet

C. H. Johnson windlass at St. Ignace waterfront park
(Authors, 1979)

75

thick, and are one of the more interesting cargos we have seen. Somewhere between St. Helena and the north shore, there are probably one or more large wooden stock anchors yet to be found.

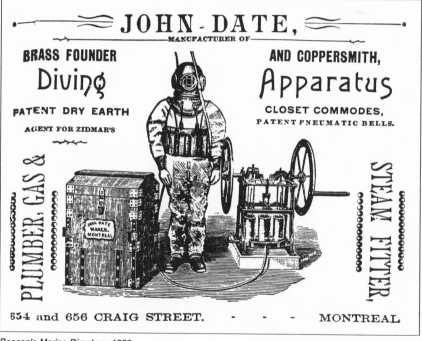

Beeson's Marine Directory, 1890

C. H. Johnson Certificate of Enrollment, 1892 *(Courtesy U.S. National Archives)*

VESSEL FACTS	Site #19
NAME:	C. H. JOHNSON
RIG:	Schooner
OFFICIAL NO.:	5833
GROSS TONS:	332
LENGTH:	137'
HULL:	Wood
BUILT:	1870, Marine City MI, by William Morley
DATE LOST:	September 23, 1895
CAUSE OF LOSS:	Stranded
LIVES LOST:	None
CARGO:	Stone Blocks
BOUND FROM/TO:	Portage Entry (Lake Superior)/Chicago
LAST ENROLLMENT:	April 4, 1892, Cleveland Custom House, #72
SURRENDERED:	September 26, 1895, Cleveland, "Vessel lost"
CONFIGURATION:	1 Deck, 3 Masts, Square Stern, Plain Stem
DEPTH:	13'

WRECK LOCATION

In Lake Michigan, 9 miles, 320 degrees from Old Mackinac Point.

LORAN: 31247.0/48061.7   LAT/LON: 45 52 20/84 50 08

WRECK CONDITION AND FEATURES

The *C. H. Johnson* is broken up. The keelson and most of the ribs are still present. Fifteen to 20 stone blocks (8' x 4' x 2') hold the remains of the hull in place. The wreck usually has lots of fish around it. This is a very good dive for novice divers and the wreck can be reached from shore.

CANISTEO

At the western end of the Straits of Mackinac lie some of the most treacherous reefs on the Great Lakes. Vessels coming down Lake Michigan must traverse a narrow course between Grays Reef

Waugoshance Lighthouse
(Authors, 1979)

and the numerous shoals off the tip of Waugoshance Island before making a right hand turn into the main channel. Until 1891,[1] when lightships were put in place on Grays Reef and White Shoals, the only aid to navigation through this area was the Waugoshance Light. It was established in 1851 and abandoned in 1912. The sailors of the day referred to it as "Wobbleshanks." During World War II, the U.S. Navy used it as a target for dive bombing practice.

Literally hundreds of vessels suffered either groundings or collisions as they made a "Grays Reef passage" by Waugoshance Light. Keepers of the Lighthouse kept journals of all wrecks occurring in its vicinity. The propeller *Canisteo* made her way into the *Waugoshance Journal* as a result of a collision with the schooner *George Murray*. The following entry, with its quaint spellings, was copied from the original *Journal* housed at the Great Lakes Historical Society Library in Vermilion, Ohio:[2]

"October 14, 1880: U. S. American Propeller. *Geo. Blackman,* Master. Crew and Passengers 22. Cargo 15,000 bushels Corn, Flaxseed, Flour and Lard. From Chicago, Ill. to Buffalo, N. Y. None lost. The propeller *Canisteo* of Buffalo, belonging to the U. S. Boat Co. Collided with a Sail Vessel opposite the Station at 3:30 a.m. The Captain run hur a shore close to the station and was seen by the 1st Asst. at 3:40 a.m. who being on watch at the time. The steamer lay about 800 feet to the North East of Station and was sunk in 18 feet of water. As soon as daylight the 1st Mate and part of the crew came to Station and asked to have one of the Keepers go along with him to Cheboygan for a Tug. His request was granted and the Second Asst. Mate and four of the crew started for Cheboygan. During the day the Captain and all of the Crew came to the Station and we rendered all possible assistance to make them comfortable. The Second Asst. and Mate returned with the Tug *Winslow* at 6 p. m. The Capt and Crew left Station on board the *Winslow* for Mackinaw. The weather being to ruff to Work at wreck. Blowing a Gale from S.W. The Steamer is gone to pieces, the cargo is all lost. Nothing remains to be seen but part of hur engine above water. The Steamer was built in 1862 and lost on the 16th October 1880."

All the keeper's entries were not correct, as the *Canisteo* actually was owned by the Union Steamboat Company.[3] The storm that tore the *Canisteo* to pieces on October 16, 1880, was one of the worst of the century, with over 90 ships wrecked and 118 lives lost. The steamer *Alpena* went down in Lake Michigan with the loss of 60 lives.[4]

For weeks after the loss of the *Canisteo*, residents of the Straits area salvaged barrels of lard that floated from the wreckage. Insurance underwriters tried to recover this cargo, but the residents successfully hid it from them.[5] Starting in 1881, salvors attempted to remove the steam engine from the wreck. Finally in August 1884, John Dodd, a hard-hat diver, succeeded in recovering her machinery.[6]

Based on research we did in 1980, we knew the approximate position of the wreck. But we never took the time to search for it until the summer of 1988. We actually located the wreck from the air with Mike Kohut of Recreational Diving Systems, Royal Oak, Michigan, as our pilot. It is interesting to note that the wreck sits about 3,000 feet east of where it originally sank. We surmise that the heavy ice pushed the wreck eastward to its current location.

VESSEL FACTS **Site #6**

NAME:	CANISTEO
RIG:	Propeller
OFFICIAL NO.:	4394
GROSS TONS:	856
LENGTH:	196'
HULL:	Wood
BUILT:	1862, Buffalo NY, by Mason & Bidwell
DATE LOST:	October 14, 1880
CAUSE OF LOSS:	Collision
LIVES LOST:	None
CARGO:	Corn and lard
BOUND FROM/TO:	Chicago/Buffalo
LAST ENROLLMENT:	April 6, 1876, Buffalo Custom House, #41
SURRENDERED:	June 22, 1881, Buffalo, "Total loss"
CONFIGURATION:	2 Decks, 1 Mast, Round Stern, Plain Stem
DEPTH:	15'

WRECK LOCATION

In Lake Michigan, about .6 miles east of Waugoshance Light.

LORAN: 31341.9/48070.8   LAT/LON: 45 47 32/85 04 75

WRECK CONDITION AND FEATURES

The *Canisteo* is broken up with some of the hull remaining. The wreckage measures 143 feet in length, much of it having been ground up by ice. The engine and other gear were salvaged from the wreck, so there is no machinery to see. The mounting platform for the engine is still intact. Double ribs were used in the construction of this vessel. The keel and several longitudinal stringers are of interest. This wreck is an excellent dive for novices. However, because of its remote location, the wreck does not merit the long boat ride. If you dive the *Cayuga* or the *Colonel Ellsworth,* you might consider stopping to dive the *Canisteo* on your return to port.

CAYUGA

Painting of the *Cayuga* by Rev. Edward J. Dowling, S.J.
(Courtesy Great Lakes Marine Collection, Milwaukee Public Library)

Hard-hat diving began on the Great Lakes as early as 1850,[1] shortly after the invention of the hard-hat diving suit by Augustus Siebe in England in 1839.[2] By the 1870s, sunken vessels over 200 feet long were being raised by "submarine divers" from depths of over 100 feet. Advertisements for submarine diver services became commonplace.[3] Their activities were followed with intense interest, as they were viewed as adventurous men who were exploring an exciting new world.

Submarine divers were a rare breed. Their occupation not only required excellence in a set of definable skills, but it also demanded a quality that defied simple explanation. In the words of contemporary author Tom Wolfe, they all had what might be termed *The Right Stuff.*[4] This enigmatic quality was possessed by a few valiant men who lived the epic times of early Great Lakes shipwreck diving.

Captain James Reid was one of those who reached the upper ledges of the ziggurat of the brotherhood of submarine divers. His first salvage job was on the barge *Plymouth* that had stranded in the Straits of Mackinac in 1876. Soon afterward, he formed the Reid Towing and Wrecking Company, and through risk taking and hard work, built the finest salvage and wrecking business extant on the Great Lakes in the latter half of the nineteenth century.[5] His fearlessness and resourcefulness in salvaging and recovering sunken vessels became legend. His successes were many — some were considered impossible. But, he had his failures. His unsuccessful attempt to raise the propeller *Cayuga* was James Reid's one great failure.

The *Cayuga* sank in a collision with the old and decrepit wooden propeller *Joseph L. Hurd*. The two vessels collided in Lake Michigan south of Grays Reef Light on May 10, 1895.[6] It was 3 a.m. and a dense fog hung over the water. The *Hurd* struck the *Cayuga* on the starboard side and tore a large hole in her hull below the water line. The *Cayuga* sank in 25 minutes in 100 feet of water. Even with 15 feet of her bow section torn away, the *Hurd* stayed afloat and

MARINE

AGAIN THE CAYUGA.

JIM REID TO TOW UP FOUR PONTOONS, MAKING EIGHT IN ALL.

With These and the Inflated Boilers and Bottom He Expects Success.

Chicago, May 5.—The wrecking tug Protector, owned by Capt. James Reid, of Bay City, is now in port making up a tow of pontoons for the wrecking of the Lehigh Valley liner Cayuga, which was sunk by collision near Skillagalee light, in the Straits of Mackinaw. The pontoons are built of one-half-inch steel plates, and measure 34 feet in length by 18 feet in diameter. They are slightly conical on the ends, and are heavily braced within by angle irons and cross timbers. There are four pontoons here and there are four others, slightly smaller, which are now fastened to the Cayuga, having been placed there last fall. It is thought the lifting power of each pontoon will be about 200 tons, so that with all eight there is a combined power of 1,500 tons, at least. In addition the water bottom of the Cayuga is filled with air, and the boilers are to be utilized in a similar manner.

If the Cayuga is raised in this manner it will be one of the most wonderful wrecking jobs ever heard of, for, in addition to the task of lifting this enormous weight, the steamer lies on her side, and in 100 feet of water, which makes it very difficult for divers to work. Wreckers all over the country have their eyes on Capt. Reid, and if the project is successful there will be endless jobs for the pontoons. It is thought the Protector will leave with her strange tow in a day or two. The work of raising the steamer will be resumed at once.

Detroit Free Press, May 6, 1897

83

Pontoons at Cheboygan used in attempt to raise the *Cayuga*
(Courtesy Ralph Roberts Collection)

was later towed into Harbor Springs, Michigan (see photo on page 234).[7]

Shortly after her sinking, bids were sought by the insurance company for the recovery of the *Cayuga*.[8] Marine experts said that Lake wreckers were unequal to the task of raising the *Cayuga*. They supported their view with two basic arguments.[9] First, the largest vessel ever recovered from this depth lay in protected waters and weighed less than one-half the weight of the *Cayuga*. The task was further complicated because the *Cayuga* rested almost all the way over on her port side and would have to be righted before she was

Tug *Protector* with barge and pontoon over *Cayuga*
(Courtesy Great Lakes Historical Society)

lifted. Secondly, no lifting equipment large enough to raise the *Cayuga* had ever been built, let alone tried out, on the Great Lakes.

In the face of this challenge, no reasonable bids were received by the insurance company for the recovery of the *Cayuga*. The summer of 1895 dragged on, and the underwriters had all but resigned themselves to abandoning the wreck. Then, on September 6, they dramatically announced that a contract had been signed with the Reid Towing and Wrecking Company of Bay City, Michigan, to raise the *Cayuga*.[10] True to form, James Reid had dared to achieve what no other salvage diver had been able to accomplish before him.

Reid's plan for raising the wreck called for using eight large air-filled steel pontoons (attached to the wreck) and a barge to raise the *Cayuga* a few feet off the bottom and then tow it to shallow water where it could be repaired and refloated.[11] With passion and relentlessness, he pursued this plan to no avail from 1895 through 1899. In the interim, one hard-hat diver lost his life and four others were

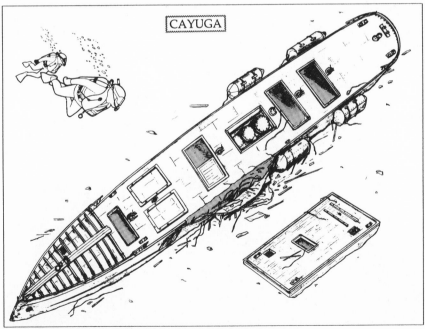

Underwater drawing of the *Cayuga*
(Copyright © 1981 Chuck & Jeri Feltner)

seriously injured, including Reid himself who suffered a serious case of the "bends."[12] The costs almost bankrupted his company.

In 1900, Reid accepted defeat and abandoned the salvage of the Cayuga.[13] He went on to other wrecking jobs, almost all of which were successful. He died in 1913 and was buried outside Sarnia, Ontario. No other attempts were made by anyone to raise the vessel. The wreck was relocated by John Steele of Waukegan, Illinois, in the early 1970s.

We dove this wreck extensively and did some filming and survey work (see drawing on page 85). The wreck lies over on its port side at an angle of about 40 degrees from the horizontal, and the spar deck at midships has a considerable sag to it. As you swim around the bow from the starboard side, a fine brass porthole swings freely in its mount when touched. Close by, and about 20 feet aft of the bow, you encounter the hole punched in the Cayuga's hull when she was rammed by the oncoming Hurd. The hull is easily penetrated and the engines and boiler provide lots of fascination to those mechanically inclined.

One of the most eerie sights on the wreck is the steel pontoons left there by Reid. Giant cables, as thick as a man's forearm, still bind them to the wreck. As you swim around these pontoons at depths of 90 feet or better, your mind readily slips backward to the turn of the century. At any moment you expect to encounter the ghost of James

Onboard the *Gemini II*, Paul Horn, Ted Sledz and Chuck Feltner after diving the *Cayuga* (Authors, 1979)

Reid, garbed in his hard-hat diving gear, making one final and desperate attempt to raise the *Cayuga.*

VESSEL FACTS	Site #3
NAME:	CAYUGA
RIG:	Propeller
OFFICIAL NO.:	126556
GROSS TONS:	2,669
LENGTH:	290'
HULL:	Steel
BUILT:	1889, Cleveland OH, by Globe Iron Works
DATE LOST:	May 10, 1895
CAUSE OF LOSS:	Collision
LIVES LOST:	None
CARGO:	Flour and grain
BOUND FROM/TO:	Milwaukee/Buffalo
LAST ENROLLMENT:	June 3, 1889, Buffalo Custom House, #72
SURRENDERED:	June 29, 1895, Buffalo, "Lost"
CONFIGURATION:	2 Decks, 4 Masts, Round Stern, Plain Stem
DEPTH:	98'

WRECK LOCATION

In Lake Michigan, 3.6 miles, 209 degrees from Grays Reef Light.

LORAN: 31390.4/48089.8   LAT/LON: 45 43 07/85 11 16

WRECK CONDITION AND FEATURES

The *Cayuga* is upright and intact. She has about a 40-degree list to the port side. All the cabins are gone and the port midsection is somewhat broken up. She is a double-decked vessel with the main deck at a depth of about 70 feet. The wreck is easily penetrable. Spare propeller blades are stored aft on her lower deck. The machinery includes a three-cylinder (24", 38" and 61" bores and 42" stroke), triple-expansion steam engine (1,500 HP at 85 RPM) and three scotch-type boilers (11' 10" D x 12' L). The starboard bow has a large collision gash. A 75-foot-long deck barge, sunk during the salvage operations, lies about 40 feet off the port midsection. Lore has it that a hard-hat diver was trapped under the barge when it sank. We have not found any evidence to confirm this suppostion. Four large "canalons" (pontoons) used in the salvage operations are still attached to the aft section of the hull. The *Cayuga* is truly one of the most exciting and unusual dive sites on the Great Lakes.

JAMES REID, President.   J. T. REID, Secretary.   W. H. REID, Treas. and Asst. Mgr.

THE REID WRECKING COMPANY, LTD.

OF

SARNIA, ONT., and PORT HURON, MICH.

WRECKING CONTRACTORS

Raft Towing, Sub-Marine Work

Divers, First-Class Tugs, American and Canadian Steam Pumps, Hawsers, Hydraulic Jacks and Lighters, etc.

WAREHOUSE AND GENERAL OFFICES

ON DOCKS, FOOT OF CROMWELL STREET

Beeson's Marine Directory, 1895

CEDARVILLE

Cedarville
(Courtesy Great Lakes Marine Collection, Milwaukee Public Library)

For all the pleasure the wreck of the propeller *Cedarville* has brought to the sport diving community, back in 1965 it brought much pain to the people of Rogers City, Michigan. On May 7, 1965, the *Cedarville* sank after a collision in a dense fog with the Norwegian freighter *Topdalsfjord*. Ten crewmen of the *Cedarville*, nine of them from Rogers City, died in the accident. Only seven years earlier, the same city was in mourning for the dead crewmen of the *Carl D. Bradley*, a sister ship of the *Cedarville*, which sank during a violent storm on Lake Michigan with the loss of 33 lives.[1] The two wrecks combined left over 80 children in Rogers City fatherless. In the case of the *Cedarville*, the grief endured by those who lost their loved ones was intensified by the knowledge that the sinking was a marine disaster that never should have occurred. Her loss was truly a tragedy.

On May 7, 1965, at 5:01 a.m., the *Cedarville* departed Calcite, Michigan, near Rogers City, enroute to Gary, Indiana, with 14,411 tons of limestone and a crew of 35, including the master, Captain Martin Joppich. After clearing the harbor at Calcite, the *Cedarville* proceeded toward the Straits of Mackinac in light fog at full speed. Reports indicated that the fog was much denser in the vicinity of the Mackinac Bridge.

About three miles from the Bridge, radio communication was established with the German vessel *Weissenberg* which was headed eastward in the Mackinac Bridge channel. A port-to-port passing arrangement was made, but confirming whistle signals were not sounded. Third mate Charles Cook manned his radar set while wheelsman Leonard T. Gabrysiak watched his compass intently. The visibility had dropped under 1,000 feet. As the tension mounted, the lookout on the *Cedarville* reported fog signals underway from the relative direction of the Mackinac Bridge.

At 9:38 a.m., the *Weissenberg* passed under the Bridge and reported to the *Cedarville* that there was a Norwegian vessel ahead of the *Weissenberg*. This came as a jolting surprise to Captain Joppich, for he had assumed that the closest target on his radar screen was the *Weissenberg* with which he had been communicating. Earlier he had spoken with the freighter *Steinbrenner,* which was running well ahead of him and been informed of a vessel that wouldn't answer by radio or whistle blast. Frantically, Captain Joppich tried to raise the *mystery* vessel on his radio. His efforts were of no avail for no answer was received. Captain Joppich was faced with the stark reality that close at hand and bearing down on him in a dense fog was a *mystery* vessel with which he could not establish communication.

Captain Joppich immediately reduced his speed and ordered a 20-degree turn to starboard. Third mate Cook looked up from his radar screen and reported the *mystery* vessel dead ahead. Terror gripped the faces of those in the pilot house. Suddenly the lookout on the bow shouted, "there she is." Wheelsman Gabrysiak spotted the bow of the Norwegian vessel only about 100 feet off his port bow. It was obvious to everyone in the *Cedarville's* pilot house that a collision was only an instant away. Joppich ordered the helm hard-to-starboard and full-speed ahead on the engines. As the *Cedarville's* bow passed ahead of the *mystery* vessel's bow, Joppich ordered the helm hard-to-port in a last desperate effort to swing the stern clear. But it was too late. The Norwegian vessel crashed into the port side of the *Cedarville*, cutting a deep gash in her side between the seventh and eighth hatch. For a brief moment, the *mystery* vessel's bow was imbedded in the *Cedarville's* side. Then, in the dense fog, they separated and disappeared from each other's sight.

Following the collision, Captain Joppich stopped the *Cedarville's* engines, sounded the general alarm, broadcast a *MAYDAY* message, and dropped the port anchor. First mate Harry Piechan reported to the bridge that they were taking a tremendous amount of water in No. 2 hold, and that efforts to cover the hole in the hull with the emergency collision tarpaulin were useless due to the size of the hole. An angry Captain Joppich radioed the *Weissenberg* asking for the name of the Norwegian vessel that struck him such a mortal blow. Back came the answer "the *Topdalsfjord.*"

Recognizing that his vessel was doomed, Joppich raised the anchor and attempted to beach the *Cedarville* at Mackinaw City. The time was 10:10 a.m. He set a course of 140 degrees, instructed the *Weissenberg* to stay out of his way, and continued to transmit *MAYDAY* messages. At 10:25 a.m., the *Cedarville*, with little freeboard remaining, suddenly rolled over to starboard and sank in 105 feet of water about 3.5 miles southeast of the center of the Mackinac Bridge. The distance traveled from the point of collision to the point of sinking was 2.3 miles. The distance remaining to the beach was two miles. Ironically, the distance from the point of collision to the shallow water of Graham Shoal was only one mile, while that to Old Mackinac Point was but 2.2 miles. The selection of the course for beaching the vessel proved to be the last fatal mistake in the tragedy of the *Cedarville*.

In the sinking, most of the crew were thrown into the water. Third mate Charles Cook was last seen attempting to don a life preserver in the wheelhouse. Chief engineer Donald Lamp, oiler Hugo Wingo and stokerman Eugene Jones, stayed at their posts in the engine room. In all, 27 crew members were picked up by life boats from the *Weissenberg*, which had followed the *Cedarville* by radar after hearing her *MAYDAY* call. Deck watchman Edmund Jungman was dead from drowning when brought aboard the *Weissenberg*, and wheelsman

Stanley Haske died shortly afterward from shock and exposure. The survivors were transferred to the U.S. Coast Guard cutter *Mackinaw*, which delivered them to the old State ferry dock in Mackinaw City.[2]

Cedarville survivors at Mackinaw City in 1965
(Courtesy Dave Rogers, Bay City Times)

Within a few days after the sinking, the bodies of five of the eight missing crewmen were recovered. The three unrecovered bodies were those of third mate Charles Cook, oiler Hugo Wingo and stokerman Eugene Jones. A year later, in 1966, scuba diver John Steele of Waukegan, Illinois, found the body of Charles Cook lying on the bottom about 200 feet off the wreck. The partial remains of one of the others was also reported near the wreck in 1976. One body is still missing.

As a dive site, the *Cedarville* has much to offer. The upper portion of her hull reaches to within 35 feet of the surface. The superstructure and the cabins can be reached at about 75 feet and a full exploration can be made at a maximum depth of about 105 feet. Most divers enjoy visiting the inside of the cabins on the bow and stern. If you like real adventure and have the experience to match, you can penetrate the engine room from a door in the side of the hull at the port stern. To be sure you are on the right wreck, visit the transom area of the stern or the side of the hull up in the bow area and there you will find the name *"Cedarville"* painted on the hull. At 588 feet in length, the wreck is indeed an awesome sight underwater.

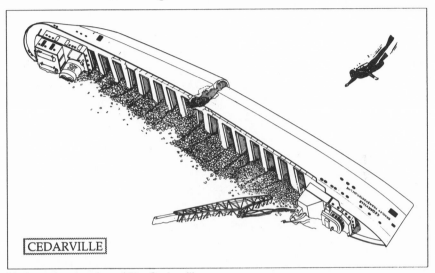

Underwater drawing of the *Cedarville*
(Copyright © 1981 Chuck & Jeri Feltner)

Chuck & Jeri Feltner prepare to dive the *Cedarville*
(Photo by Paul Horn, 1980)

93

VESSEL FACTS	Site #24
NAME:	CEDARVILLE
RIG:	Propeller
OFFICIAL NO.:	226492
GROSS TONS:	8,575
LENGTH:	588'
HULL:	Steel
BUILT:	1927, River Rouge MI, Great Lakes Engrg. Works
DATE LOST:	May 7, 1965
CAUSE OF LOSS:	Collision
LIVES LOST:	10
CARGO:	Limestone
BOUND FROM/TO:	Calcite/Gary
LAST ENROLLMENT:	January 22, 1964, New York, #178
SURRENDERED:	June 28, 1965, N.Y., "Vessel sank May 7, 1965"
CONFIGURATION:	1 Deck, 2 Masts, Round Stern, Curved Stem
DEPTH:	105'

WRECK LOCATION

In Lake Huron, 2.8 miles, 89 degrees from Old Mackinac Point.

LORAN: 31210.7/48130.6   LAT/LON: 45 47 13/84 40 13

WRECK CONDITION AND FEATURES

The *Cedarville* is intact and lying on her starboard side about 45 degrees from being upside down. The large gash from the collision is between the seventh and eighth hatch. Experienced divers will find the cabins on the bow and stern very interesting and enjoyable to explore. The vessel name is clearly discernible on the port bow and across the stern transom. A door on the port stern of the hull leads into the engine room. Extreme caution should be exercised by divers attempting to explore this compartment, as it is very confusing (almost inverted), heavily silted and littered with debris. The propeller has been cut off and lies on the bottom beneath the propeller shaft. Virtually everything of value has been salvaged from the wreck. Nevertheless, the *Cedarville* has been, and will continue to be, one of the most popular dive sites in the Straits.

CIRCASSIAN

In late November 1860, the schooner *Circassian* stranded on White Shoals in Lake Michigan during a gale accompanied by a blinding snow storm.[1] Shortly afterwards, several passing vessels reported seeing the stranded wreck with no one aboard. Since no survivors had been picked up, it was assumed that the crew had perished.[2] Twelve days later they were discovered alive on Hog Island ten miles west of White Shoals.[3]

The crew suffered considerable hardship. They had stranded about eleven o'clock at night, and every wave made a clean breach over the vessel as she pounded on the rocks. During the night, the vessel broke in two amidships. At daylight, the yawl boat was hauled alongside and the captain and crew embarked without saving any of their belongings. They rowed to Hog Island, part of the Beaver Island archipelago, and came ashore in deep snow. After walking for two miles in a bitter freezing rain, they reached a fisherman's hut and were given aid.[4] By Christmas, all vestiges of the wreck had disappeared.[5]

The *Circassian* had been purchased by William Washburn of Chicago on the very day she departed on her fatal voyage.[6]

WALTER V. METCALF,
Submarine ✦ Diver.

Contracts for Submarine work of all kinds where Divers are required; such as preparing Foundations for Piers, Abutments, Wharves, Dams, etc,. Submarine Drilling, Blasting, Removing Obstructions, and Recovering Sunken Property.

V. O. TUG OFFICE.
Main Street Bridge,   CLEVELAND, O.
TELEPHONE No. 409.

Beeson's Marine Directory, 1884

95

VESSEL FACTS	**Site #4**
NAME:	CIRCASSIAN
RIG:	Schooner
OFFICIAL NO.:	None
GROSS TONS:	366 (BOM)
LENGTH:	135'
HULL:	Wood
BUILT:	1856, Irving NY, by Charles Stevens
DATE LOST:	November 22, 1860
CAUSE OF LOSS:	Stranded
LIVES LOST:	None
CARGO:	Grain
BOUND FROM/TO:	Chicago/Buffalo
LAST ENROLLMENT:	November 20, 1860, Chicago Custom House, #90
SURRENDERED:	No endorsement
CONFIGURATION:	1 Deck, 2 Masts, Square Stern, Plain Stem
DEPTH:	12'

WRECK LOCATION

In Lake Michigan on White Shoals, 1.1 miles, 242 degrees from White Shoals Light.

LORAN: 31356.6/48033.7   LAT/LON: 45 50 09/85 09 22

WRECK CONDITION AND FEATURES

The *Circassian* is completely broken up. This wreck has been ground up by the ice and what remains offers little of interest to divers. Additionally, this wreck has been scavenged for years by divers seeking shipwreck wood for furniture making.

COLONEL ELLSWORTH

A few Great Lakes sailing vessels seemed to lead charmed lives, forever escaping a multitude of destructive forces always at work to turn them into a shipwreck. The schooner *Colonel Ellsworth*, who survived numerous mishaps and non-fatal casualties in her 35 years, was one of those. On December 1, 1867, loaded with lumber, she ran aground in Thunder Bay near Alpena, Michigan, in a blinding snowstorm.[1] Because of inclement weather and the closing in of winter, she was left there on the beach until the following spring. In April 1868, she was released and brought to Clark's Dry Dock in Detroit for a thorough overhauling.[2]

By the late fall of the same year, the *Ellsworth* was in trouble again. This time she ran upon a reef near Forty Mile Point in Lake Huron carrying a full load of coal. After much difficulty, she freed herself and proceeded to Chicago with the help of a steam pump she picked up at Cheboygan, Michigan.[3] She was involved in a minor collision with another vessel near Green Bay, Wisconsin, in May 1870.[4]

The *Ellsworth's* next brush with disaster occurred June 8, 1872, when loaded with 21,665 bushels of corn from Chicago, she ran aground and sank in shallow water about a quarter of a mile west of Point Abino, Ontario, on Lake Erie.[5] The wet corn cargo swelled and warped her decks upward. The cargo had to be off-loaded to keep the *Ellsworth* from literally bursting apart. She was finally released and towed to Detroit for repairs.[6] Yet another accident happened in September 1875, when she ran ashore near Calumet during a major gale on Lake Superior. This time she was pulled off with minor damages.[7]

For the next 12 years, she sailed a quiet life until 1895, when she was bought by William J. Farwell of Chicago for the small sum of $3,000. In the late fall of 1895, she was ashore again, this time at Whitefish Point in Lake Superior. For the second time in her career, the *Ellsworth* spent a long, lonely winter on the beach. She was released in the spring of 1896,[8] repaired, and put back to work. The *Ellsworth* had been lucky. It was indeed a rare thing for a vessel to survive two winters on the ice-clogged beaches of the Great Lakes. Few others had.

On September 2, 1896, at four o'clock in the morning, her luck ran out. In a strong southwest gale and rain storm, the *Colonel Ellsworth* collided with the schooner *Emily B. Maxwell* off Waugoshance Light.[9] The crew of the *Ellsworth* escaped in the yawl boat and was picked up by the *Maxwell* and brought to Mackinaw City. The *Ellsworth* was bound eastward through the Straits, and was reported to have sunk about four miles northeast of Waugoshance Point. She sank bow first, and the top part of her sails could be seen sticking out of the water. Diver John Dodd from Cheboygan salvaged her anchors and other usable equipment.

The wreck lay on the bottom for over 70 years before she was located by Dick Race of Chicago in 1968. The location of the wreck was shown on U.S. Lake Survey charts from about 1900 onward.

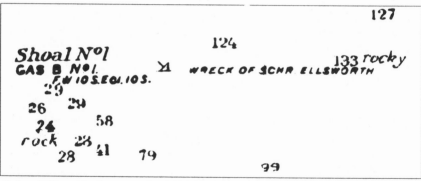

Colonel Ellsworth shown on the 1902 Straits of Mackinac U.S. Lake Survey chart
(Courtesy Burton Historical Collection, Detroit Public Library)

VESSEL FACTS Site #8

NAME:	COLONEL ELLSWORTH
RIG:	Schooner
OFFICIAL NO.:	4354
GROSS TONS:	319
LENGTH:	137'
HULL:	Wood
BUILT:	1861, Euclid OH, by William Treat
DATE LOST:	September 2, 1896
CAUSE OF LOSS:	Collision
LIVES LOST:	None
CARGO:	None
BOUND FROM/TO:	Up
LAST ENROLLMENT:	July 27, 1895, Detroit Custom House, #12
SURRENDERED:	September 23, 1896, Detroit, "Vessel lost"
CONFIGURATION:	1 Deck, 3 Masts, Square Stern, Plain Stem
DEPTH:	84'

WRECK LOCATION

In Lake Michigan 6.2 miles, 109 degrees from White Shoals Light.

LORAN: 31317.2/48067.7   LAT/LON: 45 48 26/85 01 00

WRECK CONDITION AND FEATURES

The *Colonel Ellsworth* is upright and intact. The cabin structure is gone and the aft deck is pushed up apparently by the force of the rudder striking the Lake bottom. The bow is partially broken open. Things to see include a windlass that sits on a forecastle, and a mast and mast doubler lying on the bottom off the port bow. The wreck is easily penetrable and many deck fittings are still present. The anchors have been removed. Because of her approximate 18 miles from Mackinaw City, the *Ellsworth* is not dived as heavily as other wrecks in the Straits. Being only 84 feet to the bottom and about 70 feet to the deck, the *Colonel Ellsworth* is an easy and enjoyable dive, particularly for those who like old sailing vessels.

EBER WARD

Eber Ward
(Courtesy Great Lakes Marine Collection, Milwaukee Public Library)

As daylight dawned on the morning of April 20, 1909, the routine and somewhat nondescript life of the propeller *Eber Ward* was about to come to an abrupt and tragic end. Several days earlier, she had left Chicago on her maiden voyage of the year and stopped in Milwaukee to pick up a load of 55,000 bushels of corn bound for Port Huron. Having made a Grays Reef passage with an eastward turn into the Straits of Mackinac at White Shoals, Captain Timese LeMay of Detroit[1] stood confidently on the bridge of the *Ward* and observed in the far distance what he thought to be a slushy mass of windrow ice dead ahead. At a distance of five to six miles west of Mackinaw City, the *Ward* ran directly into this ice floe and sank within ten minutes, carrying five crew members to their death. It was nine in the morning of a bright fair weather day.

In somewhat more dramatic terms, the *Detroit News* reported her loss as follows:[2] "Capt. LeMay had stood on the bridge and felt the timbers twist and crackle beneath him as the ice won in its battle with the wood; he had seen the water creep toward the deck and he saw

Shipwrecked crew of the *Eber Ward*, photo by George Coffman, 1909
(Courtesy Edna Coffman, 1980)

WRECKER FINDS STR. EBER WARD

Sunken Detroit Freight Boat
Located in 138 Feet of Water.

The wreck of the steamer Eber Ward, of Detroit has been located in the Straits of Mackinac by W. G. Smith, of Milwaukee. The location was made by sounding. He is expected to arrive at St. Ignace next week with his submarine outfit.

The boat lies in 138 feet of water, between Gros Cap and Mackinaw City, and the task of pumping the corn out of the hold of the sunken steamer will be a difficult one. Pipes will be put down and the corn will be pumped into the hold of another vessel, where it will be kept moist until it is conveyed to Chicago to be used in the manufacture of starch.

As yet none of the bodies of the five men who lost their lives when the boat collided with an ice floe have yet been recovered. Bereaved relatives are of the opinion that as soon as the work of pumping out the corn begins the suction will at least draw part of the missing number to the surface.

Detroit News June 4, 1909

five of his men sink to death beneath the jagged crust of Lake Michigan."

The *Eber Ward* was built in 1888 for Ward's Detroit and Lake Superior Line.[3] Ironically, the vessel's namesake Eber Ward was, from 1829 to 1842, keeper of the Bois Blanc Island Lighthouse located only a few miles from the wreck site.[4] Throughout her 21-year career, she plied the upper Lakes carrying both bulk and package freight without major incident.[5] Two months after she sank, her cargo of corn was salvaged by divers from the propeller *Albert Soper* and sold to a starch works.[6]

Upon finding the *Eber Ward* in 1980, we filmed it and did an underwater archaeological survey. A three-dimensional scale drawing shown in the accompanying illustration depicts the condition of the wreck as she rests on the bottom today. The *Ward* is a popular dive site for scuba divers. But her depth of 140 feet and often strong currents in the area, can make this a dangerous dive for less experienced divers. Since her discovery, there have been several serious accidents on the wreck. Experience and caution are the order of the day for divers of this shipwreck.

Artifacts from this vessel were displayed at Dossin Great Lakes Museum on Belle Isle in Detroit. Because of this display and various radio, TV and newspaper stories, relatives of some survivors of the wreck were located. These include Rose Lehman, the granddaughter of Captain LeMay. Ms. Lehman spent summers sailing on the *Ward* with her grandfather and can recite vivid memories of her experiences. We also have shared information on this wreck with a relative of Charles Lester, the *Ward's* wheelsman, whose family eventually married into the Ward family. Ironically, this relative carries both the name of the ship and the *Ward's* wheelsman. His name is Eber Ward Lester, Jr. of Royal Oak, Michigan.

EBER WARD,

Vessel Owner and Agent,

FIRE AND MARINE INSURANCE.

Representing the Following Reliable Companies:
MARINE—Ætna, of Hartford; Greenwich, of New York; Commercial Mutual, of New York.
FIRE—Milwaukee Mechanics; Transatlantic, of Hamburg; Concordia; North America; Hekla; Security, of New Haven, Conn.

Office, 51 Griswold Street,

DETROIT-   -   -   MICH.

Telephone No. 972.

Beeson's Marine Directory, 1888

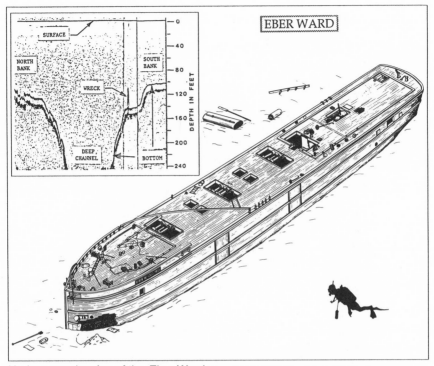

Underwater drawing of the *Eber Ward* (Copyright © 1980 Chuck & Jeri Feltner)
Chart recording shows wreck on ledge next to deep channel

Mushroom anchor on the port side of the *Eber Ward* (Authors, 1980)

VESSEL FACTS Site #15

NAME:	EBER WARD
RIG:	Propeller
OFFICIAL NO.:	136011
GROSS TONS:	1,343
LENGTH:	213'
HULL:	Wood
BUILT:	1888, W. Bay City MI, by F. W. Wheeler & Co.
DATE LOST:	April 20, 1909
CAUSE OF LOSS:	Cut by ice
LIVES LOST:	5
CARGO:	Corn
BOUND FROM/TO:	Milwaukee/Port Huron
LAST ENROLLMENT:	March 26, 1907, Port Huron Custom House, # 22
SURRENDERED:	April 23, 1909, Port Huron, "Vessel lost"
CONFIGURATION:	2 Decks, 1 Mast, Round Stern, Plain Stem
DEPTH:	140'

WRECK LOCATION

In Lake Michigan, 4.6 miles, 292 degrees from Old Mackinac Point.
LORAN: 31253.6/48096.7   LAT/LON: 45 48 13/84 49 04

WRECK CONDITION AND FEATURES

The *Ward* sits upright and is intact with the bow pointing almost due south. The cabins and transom blew off when the vessel sank. She is a double-deck vessel with her upper deck at about 110 feet. Things to see include two iron anchors on the bow and a mushroom anchor on the port side. There are two large holes in the bow where the ice cut her open. She has some unusual cargo unloading machinery in the main hatchways. Her machinery includes fore and aft compound steam engine (48" & 24," Samuel F. Hodge Co.), a scotch boiler (12' x 12.5') and a large four-blade propeller. Considerable debris and wreckage lies on the bottom, particularly around the stern. In 1987, divers located the starboard lifeboat (which capsized upon sinking) northeast of the port stern.

FRED MCBRIER

Fred McBrier
(Courtesy Ralph Roberts Collection)

During the latter half of the nineteenth century, shipbuilding flourished on the Great Lakes. For example, in 1874, the U.S. Commissioner of Navigation recorded the launching of 130 sailing vessels and 99 steam vessels.[1] Shipbuilding companies sprang up everywhere. A young man with the skill and a few thousand dollars had the opportunity to become wealthy in a few short years. One such person was Frank Willis Wheeler, the oldest son of Chesley Wheeler, himself a shipbuilder in West Bay City, Michigan. In 1877, young Frank Wheeler borrowed $3000 and, with Albert A. Crane, a Bay City hardware merchant, formed what grew to be one of the largest shipbuilding companies on the Great Lakes. From 1877 through 1894, the F. W. Wheeler Shipbuilding Company built 127 vessels.[2] Today, four of these vessels rest on the bottom of the Straits of Mackinac, all within 20 miles of each other. They are the propellers *Fred McBrier* (Hull #12), *Eber Ward* (Hull #43), *Landbo* (ex *Nyanza*, Hull #63), and *Uganda* (Hull #88).[3]

The propeller *Fred McBrier* was generally used to carry bulk cargos and, as steamers of her vintage go, was a small vessel at only 442 tons. Consequently, to be profitable, she usually towed barges behind her. The barges were most often sailing vessels, such as

Propeller *Charles H. Bradley* with schooners *Brightie, Mary Woolson* and *Goshawk* in tow c.1895
(Courtesy Institute for Great Lakes Research, Bowling Green State University)

schooners, that had been "cut down," a nautical term used when the class of a vessel was reduced.[4] This practice on the Lakes was first used in the lumber trade around 1865 and was highly successful. It involved clearing the deck amidship of masts and other gear to make room for cargo. This meant that on three-masted vessels, the center, or mainmast, was removed. Additionally, the amount of sail on the remaining masts was reduced to a minimum, leaving only enough to handle emergencies, as the vessel was always in tow. These vessels, and the steamers that towed them, became known as lumber "hookers," from the sailor's deprecative term for a clumsy or old-fashioned vessel.[5] By 1871, tow barges were introduced in the grain trade and were subsequently used to carry whatever bulk cargoes there might be.[6] Although highly economical, such configurations were often involved in collisions, as their maneuverability was limited.

By the 1880s, many so-called schooners were built specifically to be towed, often being modified to make them more useful as barges.[7] One common change was to use a straight steamer bow instead of the sharper schooner bow. In this case, the vessel had no bowsprit and the foremast stays were connected directly to the bow rail. A heavy stanchion, or samson post, was placed at the bow to accommodate a towing bridle. Top sails were eliminated, as sailors had to be paid extra to set them. These vessels were popularly called schooner-barges, but were officially registered by the Custom Houses as schooners. Some never unfurled a sail in their lifetime. Steamers, towing a string of two or three cut-down schooners or schooner-barges, were a common sight on the Lakes in the late 1800s.

The *Fred McBrier* was one such steamer. In October 1890, she was downbound with a load of iron ore. Her consorts under tow were the schooner-barges *J. B. Lozen* and *A. Stewart*. Upbound in the darkness was the propeller *Progress*, who was towing the schooner *F. A. Georger*. About ten miles west of Mackinaw City, the two steamers collided. At 442 tons, the *McBrier* was no match for the 1,596-ton *Progress*. With a giant hole in her hull, she sank quickly and without fanfare. No lives were lost.[8]

The wreck of the *McBrier* was found in 1967 by a group of divers led by Jim Ryerse from St. Ignace, Michigan. Shortly after that,

107

Mackinaw City divers Dick Campbell, Fred Leete and Dean Deliyanides, accompanied by John Steele of Waukegan, Illinois, and Dick Race of Chicago, recovered a 2,000-pound iron anchor, as well as other artifacts, from the wreck.

John Steele, Dick Campbell, and Dick Race with *McBrier* anchor c. 1967
(*Photo by Fred Leete*)

VESSEL FACTS **Site #11**

NAME:	FRED MCBRIER
RIG:	Propeller
OFFICIAL NO.:	120452
GROSS TONS:	442
LENGTH:	161'
HULL:	Wood
BUILT:	1881, W. Bay City MI, by F. W. Wheeler & Co.
DATE LOST:	October 3, 1890
CAUSE OF LOSS:	Collision
LIVES LOST:	None
CARGO:	Iron Ore
BOUND FROM/TO:	Escanaba/Cleveland
LAST ENROLLMENT:	April 10, 1890, Detroit Custom House, #71
SURRENDERED:	October 9, 1890, Detroit, "Total loss"
CONFIGURATION:	1 Deck, 2 Masts, Round Stern, Plain Stem
DEPTH:	104'

WRECK LOCATION

In Lake Michigan, 9.3 miles, 278 degrees from Old Mackinac Point.
LORAN: 31287.8/48085.3   LAT/LON: 45 48 11/84 55 09

WRECK CONDITION AND FEATURES

The *McBrier* lies upright and is mostly intact. There is considerable machinery (engines, boiler, windlass, etc.) to be explored. The manner in which the wreck is broken up presents a confusing scene to the underwater explorer. This factor, combined with a usual heavy silt, makes this wreck somewhat difficult to dive. Partly for this reason, the wreck is infrequently visited by scuba divers.

GENESEE CHIEF

The first steamship company on the Lakes, operated by a railroad company, was the Union Steamboat Company, which was established in 1852. One of the early vessels in this fleet was the *Genesee Chief*.[1] She was originally built as a twin-screw propeller with two engines, which was not unusual for vessels of this type built prior to 1853-54.[2] The propeller *Canisteo*, lost in the Straits in 1880, was also part of the Union Steamboat Line.[3]

In 1863, the *Genesee Chief* was rebuilt in Cleveland by Stevens and Presley as a single-screw propeller.[4] She burned to the water's edge at Clark's Dry Dock of Detroit in 1868, and was rebuilt this time as an unrigged barge.[5] In 1885, she was rerigged as a two-masted schooner.[6] On her last trip, she became severely waterlogged and was abandoned at the Millard D. Olds lumber docks in Cheboygan in August 1891.[7] Her documents were finally surrendered in 1897. This wreck, along with that of the propeller *Leviathan*, was towed from Cheboygan and scuttled at Duncan Bay.

Millard. D. Olds Lumber Co. dock in Cheboygan and the propeller *Argo* c.1910
(Courtesy William C. Duman)

VESSEL FACTS   Site #37

NAME:	GENESEE CHIEF
RIG:	Schooner
OFFICIAL NO.:	10243
GROSS TONS:	275
LENGTH:	142'
HULL:	Wood
BUILT:	1846, Carthage NY, by George Steers
DATE LOST:	August 24, 1891
CAUSE OF LOSS:	Abandoned
LIVES LOST:	None
CARGO:	Shingles
BOUND FROM/TO:	Naubinway/Tonawanda
LAST ENROLLMENT:	February 28, 1891, Buffalo Custom House, #40
SURRENDERED:	March 22,1897, Buffalo,"Broken up/Abandoned"
CONFIGURATION:	1 Deck, 2 Masts, Square Stern, Plain Stem
DEPTH:	10'

WRECK LOCATION

At the mouth of Duncan Bay in Lake Huron, 1.5 miles, 71 degrees from the mouth of the Cheboygan River.

LORAN: 31156.9/48227.8   LAT/LON: 45 39 71/84 26 13

WRECK CONDITIONS AND FEATURES

The *Genesee Chief* sits upright and is completely broken up. Her two mast steps are evident, but there is no evidence of a centerboard. There is not a lot of interest for the diver to see on this wreck. However, it is approximately 300 feet north of the wreck of the *Leviathan*. Both wrecks can be dived on one visit.

HENRY CLAY

When the U.S. Lake Survey party sent to the Straits of Mackinac arrived in the spring of 1851, they were undoubtedly surprised to see the brig *Henry Clay* ashore and standing high out of the water just north of Point Au Sable (now Point Nipigon). They were there to conduct the very first U.S. Government hydrographic survey of the Straits resulting in the first official navigational chart of the area.[1] Dutifully, they included the position of the *Henry Clay*

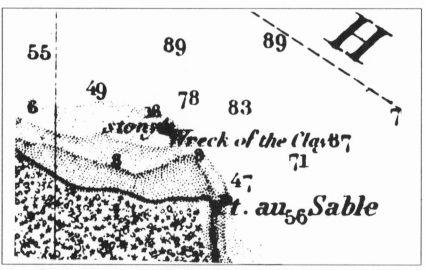

Henry Clay shown on the 1854 Straits of Mackinac U.S. Lake Survey chart
(Courtesy Burton Historical Collection, Detroit Public Library)

on their chart. Over time, the scourges of severe weather and early shipwreck looters reduced the *Clay* to a few scattered boards on the bottom of Lake Huron. Her remains lie about 150 yards offshore in ten feet of water approximately 300 feet southeast of the wreck of the schooner *Albemarle.*

The brig *Henry Clay* was built in 1842 in Huron, Ohio. Information about her activities, until she stranded in the Straits in the late fall of 1850, is sparse. News of her demise was also meager. On

December 9, 1850, Captain A. P. Dobbins of the propeller *Troy* gave the *Detroit Free Press* the following account of his trip from Chicago to Detroit. "Left Chicago Friday, November 29th. December 3rd., under lee of Mackinac blowing very hard from ESE — cold and snowing hard. Brig *Henry Clay* Ashore in south passage and abandoned. Crew came down as passengers on the *Troy*."[2]

VESSEL FACTS	Site #28
NAME:	HENRY CLAY
RIG:	Brig
OFFICIAL NO.:	None
GROSS TONS:	163 (BOM)
LENGTH:	87'
HULL:	Wood
BUILT:	1842, Huron OH, by Fairbanks Church
DATE LOST:	December 3, 1850
CAUSE OF LOSS:	Stranded
LIVES LOST:	None
CARGO:	Unknown
BOUND FROM/TO:	Unknown
LAST ENROLLMENT:	May 22, 1849, Cleveland Custom House, #32
SURRENDERED:	No endorsement
CONFIGURATION:	1 Deck, 2 Masts, Square Stern, Scroll Head
DEPTH:	10'

WRECK LOCATION

Near Point Nipigon in Lake Huron, 9.4 miles, 123 degrees from Old Mackinac Point.

LORAN: 31189.7/48183.7   LAT/LON: 45 43 33/84 32 31

WRECK CONDITION AND FEATURES

The *Henry Clay* is completely broken up with only scattered timbers remaining. Divers will not find much of interest.

ISLANDER

Islander at Les Cheneaux Islands
(Courtesy Institute for Great Lakes Research, Bowling Green State University)

The first town built near modern-day Cheboygan was Duncan City, which was on the western edge of the mouth of McLeod's Bay, slightly more than a mile east of the mouth of the Cheboygan River. The bay was originally named after the McLeod brothers who started the A. & R. McLeod Sawmill in 1846 — the first in the region. In 1851, Jeremiah W. Duncan established a major lumber mill at this location,[1] and the town and the bay adopted the Duncan name, becoming known as Duncan City and Duncan Bay, respectively.

Duncan City was originally established as a refueling dock for wood-burning steamboats. The first steamer to stop there was the side-wheeler *General Scott* in 1847. She delivered a yoke of oxen from St. Helena Island that were thrown overboard and made to swim to shore.[2] Between 1850 and 1860, the village of Cheboygan sprang up along the eastern banks of the Cheboygan River and by 1867, with the dredging of the Cheboygan River,[3] much of the marine traffic shifted to this more protected harbor. Meanwhile, the lumber industry around Cheboygan boomed and an extensive set of lumber docks were built at Duncan City, as well as along the Lake Huron shoreline to the west of the Cheboygan River (see drawing below). Lumbering reached its peak in the Cheboygan region in 1897 with 200 million board feet being produced.[4]

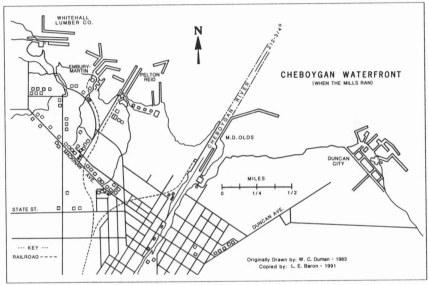

Cheboygan waterfront showing sawmills c. 1895
(Courtesy William C. Duman, 1983)

This "inexhaustible" resource soon disappeared, and by 1920 most of the mills had closed. Consequently, in the early part of the twentieth century, the docks on Duncan Bay and the bay itself became little used. Abandoned and sunken vessels that got in the way of progress at the Cheboygan docks, such as the *Genesee Chief* and the *Leviathan*, were towed to Duncan Bay and scuttled. Others, such as the *Islander*, were taken to the Duncan City dock and abandoned. Over time and with the stress of weather, the propeller *Islander*, along with the Duncan City docks, disintegrated.

Throughout her lifetime the *Islander* operated as a ferry boat for the Arnold Transit Company. She made regular trips from Mackinac to the Les Cheneaux Islands.[5] She usually left Mackinac for Les Cheneaux at 9:00 a.m. and returned at 1:30 p.m., with a second trip

Islander (I) at Cheboygan dock in 1942 with Captain LaWay's vessel *M. H. Stuart*
(Courtesy Institute for Great Lakes Research, Bowling Green State University)

scheduled for a 2:00 p.m. departure and a 6:15 p.m. return. The roundtrip fare was 50 cents. On occasion she was called upon to serve as an ice-breaker as was the case for many of the ferry boats that ran in the Straits area.[6] At the end of her career she was sold to Captain E. J. LaWay, who towed her to Cheboygan in 1941 for conversion to a barge. Instead, in 1942, she was partially dismantled and abandoned at the south end of the Millard D. Olds dock on the east side of the Cheboygan River.

Islander being towed by the U.S. Coast Guard in 1945
(Courtesy William C. Duman)

In 1945 the U.S. Coast Guard raised the *Islander* to clear the harbor area directly in front of their present-day mooring facility. She was moved to the Duncan City docks and abandoned. Here, the *Islander* settled to the bottom and eventually went to pieces.

VESSEL FACTS	**Site #35**
NAME:	ISLANDER
RIG:	Propeller
OFFICIAL NO.:	100601
GROSS TONS:	210
LENGTH:	138'
HULL:	Wood
BUILT:	1895, Benton Harbor MI, by Edward W. Heath
DATE LOST:	1942
CAUSE OF LOSS:	Abandoned
LIVES LOST:	None
CARGO:	None
BOUND FROM/TO:	At dock
LAST ENROLLMENT:	June 10, 1929, Mackinac #41
SURRENDERED:	March 14, 1940, Sault Ste. Marie, "Out of doc."
CONFIGURATION:	2 Decks, No Masts, Plain Stem, Round Stern
DEPTH:	10'

WRECK LOCATION

In Lake Huron on the west side of the mouth of Duncan Bay, one mile east of the mouth of the Cheboygan River.

LORAN: 31158.9/48231.3   LAT/LON: 45 39 29/84 26 35

WRECK CONDITION AND FEATURES

The *Islander* sits upright and is completely broken up. All of the machinery and other mechanical gear has been removed from the wreck. Her keel and some of her ribs are still present. This wreck offers little of interest to the diver. However, for those who enjoy diving old dock sites, there is much to see. Submerged dock pilings are a hazard to dive boats.

J. A. SMITH

J. A. Smith
(Courtesy Great Lakes Marine Collection, Milwaukee Public Library)

As previously noted, the schooner *J. A. Smith* stranded alongside the schooner *Anglo Saxon* on September 8, 1887.[1] The *Smith* did not break up immediately and attempts were made to refloat the vessel. Two steam pumps had been placed aboard the *Smith* by the salvage tug *Leviathan*. During the salvage operations, one pump broke loose, rolled across the deck and crushed Captain Ulysses B. Searles of the *Smith* against the ship's rail. He died shortly after that.[2] Salvage efforts stopped and the salvors abandoned the *J. A. Smith*. Several years later, she was reportedly burned to the waterline.

SHIPWRECKS OF THE STRAITS OF MACKINAC

The *Smith* was built as a scow-schooner, which had a somewhat unusual hull shape. The bottom of the hull was nearly flat allowing the vessel to navigate very shallow water.[3] In the 1870s, she towed behind the propeller *R. Holland* with her consort the schooner *Genesee Chief* described earlier in this book.[4]

VESSEL FACTS	Site #10
NAME:	J. A. SMITH
RIG:	Schooner
OFFICIAL NO.:	45966
GROSS TONS:	255
LENGTH:	138'
HULL:	Wood
BUILT:	1871, Algonac MI, by Thomas Arnold
DATE LOST:	September 8, 1887
CAUSE OF LOSS:	Stranded
LIVES LOST:	1
CARGO:	Cedar wood
BOUND FROM/TO:	Cockburn Island/Chicago
LAST ENROLLMENT:	April 24, 1886, Detroit Custom House, #52
SURRENDERED:	February 25, 1888, Detroit, "Abandoned"
CONFIGURATION:	1 Deck, 2 Masts, Square Stern, Plain Stem
DEPTH:	12'

WRECK LOCATION

In Lake Michigan, 12.3 miles, 260 degrees from Old Mackinac Point.

LORAN: 31309.6/48102.8   LAT/LON: 45 45 24/84 57 25

WRECK CONDITION AND FEATURES

The *J. A. Smith* is completely broken up. Only scattered timbers remain. The wreckage is mingled with that of the schooner *Anglo Saxon*. Divers can reach both wrecks from the shore. However, there is very little of interest to see.

J. H. OUTHWAITE

J. H. Outhwaite at the Soo Locks
(Courtesy Ralph Roberts Collection)

James Reid, salvor diver, made a valiant effort to salvage the *Cayuga* (described earlier) in the period 1895 to 1899. In the spring of 1898, he interrupted those efforts to salvage the propeller *J. H. Outhwaite* and her consort, the schooner *H. A. Barr*. The *Outhwaite*, with the *Barr* in tow, ran aground at False Presque Isle in Lake Huron during a heavy easterly gale. In a heroic rescue effort, the crews of both vessels were brought ashore by the U.S. Life Saving Service crew from Middle Island.[1] Initial efforts to salvage the *Outhwaite* failed and the owners abandoned her.[2] On May 5, 1898, Captain Reid received the contract to salvage both vessels.[3] As usual, Reid salvaged the vessels in short order and by June 4, 1898, they sat at the dry docks in Detroit.[4] He received much praise in the newspapers of the day for such a successful and expeditious wrecking operation.[5] Extensive repairs were made to the *Outhwaite* by James Davidson's Shipyard in West Bay City, and she was put back in service by the end of the year.[6]

By all accounts, the worst storm ever on the Great Lakes occurred in November 1913.[7] Before that, the great storm of November 1905 held this dubious title. It was during this storm that the *J. H. Outhwaite* found her permanent resting place on the bottom of the Straits of Mackinac.

The 1905 storm began Monday, November 27, and reached its peak on Lake Superior the next day. Winds blew between 70 and 80

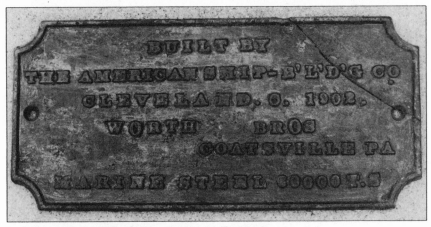

Builder's plate from the boiler of the *J. H. Outhwaite*
(Courtesy Phil Spencer, photo by Craig Warren)

miles per hour. Temperatures dropped to 12 below zero. Blinding snow storms reduced the visibility to zero. Over 40 vessels were wrecked and 36 lives were lost. The most tragic wreck was that of the steamer *Mataafa*, which struck a pierhead and settled in shallow water while trying to enter Duluth Harbor. Although only a few hundred yards from shore, rescue of the crew was impossible until the storm subsided. Overnight, with thousands watching from shore, nine men in the aft section of the *Mataafa* froze to death. Fifteen in the forward part survived.[8]

Life Saving crew rescuing survivors of the *Mataafa* in 1905 storm
(Courtesy Ralph Roberts Collection)

Coming down from Escanaba with a load of iron ore, the *J. H. Outhwaite*, with the schooner *Mary Mitchell* in tow, fought her own losing battle with this fierce storm. Abreast of Old Mackinac Point, she lost her steering gear. At 2 a.m. on November 28, she was driven ashore at Point Au Sable (now Point Nipigon) in Lake Huron. The crew made it ashore at daylight. They had built a fire aboard the vessel to keep warm during the night. After they left, the fire flared up and burned the vessel to the waterline.[9] Captain E. J. LaWay salvaged the anchors, engines and boilers from this wreck.

For many years, this wreck was mistakenly called the *Uganda*. Measurements and other data confirm she is the *J. H. Outhwaite*.

According to the *Great Lakes Register*, a new boiler, manufactured by the American Ship-Building Company, was installed in the *Outhwaite* in 1902.[10] In the 1970s, divers recovered the builder's plate from this boiler (see photo on page 121). This plate clearly shows that the boiler was produced by the American Ship-Building Company in 1902, providing convincing evidence that this is the wreck of the *J. H. Outhwaite*.

Beeson's Marine Directory, 1888

VESSEL FACTS	Site #30
NAME:	J. H. OUTHWAITE
RIG:	Propeller
OFFICIAL NO.:	76636
GROSS TONS:	1,304
LENGTH:	224'
HULL:	Wood
BUILT:	1886, Cleveland OH, by W. H. Radcliffe
DATE LOST:	November 28, 1905
CAUSE OF LOSS:	Stranded and burned
LIVES LOST:	None
CARGO:	Iron ore
BOUND FROM/TO:	Escanaba/Cleveland
LAST ENROLLMENT:	March 2, 1903, Cleveland Custom House, #59
SURRENDERED:	December 6, 1905, Cleveland, "Vessel lost"
CONFIGURATION:	2 Decks, 3 Masts, Round Stern, Plain Stem
DEPTH:	30'

WRECK LOCATION

Near Point Nipigon in Lake Huron, 9.7 miles, 122 degrees from Old
Mackinac Point.

LORAN: 31187.3/48184.3   LAT/LON: 45 42 28/84 33 18

WRECK CONDITION AND FEATURES

The *J. H. Outhwaite* rests upright and intact but almost completely
buried in a sand bank. The wreck lies almost north-south, with the
starboard side facing westward into the sand bank. Over the years,
west to east littoral drift has almost covered the entire vessel. The
port side is downstream and is visible. The smoke stack and other
debris lie off the port side about midship. This is an easy dive for
beginners, but there is not a lot to see.

J. H. TIFFANY

The masts of the average sailing vessel on the Great Lakes stood more than 100 feet above the deck of the vessel.[1] With a depth-of-hold of 10 to 15 feet, the total distance from the underside of the keel to the very top of the mast was at least 110 to 115 feet. Clearly, if the vessel sank in a water depth less than this total distance, the tops of the masts would stick out of the water. If no other escape route was available, sailors on a sinking vessel would often climb to

Skillagalee (Ile Aux Galets) Light
(Authors, 1979)

the top of masts, lash themselves in place and hope the water was no deeper than the height of their perch. There they would wait and pray for a speedy rescue. If the rescue was not quick, their fate would be death, either from exposure or from drowning, in the event that the mast broke.

The thought of either fate was not in the minds of the sailors aboard the schooner *J. H. Tiffany* as they passed through the Straits of Mackinac in late November 1859. A violent collision with the propeller *Milwaukee* would soon change this state of mind. The collision happened about half past midnight at a point four miles northwest of Skillagalee (Ile Aux Galets) Light.[2] The *Milwaukee* was bound for Buffalo with the propeller *Free State* running alongside in company with her. When the *Free State* first spotted the *Tiffany*, she was on a tack directly across the propeller's bow. Since the *Free State* was between the *Milwaukee* and the schooner, neither of these two vessels could see each other. The *Free State*, on seeing the schooner, reversed her engines, barely avoiding a collision as the *Tiffany* passed close under her bow.

The *Milwaukee* was not so lucky. She struck the *Tiffany* nearly abreast of the foremast, badly shattering the schooner, and in extricating herself, had a big gash cut in her when the schooner swung around upon her. The crew and passengers of the *Milwaukee*, about 30 people, barely had time to launch the boats and get away from her before she went down. They were picked up immediately by the *Free State* that was standing close by.

The crew of the *Tiffany* tried to save their rapidly sinking vessel by beaching it on Skillagalee Reef. Enroute, they took down the fore-topsail and got it under the hull in an attempt to stop the leak. When this failed, they turned their attention to the yawl boat that was found to have been badly damaged in the collision. It was dragging at the stern, upsidedown, with a large hole in it. As the water crept over the deck of the sinking schooner, panic set in and the crew took to the rigging.

One of the sailors, in running to the shrouds, was overtaken by the water and drawn under with the sinking craft. Upon surfacing, he was near exhaustion but managed to swim to the main-topmast. There were several of the crew already upon it, and others, in attempting to get upon it, overloaded it and it broke, dumping them all back in the water. The foremast was still standing and they all swam for it. It was, however, a fearful swim for life, and in the dramatic words of the *Detroit Free Press*:[3] "Each individual, in the desperation of the moment, cared only for himself, and in their frantic efforts grasped one another for support, and struggled against each other until several were hopelessly strangled and sank to rise no more." Of the crew of ten, the five who made it lashed themselves to the rigging and were resigned to whatever fate might await them.

Meanwhile, the *Free State*, having completed the rescue of those aboard the *Milwaukee*, turned her attention to the disabled schooner that had disappeared in the darkness. However, a course was taken as nearly in the direction in which she was last seen, and after searching for about an hour, the shouts of the men upon the mast were heard. When the five survivors were brought aboard, they were in a state of exhaustion and some near death from exposure to the cold November water and weather. Nevertheless, they had beaten the odds and survived both of the dreaded fates of a shipwrecked sailor clinging to a mast.

Hard-hat divers c.1900
(Courtesy Wally Hirthe)

In April 1860, six months after the *Tiffany* had sunk, the schooner *Surprise* reported seeing her masts sticking out of the water.[4] Later that year in December, the schooner *Plover* observed that they were still standing.[5] In 1873, hard-hat diver Peter Falcon found the wreck of the *Tiffany* in 105 feet of water.[6] During 1873 and 1874, he salvaged most of the 356 tons of railroad iron she was carrying and sold it for $35 a ton. In course of the salvage operations, William Wright, one of Falcon's hard-hat divers, got a serious case of the bends and died.[7]

While carrying on his salvage work in 1874, Falcon's salvage vessel nearly got hit by several vessels, as the wreck lay directly in the commonly-traveled steamer track. To warn other vessels, he published a notice of his work in the marine column of the major port newspapers. For example, the June 19, 1874, edition of the *Chicago Tribune* stated:[8] "The wrecking schooner *Active* has again commenced work upon the wreck of the *Tiffany*, which lies 4 miles N.W. 1/2 N. from Aux Galet light, and 8 miles S.W. 3/4 W. from Waugoshance light. This is in the direct track of vessels. Anchor lights will be displayed at night and a large bell will admonish vessels coming too near to keep off."

Armed with this detailed information on the wreck's location and depth, we set out in the summer of 1982 to find the wreck of the *Tiffany*. We were accompanied on our boat, the *Gemini II*, by Ben Cline of Westland, Michigan, and assisted by Stan Stock of Gaylord, Michigan, on his boat, the *Narcosis*. We ran extensive search patterns in the area but were unable to find the wreck. We surmised that the wreck had been flattened on the bottom by Falcon's salvage efforts, and, thus, our chart recording depth sounders could not "see" the limited-height profile of the wreck.

To overcome this problem, a 2,000-foot long drag line was set up between the two boats and was pulled along the bottom in hope of snagging the wreck. This was the same technique employed over 100 years earlier by Peter Falcon when he first located the *Tiffany*. After several days of painstaking searching with this drag line, we finally snagged an object that brought both boats to a stop. However, a severe storm forced us to retrieve our line and run to port. Other projects occupied us and before we could return to dive the site, other divers had located the wreck of the *Tiffany* as well as the propeller *Milwaukee* (described later). The wreck position we had determined using the drag line subsequently proved to be correct.

The wreck of the *Tiffany* was found in 1985 by divers Brian Scott, Craig Scott, Dave Scott, George Manning and Bill Salsbury, all from Muskegon, and John Makuch of Detroit. Interestingly, the wreck location given by Falcon in his notice to mariners was only about 1,000 feet from the actual wreck site.

VESSEL FACTS   **Site #2**

NAME:	J. H. TIFFANY
RIG:	Schooner
OFFICIAL NO.:	None
GROSS TONS:	371 (BOM)
LENGTH:	137'
HULL:	Wood
BUILT:	1856, Cleveland OH, by Lafrinier & Stevenson
DATE LOST:	November 29, 1859
CAUSE OF LOSS:	Collision
LIVES LOST:	5
CARGO:	Rail iron
BOUND FROM/TO:	Oswego/Chicago
LAST ENROLLMENT:	April 27, 1859, Oswego Custom House, #6
SURRENDERED:	Oswego, "Vessel lost"
CONFIGURATION:	1 Deck, 2 Masts, Square Stern, Plain Stem
DEPTH:	103'

WRECK LOCATION

In Lake Michigan, 4.8 miles, 232 degrees from Grays Reef Light.

LORAN: 31402.0/48081.7   LAT/LON: 45 43 37/85 13 76

WRECK CONDITION AND FEATURES

The *J. H. Tiffany* is upright but completely broken up due to salvage efforts and lies flattened on the bottom. The cargo, and most of the wreck's equipment, was salvaged. There is very little left of this wreck for the diver to enjoy.

JAMES R. BENTLEY

Many people are unaware that numerous words and phrases used in everyday conversation are derived from nautical terms. Examples abound: *Bitter end* (the last link in an anchor chain), *pipe down* (a call on a boatswain's pipe or whistle to observe silence), *jury rig* (makeshift rig of sails or masts to replace damaged equipment), *blazer* (a special jacket worn by sailors on the ship *HMS Blazer*), and *scuttle butt* (a barrel of fresh drinking water placed on deck around which sailors exchanged news and gossip), are but a few.[1]

The devil to pay is a shortening of the nautical saying *The devil to pay and no pitch hot*, which meant an apparently insoluble predicament. The "devil" was a caulker's name for the difficult to get at and outermost deck seam, next to the hull, which a sailor had to *pay*, i.e., seal with pitch. The side of the hull was obviously the only thing between *the devil and the deep blue sea*, clearly a dangerous spot to be.

Pouring oil on troubled waters is an oft-used phrase that generally means to smooth things over. In actuality, an oil slick on a rough sea will prevent waves from breaking. For centuries, sailors have used this phenomenon in cases of distress when trying to bring a small boat alongside a ship in a heavy sea. *Oil bags*, attached to lines, were heaved over the side and the oil oozed from them forming the becalming slick. The bags were made of canvas, contained oakum or cotton waste saturated with oil, and were punctured in several places to allow the oil to drip out slowly.[2] Were it not for oil bags, the crew of the schooner *James R. Bentley* may not have survived.

The *Bentley*, Captain Charles Hamilton in command, sailed from Chicago on the morning of November 9, 1878, bound for Buffalo and carrying 36,288 bushels of rye. Her voyage was uneventful up to the time she entered the Straits of Mackinac. When abreast of Cheboygan, between Lighthouse Point and Bois Blanc Island, she struck a reef with great force but bounded off and continued on her course. This happened at 4:45 on the morning of November 12.

The shock of the collision brought all the crew on deck, and a damage check showed that the centerboard was jammed up in its box, and the vessel was taking on water. The pumps were put in motion, and Captain Hamilton attempted to beat back into the passage for shelter to try to save the vessel and cargo. But, with the centerboard jammed up and a strong gale blowing from the north-northwest, they could not turn the *Bentley* around. After three and one-half hours of intense effort to save the vessel, and with the hold filled with water, Captain Hamilton reluctantly gave the order to abandon ship.[3]

The yawl boat was brought under the port quarter, and the Captain and his eight crew members scrambled aboard in a heavy sea. Within minutes, the *Bentley* went down, bow first. Fortunately for the men of the *Bentley*, their plight was observed by two other vessels, the bark *Erastus Corning* and the schooner *Groton*.[4] The *Corning*, under the command of Captain George H. Clarke, hove to and attempted to pick up the survivors. In the rough sea, the yawl boat was in danger of being swamped. Recognizing the problem, Captain Clarke had the crew of the *Corning* throw oil bags overboard to calm the sea.[5]

> **POURING OIL ON THE WATER.**
>
> **Captain Clarke's Rescue of the Crew After the J. R. Bentley Sank.**
>
> To the Editor of The Inter Ocean.
>
> BUFFALO. N. Y., Nov. 17.—We wish to return our best thanks to Clarke, of the Erastus Corning, his officers, and crew for rescuing us. Captain Clarke poured oil on the water to smooth the sea down when our heavily-laden boat (nine in it) was approaching his vessel that the sea might not swamp her. He did all he could with all his officers and crew to make us all comfortable, and brought us to Buffalo. He is a true sailor, noble in character, and we again wish to return to him and his officers and crew our warmest thanks for his kindness.
>
> CHARLES HAMILTON,
>
> Master schooner Bentley, for himself, his officers, and crew.

Chicago Inter-Ocean November 19, 1878

With the seas diminished by the oil, the yawl was brought alongside and the *Bentley's* crew was pulled aboard the *Corning*. The only injury amongst the crew was a broken arm suffered by first mate William Derby that occurred when the *Bentley* struck the reef.

The wreck of the *James R. Bentley* was discovered by John Steele of Waukegan, Illinois, in the summer of 1984. Because of its out-of-the-way location, its depth, and the often poor visibility, few sport divers visit this wreck.

VESSEL FACTS **Site #40**

NAME:	JAMES R. BENTLEY
RIG:	Schooner
OFFICIAL NO.:	12720
GROSS TONS:	574
LENGTH:	178'
HULL:	Wood
BUILT:	1867, Fairport OH, by Bailey Brothers
DATE LOST:	November 12, 1878
CAUSE OF LOSS:	Foundered
LIVES LOST:	None
CARGO:	Rye
BOUND FROM/TO:	Chicago/Buffalo
LAST ENROLLMENT:	April 19, 1872, Buffalo Custom House, #114
SURRENDERED:	December 31, 1878, Buffalo, "Vessel wrecked"
CONFIGURATION:	1 Deck, 3 Masts, Square Stern, Figurehead
DEPTH:	150'

WRECK LOCATION

In Lake Huron, 9.9 miles, 93 degrees from Poe Reef Light.

LORAN: 31057.7/48251.1   LAT/LON: 45 41 45/84 09 12

WRECK CONDITION AND FEATURES

The *James R. Bentley* sits upright and is intact with the mizzenmast still standing. The foremast and the mainmast lie across the starboard side with their top ends stuck in the Lake bottom. Over time, they were apparently loosened and pulled out of their steps by the current. The foremast fife rail, with belaying pins in place, is intact and surrounds the foremast hole. The ship's wheel and steering mechanism are identical in design to those produced by the Boston Steering Gear Company. The vessel name is carved into the gunwales near the bow in letters eight to ten inches high. Her groundtackle, anchors and windlass are present. Under the bowsprit sits the figurehead. The wreck is heavily silted and visibility is often very poor.

L. B. COATES

L. B. Coates at Oconto, Wisconsin, in 1917
(Courtesy Freshwater Press, Inc.)

Hard-hat diving, or submarine diving as it was originally known, was a high expertise, specialty profession, knowledge of which was often handed down within families, if not directly from father to son. Examples in this book include Peter Falcon and his sons (see the propeller *Milwaukee*), James Reid and his son Tom Reid (see the propeller *Cayuga*), and Fred Ryerse and his great-grandson, Jim Ryerse (see the propeller *William H. Barnum*). Such was the case for William C. Duman of Cheboygan.

William C. Duman was born in 1924 in a home on Mackinaw Avenue on the west side of Cheboygan, only a short distance from the Whitehall Lumber Company docks on Lake Huron — the final resting place of the abandoned schooner *L. B. Coates.* His father, Lawrence Duman, as well as his great uncle, John Dodd, were submarine divers. From this heritage, Bill Duman became a submarine diver. As natives of the Straits area, he, his father and great uncle, were an intimate part of the infrastructure that supported the maritime commerce of the region. These three generations of submarine divers were living threads in the fabric of shipwreck history of the Straits of Mackinac. Tracing their activities reveals much of the richness of this history.

L. B. Coates at Whitehall Lumber Co. dock with Lawrence Duman in the crow's nest (propeller *Myrtie M. Ross* alongside) c.1923
(Courtesy William C. Duman)

John Dodd was a tough man — even signing his letters to his sister Mary Duman "From your hard case of a brother — John Dodd."[1] He was born in 1857, the son of Samuel Dodd and Maria Kavanagh. His family had homesteaded 40 acres of land west of Cheboygan in 1865. By January 1882, John Dodd and his wife were living in St. Ignace where he had bought a house for $1,200 cash.[2] How he learned to dive is unclear but, by the summer of 1882, news of his diving exploits appeared in the Cheboygan newspapers. While working for Wilson Newton, he did extensive diving and salvage work on the schooner *Lawrence* that was sunk in the Straits west of St. Helena Island.[3] Wilson Newton, along with his brother Archie, owned St. Helena Island and lived

John Dodd c.1885
(Courtesy William C. Duman)

there at the time the *Lawrence* sank.[4] The following year, 1883, Dodd recovered the ground tackle and machinery from the propeller *Canisteo* sunk in 1881 off Waugoshance Light.[5]

In his travels around the Lakes, John Dodd regularly wrote letters to his sister Mary Duman and the contents of these relate much about his personality.[6] For example, in a letter from Grand Haven, Michigan, on September 20, 1886, he wrote, "I have made hundreds of dollars this summer but not a cent of it went for whiskey," and again in the same letter regarding his diving ability, "I am a good man at my own trade and the people all over the United States know it." In a letter dated July 18, 1886, he told of diving on wrecks around Frankfort, Michigan, while working on the tug *Leviathan* and noted "I am proud to think I have the nerve and constitution to stand the hard work." By 1886, Dodd had set up his own independent business

JOHN DODD,

MARINE DIVER.

WRECKING TUG, SUEAM PUMPS AND HAWSERS AT SHORT NOTICE.

John Dodd's letterhead c.1886
(Courtesy William C. Duman)

135

Lawrence Duman's tug *G. C. Duman*, Thursa Duman on bow, 1921
(Courtesy William C. Duman)

(see letterhead).[7] In 1890, he worked for the Reid Towing and Wrecking Company in St. Ignace. In 1896, he salvaged equipment from the wreck of the schooner *Colonel Ellsworth*. Finally, on May 11, 1916, Mary Duman wrote a letter to her son Lawrence Duman who was in Hessel, Michigan, stating, "Well Lawrence they buried Uncle John in St. Ignace – they all took it pretty hard."[8]

Lawrence Duman (right) and brother John Duman with the *L. B. Coates* and *Myrtie M. Ross* in background c.1930
(Courtesy William C. Duman)

Lawrence Duman took up submarine diving about the time he acquired John Dodd's hard-hat diving equipment in an estate sale. Born in 1897, he was married to Thursa Werner, part of a prominent Cheboygan family. Together they shared Lawrence's interest in boats — he having owned the tug *G. C. Duman* (see photo), propeller *Helen Taylor*, tug *Home*, and the hull of the tug *James E Sanford*. In 1923, he was the captain and owner of the *Helen Taylor* when she sank in a storm off St. Helena Island.[9] Aside from operating his own boats, Lawrence Duman worked as a crewman on a number of Great Lakes vessels including the propellers *Edward Buckley*, *Maruba*, *Moses Taylor*, *Amasa Stone* and *Western States*. Most of his career was spent in diving doing salvage and

Lawrence Duman and son, diver Bill Duman, working on the Arnold Line ferry *Mackinac Islander* in 1945
(Courtesy William C. Duman)

repair work. His business letterhead read simply, "L. Duman, The Diver, Sub Marine Work, Cheboygan, Michigan." He, for example, did the diving required in the raising of the propeller *Algomah* from the Cheboygan River in 1944. Lawrence Duman and the well-known Edward J. LaWay of Big Stone Bay west of Mackinaw City (see schooner *Anglo Saxon*) were good friends and occasionally collaborated on marine projects. Lawrence Duman passed away in 1972. His widow, Thursa, still lives in Cheboygan today.

By the time he was 14 years old, Bill Duman had learned submarine diving from working with his father Lawrence. He was the third generation in his family to do so. During World War II, he was a machinists mate in the U. S. Navy but did do some hard-hat diving. After the War, Bill worked for a while as a fireman on the ferry boat *Algomah II*. In 1946, he took a full-time job in the southeast Michigan area which limited his diving activities in the Straits to part-time work. By 1957, Bill had purchased and started to use SCUBA diving equipment in his work. Bill Duman is now retired and lives with his wife Nathalie in Ortonville, Michigan. Although, he made his last dive in 1975, he continues to follow diving and maritime events around the Lakes and is a frequent visitor to his home in Cheboygan.

As a child, young Bill and his friends played on the schooner *L. B. Coates* and the propeller *Myrtie M. Ross*, both abandoned at the Whitehall Lumber Company dock not far from his home. He recalls that the *Coates* caught fire in 1930 and was partially burned. Over the years he watched this vessel disintegrate under the stress of weather and slowly disappear beneath the waters of Lake Huron.

The *Coates* was built in Saugatuck, Michigan, in 1874 and was named after Captain Linsford Baines Coates who was a part owner of the Saugatuck Lumber Company.[10] This schooner was built to serve their transportation needs and had a carrying capacity of 245,000 board feet of lumber. Captain Coates lived on Mackinac Island and in 1878, with George T. Arnold, formed the Coates and Arnold Steamship Company,[11] the predecessor of today's Arnold Transit Company that provides ferry service in the Straits area.

Around 1880, Captain Coates established a fishery on the southwestern tip of Marquette Island,[12] the largest island in the Les Cheneaux Islands that lie several miles to the northeast of Mackinac Island. The point of land where his fishery was located was named after him (Coats Point — the "e" was dropped).[13] He enticed his partner to purchase land on the northern point of nearby Little LaSalle Island. That point is now named Arnold Point.[14] Sometime later, the Arnold ferry boats began serving the Les Cheneaux Islands (see the propeller *Islander*). In a strange twist of history, the man, Bill

Duman, who as a child, played on the schooner *L. B. Coates*, also wound up working as a submarine diver repairing boats for the company cofounded by Captain Coates (see photo on page 137).

The *L. B. Coates* had several owners throughout her lifetime and was last owned by Ben Pardee of Bay City, Michigan. She was abandoned at the Whitehall Lumber Company dock circa 1921. Today, the wrecks of the *Coates* and the *Myrtie M. Ross* lie within 200 feet of each other. It is ironic — and as best we can determine, coincidental — that both vessels were constructed by the same builder, John B. Martel of South Haven, Michigan.

VESSEL FACTS	Site #33
NAME:	L. B. COATES
RIG:	Schooner
OFFICIAL NO.:	15970
GROSS TONS:	189
LENGTH:	116'
HULL:	Wood
BUILT:	1874, Saugatuck MI, by John B. Martel
DATE LOST:	1922
CAUSE OF LOSS:	Abandoned
LIVES LOST:	None
CARGO:	None
BOUND FROM/TO:	At Cheboygan dock
LAST ENROLLMENT:	July 12, 1917, Pt. Huron Custom House, #2
SURRENDERED:	August 18, 1921, Port Huron, "Abandoned"
CONFIGURATION:	1 Deck, 2 Masts, Square Stern, Plain Stem
DEPTH:	8'

WRECK LOCATION

In Lake Huron, approximately 400 feet offshore at a spot 1,500 feet west of the mouth of the Little Black River near Cheboygan.

LORAN: 31174.2/48219.0   LAT/LON: 45 39 85/84 29 02

WRECK CONDITION AND FEATURES

The *L. B. Coates* sits upright and is completely broken up. Slightly over 100 feet of her keel is still present. The centerboard box of the *Coates* comes within one foot of the surface of the water. The construction of this vessel is unusual in that the centerboard box structure extends the entire length of the vessel. The centerboard itself is 22 feet in length and is housed in the centerboard box with the front end being approximately 30 feet aft of the bow of the wreck. This unusual centerboard box construction may be of interest to divers who are concerned with vessel construction. Otherwise, there is little of interest to the diver on this dive site. However, it is only 200 feet south of the wreck of the *Myrtie M. Ross.* Both wrecks can be visited on a single dive. Boat access to this wreck is guarded by the submerged pilings of the old docks of the Whitehall Lumber Company and the Embury-Martin Lumber Company.

The MORSE Diving Apparatus

Nine styles, ranging in capacity from 15 to 187 feet.

Our Apparatus is the Official Standard for the United States Navy, and has been adopted by the Corps of Engineers, United States Army.

The MORSE Monitor Nozzle

A permanent fire protection for buildings and for use on tugs in fire fighting, as well as fire boats, and rolling stock of Fire Departments.

MANUFACTURED ONLY BY

ANDREW J. MORSE & SON, Inc.

221 High St., BOSTON, MASS.

CATALOGUE ON APPLICATION.   See Page 181.

Polk's Marine Directory, 1891

LANDBO

Landbo
(Courtesy Great Lakes Marine Collection, Milwaukee Public Library)

The propeller *Landbo* was originally named *Nyanza* (American #130462, 1,888 gross tons).[1] She was sunk in a collision with the propeller *Northern King* at the foot of Sugar Island in the St. Mary's River on July 15, 1895. She was subsequently raised and repaired at the American Steel Barge Company dry dock in Superior, Wisconsin. The *Nyanza* was sold to Canadian owners in 1916 and renamed *Landbo*, a twist of the name Boland.[2]

The *Landbo* foundered near Point Au Sable (now Point Nipigon) with a cargo of 3,000 tons of coal on August 8, 1919. She was purchased by the Great Lakes Towing Company for $4,000 where she lay. After she was raised, they sold the coal cargo for $12,000.[3] Some difficulty was encountered during the salvage operation, as six pieces of floating equipment were required to raise her.[4]

The *Landbo* was used for a few months by the Great Lakes Towing Company as a lighter and then sold on June 21, 1920, to J. B. Lund's Sons Company of Cheboygan. They planned to use the hull of the vessel as dry dock for their boat repair business. She was tied up at the Millard D. Olds Lumber Company dock on the east side of the

Cheboygan River while a slip was built for her alongside the Lund Foundry frontage further up the River.[5]

The Lund plan was slow to develop, and around 1925 a fire broke out on the vessel and she was burned. After that the *Landbo* was abandoned at the Olds dock. She was stripped of her remaining machinery by Howard Carney who runs a scrapyard business in Cheboygan. The remains of the *Landbo* lie buried in the silt of the Cheboygan River about 1,000 feet in front of the dock of the U.S. Coast Guard cutter *Mackinaw.* For many years, the position of the wreck was shown on NOAA charts of the Cheboygan River Harbor.

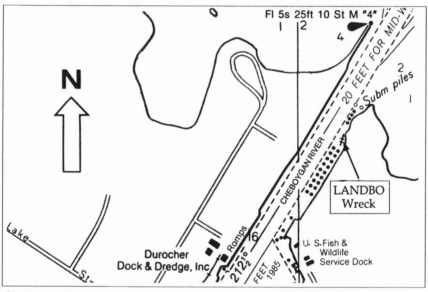

Cheboygan River harbor map showing *Landbo* location

VESSEL FACTS	Site #34
NAME:	LANDBO
RIG:	Propeller
OFFICIAL NO.:	134519 (Canadian)
GROSS TONS:	2,292
LENGTH:	280'
HULL:	Wood
BUILT:	1890, W. Bay City MI, by F. W. Wheeler & Co.
DATE LOST:	September 1920
CAUSE OF LOSS:	Abandoned
LIVES LOST:	None
CARGO:	None
BOUND FROM/TO:	At dock
LAST ENROLLMENT:	1917, Sarnia
SURRENDERED:	September 8, 1920, "Abandoned"
CONFIGURATION:	1 Deck, 2 Masts, Round Stern, Plain Bow
DEPTH:	8'

WRECK LOCATION

On the east side of the Cheboygan River, 1,000 feet northeast of the U.S. Coast Guard mooring facility.

LORAN: 31167.7/48227.8   LAT/LON: 45 29 39/84 27 91

WRECK CONDITION AND FEATURES

The *Landbo* sits upright and is broken up. Her keel, ribs, and some of the hull are present, but these remains are mostly buried in mud and silt. This factor, combined with the poor visibility in the Cheboygan River, makes this a rather uninteresting dive site.

LEVIATHAN

Leviathan
(Courtesy Great Lakes Historical Society)

The twin-screw propeller *Leviathan* was the best-known salvage and wrecking tug ever to run on the Lakes.[1] She saved more vessels from becoming total wrecks than any other wrecking tug and was recognized as the "Guardian Angel" of the Lakes. Commonly called the "boss wrecker"[2] — she was the toughest — and so were her crews. The September 22, 1879, issue of the *Milwaukee Sentinel* newspaper carried the following brief item in the Marine News column:[3] "Late Friday night the crew of the tug *Leviathan* had a bloody fight near Sherman's Tannery. A fellow named Kline was badly pounded."

She saved many a vessel in the Straits and was permanently stationed at Mackinac Island and Cheboygan from 1858 onward.[4] Always the winner against the treachery of the Great Lakes, she succumbed to an onboard fire in 1891 while docked at Cheboygan. The December 3, 1891, issue of the *Cheboygan Tribune* newspaper very simply stated:[5] "She is a total loss, what remains of her hull rests on the bottom of the river at Brannack's Dock." Today, the *Leviathan* sits at the mouth of Duncan Bay just southeast of Cheboygan. She was raised, stripped of her gear, towed to this point and then scuttled.

Wm. Moran,

Junk Dealer and Wrecker,

SUBMARINE ARMORS TO RENT.

———

389 Atwater Street,

DETROIT, MICH.

Beeson's Marine Directory, 1884

VESSEL FACTS   **Site #36**

NAME:	LEVIATHAN
RIG:	Propeller
OFFICIAL NO.:	14612
GROSS TONS:	232
LENGTH:	126'
HULL:	Wood
BUILT:	1857, Buffalo NY, by Benjamin B. Jones
DATE LOST:	November 12, 1891
CAUSE OF LOSS:	Burned at dock
LIVES LOST:	None
CARGO:	None
BOUND FROM/TO:	At Cheboygan dock
LAST ENROLLMENT:	March 30, 1887, Detroit Custom House, #52
SURRENDERED:	February 15, 1892, Detroit, "Vessel lost"
CONFIGURATION:	1 Deck, 1 Mast, Round Stern, Plain Stem
DEPTH:	12'

WRECK LOCATION

At the mouth of Duncan Bay in Lake Huron, 1.5 miles, 71 degrees from the mouth of the Cheboygan River.

LORAN: 31156.5/48228.0   LAT/LON: 45 39 65/84 25 95

WRECK CONDITION AND FEATURES

The *Leviathan* sits upright and is broken up. Pillow blocks and other supporting structure for the two propeller shafts are visible. Being a tug, the vessel was constructed with very heavy timbers. These massive timbers are evident in the wreckage. This is an excellent dive site for less experienced divers. The location just inside the mouth of Duncan Bay provides good protection from the weather. The visibility is generally good and enough of the vessel remains to make for an interesting dive. Three hundred feet in front of the *Leviathan* sits the remains of the *Genesee Chief*.

M. STALKER

M. Stalker painting
(Courtesy Great Lakes Historical Society)

Milan, Ohio, the launching place of the schooner *M. Stalker*, is a quiet little inland town located several miles from any ship's dock. Anyone passing through this hamlet today would find it hard to believe that Milan was once reputed to be the greatest grain port in the world. Thomas Alva Edison was born here in 1847 when Milan was at its zenith as a bustling port. That year over 1.1 million bushels of grain were exported along with 3.3 million board feet of lumber and various other products including flour, wool, wine and clover seed.[1]

After the War of 1812, grain production in Ohio grew rapidly to the point where surpluses existed. The problem was lack of transportation to markets. The railroads had not yet arrived. The citizenry of Milan came up with a plan to build a three-mile-long canal from the town to the Huron River, which meandered several miles northward to Lake Erie. Through this waterway, the surplus grain from the countryside south of Milan could be shipped to major markets such as Buffalo. The charter for building the canal was granted January 24, 1827, and after many delays, the first vessel, the schooner *Kewaunee*, arrived at the city docks on July 4, 1839.[2]

Centerboard winch on the *M. Stalker*
(Authors, 1980)

In the years that followed, Milan prospered and other industries sprang up, including shipbuilding. In the period from 1841 to 1867, between 75 and 80 vessels were built in the Milan yards.[3] It was here on March 19, 1863, that the schooner *M. Stalker* was launched.[4] She was owned by Augustus P. Mowry of Milan and was under the command of Captain Martin Stalker, her namesake. The last vessel built was the schooner *Exile* launched in September 1867. By this time, the railroads were in full operation and commerce through Milan had all but died. In March 1868, the dam on the Huron River that supplied water for the canal was washed out and the canal was abandoned.[5] Today it is difficult to imagine that this modest town was such a thriving port let alone trace the bed of the old canal.

The *Stalker* spent most of her life in the iron ore trade. In August 1869, she was damaged slightly in a gale while docked at the Marquette ore docks on Lake Superior.[6] She underwent a rebuild in 1875 and received major repairs in 1885.[7]

During a severe November gale in 1886, the *Stalker* anchored off Mackinaw City to ride out the storm. About two in the morning, she

Debbie Gammage examines the windlass on the *M. Stalker* *(Photo by Mark Gammage, 1979)*

was struck on the starboard bow by the Canadian barge *Muskoka* in tow of the propeller *Isaac May*.[8] The collision tore away the *Stalker's* headgear and she began to take on water. The *Isaac May*, with two other barges in tow, i.e., the *Waubaushene* and the *Severn*, did not stop, though the *Stalker* lit and waved a distress torch.

The crew of the *Stalker* tried desperately to keep the water from rising by means of the bilge pumps. Realizing their vessel was about to sink, they hauled in the anchor and ran for shore in an attempt to beach her. When it became apparent they were not going to make it, they abandoned ship in their yawl boat and watched as the *Stalker* slipped beneath the waves.[9] Later that morning, the crew came ashore in their boat near Mackinaw City. Having sunk in 15 fathoms of water, the foremast of the *Stalker* was visible above the surface. Her mainmast came loose and washed ashore on Bois Blanc Island.[10] Curiously, her cargo was consigned to the J. H. Outhwaite Company of Cleveland, the namesake of the propeller *J. H. Outhwaite* that sank only five miles away in 1905.

The *Stalker* was found by divers Dick Campbell, Fred Leete, Dick Race and John Steele in July 1967. They recovered her nameboards, so her identity is not in question. The *Stalker* is an easy dive, but a sharp lookout should be maintained as the wreck lies directly on the Mackinac Island ferry boat course.

VESSEL FACTS	Site #23
NAME:	M. STALKER
RIG:	Schooner
OFFICIAL NO.:	17211
GROSS TONS:	267
LENGTH:	135'
HULL:	Wood
BUILT:	1863, Milan OH, by Henry Kelley
DATE LOST:	November 5, 1886
CAUSE OF LOSS:	Collision
LIVES LOST:	None
CARGO:	Iron ore
BOUND FROM/TO:	Escanaba/Cleveland
LAST ENROLLMENT:	April 9, 1882, Sandusky Custom House, #19
SURRENDERED:	January 20, 1887, Sandusky, "Wrecked"
CONFIGURATION:	1 Deck, 2 Masts, Square Stern, Plain Stem
DEPTH:	85'

WRECK LOCATION

In Lake Huron, 2.3 miles, 79 degrees from Old Mackinac Point.

LORAN: 31213.6/48125.9   LAT/LON: 45 47 38/84 41 04

WRECK CONDITION AND FEATURES

The *M. Stalker* is upright and intact with her bow pointing slightly west of north. The stern section is broken apart. This is an excellent dive. It is close to shore, and most of the features of an old sailing vessel can be observed. Such features include a windlass, centerboard, bilge pump, some mast sections, wire rigging, centerboard winch, etc. Being close to the main Straits channel, there is often a current and heavy silt on the wreck.

MAITLAND

Identifying a shipwreck often can be more difficult than finding one. In the absence of a nameboard or a capstan cover bearing the vessel's name, circumstantial evidence must be used to establish the identity of a wreck. This means gathering facts from the wreck itself and comparing it with historical information on vessels known to have sunk in the area. Sometimes a wreck is wrongly identified, usually being given the name of another somewhat similar vessel that also sank in the same general area. The bark *Maitland* is one of these, having been mistakenly called the *Northwest* for many years.

In the spring of 1980, we conducted an underwater survey on the *Maitland* that resulted in the scale deck plan drawing shown on page 153. Our measurements showed she was about 134 feet in length. She had one deck, three masts, a plain stem and a square stern. A sharp collision gash was found in the starboard bow area. Her bowsprit is broken off where it attaches to the hull. There was no evidence of any cargo. Curiously, no masts were found anywhere in the vicinity of the wreck. Nor were there any remains of rope or the braided wire used for rigging. The rudder was locked in a hard-to-port position. But was she really the bark *Maitland*? Compare this wreckage information with an account of her loss in the next four paragraphs, gleaned from several sources.[1]

On Friday, June 9, 1871, the *Maitland* cleared Chicago loaded with 18,000 bushels of corn for delivery in Buffalo. By Sunday night, June 11, she was making her passage eastward through the Straits of Mackinac. Although it was dark, visibility was good as there was no fog. The wind was light from the north-northwest. Around 10 p.m., when abreast of Big Stone Bay, the lookout on the *Maitland* spotted a schooner approaching from the opposite direction. To the dismay of Captain Brown of the *Maitland*, the two vessels were on a collision course and were closing fast. He quickly ordered the *Maitland* turned hard-to-port to avoid the oncoming schooner *Golden Harvest*. The corrective action was too little, too late, and the two vessels collided starboard to starboard with a grazing blow.

Unknown to the crew of the *Maitland*, the schooner *Mears* was running off the starboard side and slightly behind the *Golden Harvest*. Following the first collision, the *Maitland* staggered onward in her hard-to-port turn, fully exposing her starboard side to the oncoming *Mears*. With a sickening thud, the *Mears* cut into the starboard front quarter of the *Maitland* causing her to sink in less than five minutes. The crew of the *Maitland* escaped in the yawl boat and safely reached Mackinaw City.

Diver Rose Armstrong peers through a mast hole on the *Maitland*
(Photo by Mark Gammage, 1980)

Those on board the *Golden Harvest* did not fare so well. In the first collision, the bowsprit and starboard anchor of the *Maitland* caught the weather rigging of the *Golden Harvest* and carried it away causing both masts on the *Harvest* to go by the board. This tremendous force broke the bowsprit off the *Maitland*. In the process, the second mate and brother of the *Harvest's* captain, a Mr. Higgie, suffered a serious skull fracture and was not expected to live. The lookout forward had a leg broken and the man at the wheel had several ribs fractured. The vessel itself, although seriously damaged, was towed to Racine, Wisconsin, for repairs by the wrecking tug *Leviathan*.[2] The *Mears* lost her jib-boom and head gear and her stem was split. She was towed through to Chicago for repairs by the wrecking tug *Magnet*.

The *Maitland* had sunk about seven or eight miles west of Mackinaw City and her masts could be seen sticking out of the water. About two weeks after the sinking, Captain Peter Falcon commanding the schooner *Barber*, salvaged the masts and rigging from the *Maitland* and brought them into Mackinaw City.[3] Falcon was a well-known salvor on the Great Lakes (see *Milwaukee*, page 155), and he knew the masts could be sold for a good price.

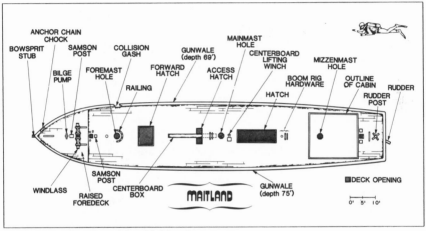

Underwater drawing of the *Maitland*
(Copyright © 1981 Chuck & Jeri Feltner)

To us it was clear that the wreck we had surveyed was indeed the *Maitland*. The location, the collision gash, the broken bowsprit and the hard-to-port position of the rudder on the wreck correlated with the circumstances of the sinking. The configuration of one deck, three masts, plain stem and square stern, were also convincing. The measurements of length and breadth of the wreck were essentially identical to those of the *Maitland*. The lack of cargo is consistent with a corn cargo that would have decayed over time and washed out of the hull. Finally, the lack of masts on the wreck was undoubtedly due to the fact that those on the *Maitland* had been salvaged by Peter Falcon. The near-perfect correlation of underwater archaeological information with that from historical research leaves little doubt that this wreck is the bark *Maitland*.

VESSEL FACTS   Site #12

NAME:	MAITLAND
RIG:	Bark
OFFICIAL NO.:	16320
GROSS TONS:	252
LENGTH:	133'
HULL:	Wood
BUILT:	1861, Goderich ON, by Henry Marlton
DATE LOST:	June 11, 1871
CAUSE OF LOSS:	Collision
LIVES LOST:	None
CARGO:	Corn
BOUND FROM/TO:	Chicago/Buffalo
LAST ENROLLMENT:	May 7, 1867, Buffalo Custom House, #87
SURRENDERED:	Buffalo, "Copy in place lost document"
CONFIGURATION:	1 Deck, 3 Masts, Square Stern, Plain Stem
DEPTH:	84'

WRECK LOCATION

In Lake Michigan, 7.1 miles, 280 degrees from Old Mackinac Point.
LORAN: 31273.1/48092.7   LAT/LON: 45 48 20/84 52 29

WRECK CONDITION AND FEATURES

The *Maitland* is upright and intact. Divers can easily penetrate this wreck. There is a raised forecastle. The windlass is in excellent condition. Many deck fittings are present. There is a bilge pump forward of the windlass and a centerboard lifting winch near the center of the vessel. The centerboard is off-center to the starboard side and does not pass through the keel. This was a low-cost construction method that did not weaken the keel. For those who like old wooden sailing vessels, the *Maitland* is one of the best dive sites in the Straits.

MILWAUKEE

The sinking of two vessels as the result of a collision was not very common. Usually the vessel that was hit was the most likely to be lost, the striking vessel more often than not survived. An exception was the propeller *Milwaukee* that rammed the schooner *J. H. Tiffany* in November 1859. Both vessels sank within approximately 3,000 feet of each other. The complete story of this disaster is recounted in the narrative of the sinking of the *Tiffany* (page 125). What is even more unusual is that both vessels, although sunk in moderately deep water, underwent significant salvage operations. This was a consequence of the actions of Captain Peter Elias Falcon, one of the most extraordinary men to sail the Great Lakes.[1]

Peter Falcon was remarkable for the fact that he raised scores of sunken vessels in their entirety from deep water in the period 1861 to 1891. He was an innovator and played a key role in the invention

Joseph G. Falcon, son of Peter Falcon, dons a helmet c. 1916
(Courtesy Falcon Marine Company)

of the technology for raising sunken vessels. Born in Norway in 1822, Falcon went to sea as a cabin boy at the age of 13, and for the next 20 years, he sailed the world over. By the age of 35, Falcon had, as he put it, "committed matrimony" and settled in Cohasset, Massachusetts, a small coastal town south of Boston. In 1858, he took up hard-hat diving and went into the salvage business.

Falcon was impatient with the techniques in use at that time for carrying out salvage operations. Very quickly he invented several new approaches, including a method for removing bulk cargo, such as coal or grain, from sunken vessels (U.S. Patent No. 49026, July 25, 1865) and an apparatus for overcoming the adhesion of a sunken vessel to the mud in which it was imbedded (U.S. Patent No. 49342, August 8, 1865).

Undoubtedly his most significant invention was the technique for raising sunken vessels from deep water in an intact condition (U.S. Patent No. 37438, January 20, 1863). The method involved the use of large casks filled with water and attached to the sunken vessel.

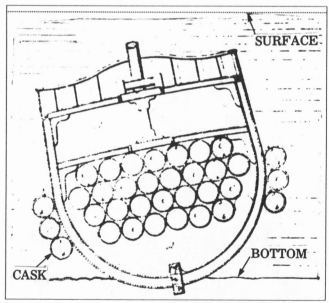

Sketch showing Falcon's method of raising sunken vessels, Patent No. 37438, January 20, 1863
(Courtesy Falcon Marine Company)

They were attached to the vessel so that the bunghole was in a downward position. The casks were filled with air from the surface using a hose of somewhat smaller dimensions than the diameter of the bunghole, thus allowing the excess air to escape once the cask was filled. Additionally, as the vessel would rise to the surface, the casks would not explode, as the rapidly expanding air could escape through the bunghole. Obviously, the air-filled casks provided the lifting force to raise the vessel, or other objects for that matter.

The principle involved in Falcon's method was the same employed by James Reid in his use of the large steel pontoons in his attempts to raise the *Cayuga* (page 82). Moreover, the "lift bags" in use today operate on the same principle, the bag simply being a flexible version of Falcon's wooden casks. Although the idea seems simple in the retrospection of over 100 years, Falcon was the first to patent it and use it extensively in the raising of sunken vessels from deep water. This invention immediately and forever changed the face of the commercial salvage business.

Falcon moved to Chicago in 1865 and promptly set to work recovering vessels.[2] His first success was the recovery of the bark *Ocean Wave* in 1866 from 113 feet of water in Lake Michigan.[3] He

Chuck Feltner (left) with Jeremiah Lapish, President of Falcon Marine Co. in 1981 *(Authors)*

raised the propeller *City of Boston* in 1870 from 100 feet of water about a half mile from where the *Milwaukee* sank.[4] Other notable successes included the recovery of the schooner *Marquette* from 90 feet of water in 1870, and the retrieval of the Canadian propeller *Oliver Cromwell* from 113 feet of water in 1871, both from the Straits of Mackinac.[5]

By 1874, Peter Falcon had perfected his underwater mechanical capability for disconnecting the engines and boilers from the hull of deep-water wrecks. He then employed his casks to raise this machinery to the surface where it could be lifted onto a barge or towed to shore and lifted onto a dock. In this way, he recovered the engine and boiler from the propeller *Milwaukee* in 1874 and took them to Chicago where they were sold.[6]

The last time Peter Falcon put on his submarine armor and made a dive was in May 1900. He had been hired to inspect a leak in a dam in the Chicago Canal and advise the foreman on how to fix it. He was then 78 years old. On May 31, 1906, in Chicago, Peter Elias Falcon, the world's pioneer in sunken ship recovery, died in the 84th year of his life. Falcon's son, Joseph Guilford Falcon, had worked extensively with his father and was also an accomplished diver (see photo on page 155). He carried on the family business until his retirement in 1922. His son, Guilford Ward Falcon, a fighter pilot in World War I, led the company in the 30s and 40s. The Falcon Marine Company is still in business today. They are located in Waukegan, Illinois, and led by Jeremiah Lapish, their president.

The wreck of the *Milwaukee* was rediscovered by the same divers who found the schooner *J. H. Tiffany*. If you dive the *Milwaukee*, take a good look around. Perhaps you'll find an old wooden cask left behind by Peter Falcon.

VESSEL FACTS **Site #1**

NAME:	MILWAUKEE
RIG:	Propeller
OFFICIAL NO.:	None
GROSS TONS:	616 (BOM)
LENGTH:	185'
HULL:	Wood
BUILT:	1853, Cleveland OH, by Luther Moses
DATE LOST:	November 29, 1859
CAUSE OF LOSS:	Collision
LIVES LOST:	None
CARGO:	Wheat
BOUND FROM/TO:	Milwaukee/Buffalo
LAST ENROLLMENT:	May 3, 1855, Buffalo Custom House, #38
SURRENDERED:	Buffalo, "Lost 1860"
CONFIGURATION:	1 Deck, 1 Mast, Round Stern, Scroll Stem
DEPTH:	96'

WRECK LOCATION

In Lake Michigan, 5.2 miles, 238 degrees from Grays Reef Light.
LORAN: 31407.2/48077.8   LAT/LON: 45 43 50/85 14 85

WRECK CONDITION AND FEATURES

The *Milwaukee* is upright but broken up. Only a section of the hull on the starboard stern is still standing. The rest of the hull has fallen outward onto the bottom, with the deck having fallen down into the bilge. The propeller and the windlass are still present, all the other machinery having been removed by Falcon. The wooden wheel with a rope barrel lies about 40 feet off the starboard side near the stern. The wreck is about 25 miles from Mackinaw City but is only 2.75 miles west of the *Cayuga*. If you are in the area to dive the *Cayuga*, a stop at the *Milwaukee* is worthwhile.

MINNEAPOLIS

Minneapolis as a passenger vessel entering Grand Haven Harbor in 1874
(Courtesy Great Lakes Marine Collection, Milwaukee Public Library)

Perhaps it was a premonition of worse things to come when the 1894 season of navigation was officially declared open on "April Fools" day. Of the many vessels moored in the Chicago River Harbor, most were reluctant to leave. The first to head out was the big steel propeller *E. M. Peck*. She was followed by a slower starting group of boats, 19 total, all strung out in a long line resembling a somber naval parade. Among the 19 was the propeller *Minneapolis* and her consorts, the schooners *San Diego* and *Red Wing*. Also in this opening parade of ships was the propeller *William H. Barnum*, who ironically was to meet her fate in the Straits of Mackinac one day sooner than the *Minneapolis*.[1]

The *Minneapolis*, laden with 48,577 bushels of wheat and pulling her grain-laden consorts, made slow time as she labored out onto Lake Michigan and headed for the Straits. The *Barnum* raced ahead and obviously thought she would beat the *Minneapolis* through to Buffalo by a wide margin. Enroute on the open Lake, the weather began to worsen. When the *Minneapolis* reached the western entrance to the Straits of Mackinac, a heavy gale was blowing and considerable ice was running, making the situation very dangerous.

The first signs of trouble were detected by first mate Sidney S. Percy at 3 a.m. Wednesday, April 4, who noticed the vessel was loggy and answered her wheel with some difficulty.[2] He made a quick inspection and discovered the hold was rapidly filling with water. All the pumps were put to use by engineer John Morgan, but could not stem the flow. He awakened the master, Captain H. W. Bogart, and the remainder of the crew of 14, who hurried from their cabins into the cold night air. The rising water soon put out the boiler fires and the *Minneapolis* ceased to make headway. Lanterns were frantically waved to gain the attention of the *San Diego,* which by now was near astern. The *San Diego's* captain steered his craft deftly into a position directly against the stern of the *Minneapolis* and the crew was hurriedly transferred aboard. The last crewmember had scarcely boarded the *San Diego* when the steamer sank to the bottom in 20

Minneapolis c.1894
(Courtesy Great Lakes Marine Collection, Milwaukee Public Library)

fathoms of water a mile-and-a-half north of Mackinaw City. Six miles away and 24 hours earlier, the *William H. Barnum* had met a similar fate, and thus would not beat the *Minneapolis* to Buffalo.

The general assessment was that the heavy ice had cut the hull of the *Minneapolis* causing her to sink. A young fireman from the crew, Oscar Faust, was later interviewed at Rice's Hotel in Cheboygan and gave this account of the sinking:[3]

"I was working in the fire hole when we were about 14 miles from Cheboygan. The mate called down that he wanted everybody to get up on deck right away. We thought he was only joking, but he called out a second time — 'get up on deck, we're sinking.' Then we went up. I hurried to my quarters to get what belonged to me, but I had only time enough to get this suit of clothes I am wearing. The *San Diego* lay against our stern and her captain was standing over the rope, which held her to us, with an ax in his hands. He was going to cut the line when our captain called out to wait as all of us had not left the *Minneapolis.*

"When I got aboard the *San Diego*, the line was cut and the *Minneapolis* veered over to starboard just afterwards. With her bows plunged down and her stern went away up in the air, her wheel tore away a chunk of the *San Diego's* bow when she took the header, then she broke in two about the waist and down she went. That's all there was to it. I haven't any complaint to make but when they took some of her iron plates off to caulk her over, and they never put them back. That left the wooden part of her hull exposed at the bows and the ice just chawed its way through. I always was dead leery about putting that iron back again where it belonged."

The location of the wreck was known for many years by George Coffman and Captain Edward LaWay, both members of pioneer Straits area families.[4] During the winters they would go out on the ice and fish on the *Minneapolis.* In 1963, local Mackinac divers Dick Charboneau and Fred Leete relocated the wreck. Their detailed exploration of the wreck showed no evidence that the vessel broke in two as stated by fireman Faust at the time of her sinking. The wreck is located only about 500 feet southwest of the main south tower of the Mackinac Bridge. It can be a challenging dive, as strong currents and poor visibility are often encountered on the wreck.

VESSEL FACTS Site #21

NAME:	MINNEAPOLIS
RIG:	Propeller
OFFICIAL NO.:	90524
GROSS TONS:	1,072
LENGTH:	226'
HULL:	Wood
BUILT:	1873, Marine City MI, by James Doran
DATE LOST:	April 4, 1894
CAUSE OF LOSS:	Cut by ice
LIVES LOST:	None
CARGO:	Wheat
BOUND FROM/TO:	Chicago/Buffalo
LAST ENROLLMENT:	March 27, 1890, Detroit Custom House, #56
SURRENDERED:	June 11, 1894, Detroit, "Vessel total loss"
CONFIGURATION:	1 Deck, 3 Masts, Round Stern, Plain Stem
DEPTH:	124'

WRECK LOCATION

In Lake Michigan, 1.5 miles, 357 degrees from Old Mackinac Point.

LORAN: 31226.2/48111.2   LAT/LON: 45 48 32/84 43 54

WRECK CONDITION AND FEATURES

The *Minneapolis* is upright and mostly intact. Her bow section is broken off. Items of interest on the wreck include a large fire box boiler, a single-cylinder low-pressure steam engine, a 12-foot diameter four-blade propeller and a donkey steam engine amidships. Her smoke stack is still standing and rises to a depth of 75 feet. There is often a very strong current and heavy silt on the wreck. Extreme caution should be exercised in diving this wreck.

MYRTIE M. ROSS

Myrtie M. Ross c.1893
(Courtesy Institute for Great Lakes Research, Bowling Green State University)

Where do elephants go to die? The same question can be asked about ships who escaped accidental loss and lived to an old age!

With age, some vessels were simply too costly to rehabilitate to working condition and thus were retired. Others, although still in good shape, were temporarily retired because they could no longer economically fulfill their primary intended purpose. Some just pulled into the nearest port and docked because they could go no further.

When retired from the mainstream, the opportunities to do constructive work were limited. They could serve as work barges, trash haulers from Mackinac Island to the mainland, or reserve boats ready to go in as a substitute whenever needed. Possibly the need existed for a floating dry dock as in the case of the propeller *Landbo*.[1]

164　　　　　　　　　　　　　　　*SHIPWRECKS OF THE STRAITS OF MACKINAC*

Or perchance they could perform as a floating museum, assiduously satisfying the interests of those with a maritime bent. Such is the case of the freighter *Valley Camp* now permanently docked at Sault Ste. Marie, Michigan. Some, like the schooner *Lily E.*, served as floating clubhouses for maritime groups like the South Shore Yacht Club of Milwaukee.[2] No matter their role, it always involved accepting a position that was of considerably reduced status, albeit in a working capacity.

After 1900, the retirement home for many vessels in the Straits was at the docks in the vicinity of the city of Cheboygan. For here there was a large number of docks, from Little Black River to Duncan Bay, that had fallen into disuse. As a result of the decline of the lumber business and the replacement of smaller vessels with larger ships able to travel large distances, Cheboygan became a port that most vessels could afford to bypass. With the growing quiet, Cheboygan gradually collected abandoned vessels at her deserted docks — and the longer they sat idle, the less likely they were to return to active duty.

When all opportunity to contribute had faded, many of these abandoned vessels were mercifully done away with by scuttling in deeper water. Sometimes their scuttling was done with splendor as they were towed to open water and set afire to commemorate some important occasion. Thus passed out the barge *Elva* (described later) when she was burned off Mackinac Island to solemnize the breaking of ground for the building of the Mackinac Bridge. Metal vessels were generally cut up for scrap. Some vessels were used to form the foundation of breakwalls and docks — acting much like a floating crib ready to be filled with stone and dirt. This was the demise of the propeller *Algomah*. Finally, many vessels were left to die a slow death at a crumbling dock. Such was the fate of the propeller *Myrtie M. Ross*.

The *Ross* was built in South Haven, Michigan, in 1890 as a general freight vessel for Volney Ross and was named after his daughter.[3] When built, she was 89 feet in length but only one year later, in 1891, was lengthened to 113 feet. Under the command of Captain Joseph Smith of South Haven, the *Ross* carried lumber, stone, produce and other goods from port to port. In the season of 1892, she made 61 round trips transporting lumber from Manistee to Benton Harbor.[4] At the start of 1894, business went well and Captain Smith's son, Frank Smith, worked on the *Ross* with his father. On July 10, 1894, tragedy befell the *Ross* at the South Haven dock when a fire broke out on the vessel at night and the Captain's son and two other crew members were trapped in the vessel and died.[5] The *Ross* was repaired and, with sorrow in his heart, Captain Smith resumed command.[6]

Myrtie M. Ross being built at South Haven, Michigan, in 1890
(Courtesy Michigan Maritime Museum)

On August 8, 1900, while at a Windsor, Ontario, dock with a load of coal, swells from a passing steamer lifted the *Ross* up and dropped her on some submerged pilings which punched holes in her bottom. She sank but was repaired and quickly put back in service.[7] Later the same year, on November 22, The *Ross* foundered during a gale on Lake St. Clair. Her crew of eight was rescued by the propeller *Walter L. Frost* and taken to Detroit.[8] The following year, having been declared abandoned, she was raised by the McMorran Wrecking Company and sold to them at a Marshall's auction on July 25, 1901, for $900. The *Ross* was repaired and put back in service by this company in 1902.[9]

In the spring of 1912, while at Cheboygan, the *Myrtie M. Ross* was sold to the Berst Manufacturing Company of Saginaw. They took her to Saginaw where she was reported sunk at the docks on December

14, 1912. On October 28, 1913, during a regular inspection in Cheboygan by the U.S. Steamboat Inspection Service, her license was refused due to faulty boilers and hull.[10] The *Ross* was left at the Whitehall Lumber Company docks in Cheboygan and, on September 8, 1916, her final *Certificate of Enrollment* was surrendered, the vessel having been declared "abandoned – unfit for service."

The *Myrtie M. Ross* eventually settled to the bottom at the Whitehall docks and she became a favorite playground for children who lived nearby. One of these was William C. Duman who recalls being chased by a watchman from the decaying wreck in the 1930s. By his recollection, the wreck had broken up completely by 1945 when the propeller was salvaged from her by local scrap dealers.

VESSEL FACTS	**Site #32**
NAME:	MYRTIE M. ROSS
RIG:	Propeller
OFFICIAL NO.:	92177
GROSS TONS:	156
LENGTH:	113'
HULL:	Wood
BUILT:	1890, South Haven MI, John B. Martel
DATE LOST:	September 8, 1916
CAUSE OF LOSS:	Abandoned
LIVES LOST:	None
CARGO:	None
BOUND FROM/TO:	At Cheboygan dock
LAST ENROLLMENT:	October 18, 1912, Port Huron Custom House, #5
SURRENDERED:	September 8, 1916, Port Huron, "Abandoned"
CONFIGURATION:	1 Deck, 1 Mast, Plain Stem, Round Stern
DEPTH:	10'

WRECK LOCATION

In Lake Huron, approximately 600 feet offshore at a spot 1,500 feet west of the mouth of the Little Black River near Cheboygan.

LORAN: 31174.9/48218.8   LAT/LON: 45 39 90/84 28 98

WRECK CONDITION AND FEATURES

The *Myrtie M. Ross* sits upright and is completely broken up. All of the machinery has been removed with the exception of a part of the propeller shaft that measures 5.5 inches in diameter. Virtually all of the keel, except for the stempost, is present and what remains measures 109 feet in length. Part of the stempost and bow lies about 20 feet in front of the main part of the wreckage. Some bow sheathing material is in this area. The keel of the *Ross* stands about three feet high and the center two-thirds is slotted. Through this slot run ribs. They are a single piece and extend to both the port and starboard side of the wreck. This unusual construction may be of interest to divers who are concerned with vessel construction. Otherwise the wreck provides little of interest to divers. The wreckage is well inside the remains of several old docks. Numerous subsurface pilings are a danger to dive boat hulls.

J. W. Westcott & Co.,
Marine Reporters, Vessel Agents and Owners.
OFFICE, FOOT OF WOODWARD AVENUE,
DETROIT, MICH.
River and Harbor Tug Office, Steam Pumps
and Lighters.
MARINE COLLECTIONS A SPECIALTY.
SPECIAL ATTENTION TO
Ore, Lumber and Coal Cargoes.
———
OFFICE TELEPHONE, No. 55.
RESIDENCE OF J. W. WESTCOTT, TELEPHONE No. 4111.

Beeson's Marine Directory, 1890

NORTHWEST

Northwest at Wolf & Davidson Dry Dock, Milwaukee, 1883
(Courtesy Great Lakes Marine Collection, Milwaukee Public Library)

169

Finding shipwrecks can be a painstaking process, often requiring months of library research and hundreds of boring hours on the water running search patterns. On other occasions, the ever-watchful are rewarded with instant success. Such was the case when we found the wreck of the schooner *Northwest*. Following is an excerpt from a story we wrote in 1981 for *Diving Times*, a newspaper about diving, published by Recreational Diving Systems of Royal Oak, Michigan:[1]

"In the fall of 1978, my wife, Jeri, and myself found ourselves on our boat headed west of the Mackinac Bridge to make a dive on a shipwreck called the *Northwest*. It was Sunday, October 1, and we had been 'blown off' the propeller *Pewabic* the day before at Alpena. Jeri was at the wheel holding a cruising speed of about 25 mph, which was making quick work of the eight-mile trip from Mackinaw City to the *Northwest*. I was making minor adjustments to the bottom recorder while, at the same time, trying to rebut Jeri's chiding remarks about why I let the chart recorder run all the time and wasted so much chart paper!

"As I studied the craggy bottom, it gradually smoothed out to the point where minor changes in bottom structure were more distinguishable. It was then that a rather noticeable 'blip' in the bottom structure appeared with an equally quick return to a flat profile. My mind struggled briefly with this bit of confusing information. The mental circuits were still searching through the memory bank trying to find a correlation when I yelled at Jeri in a thunderstruck tone to 'stop the boat!' A wave of emotion swept over me as I realized we had most likely run over a wreck where there wasn't supposed to be one! We radioed the dive boat *Lisa Ann* that was nearby with George Dunkelberg, Rose Armstrong, Al Rau and crew and told them of our 'blip,' and, with dive gear close at hand, it didn't take Al long to verify that we had discovered a virgin shipwreck. It was an old wooden schooner sitting in 73 feet of water about 4-1/3 miles west of McGulpin Point."

Having inadvertently found this wreck, we now tried to identify it. The process took over two years of careful research. Ironically, the wreck turned out to be the real *Northwest*, whereas the wreck we had set out to dive was, in fact, the bark *Maitland* (page 151). The *Maitland* had been misidentified as the *Northwest*. Through the serial number on the wreck's compass, we learned from Ritchie Compass Company in Pembroke, Massachusetts, that the compass was sold to Upson, Walton and Company, a defunct ship chandler in Cleveland. Next, with the help of C. Patrick Labadie, we located the 1873 records of Upson, Walton and Company at Canal Park Museum in Duluth, Minnesota. From these we determined that they had put this compass on the schooner *Alexander B. Moore*. Certificates of Enrollment from the National Archives in Washington, D.C., showed that the *Alexander B. Moore* was renamed as the *Northwest* when she was rebuilt in 1883. Voila! A strange tale of two ships that took much longer to unravel than to find the wreck in the first place.

Diver Al Rau at the *Northwest's* wheel
(Photo by George Dunkelberg, 1978)

The sinking of the *Northwest* in 1898 was a nonevent. She was passing through the Straits on a cold April morning in tow of the propeller *Aurora* when she struck some submerged ice and began to take on water. The *Aurora* attempted to tow her to shallow water but was blocked by the ice. This effort was continued until the *Northwest* finally went down. The crew was rescued by the *Aurora*.[2] The newspapers reported that "The grain laden *Northwest* lies in 12 fathoms of water three miles south of west from St. Helena Island Light and five miles west of McGulpin Point Light."[3] Although this position was almost a mile off, the depth was correct. The wreck is shown on the 1910 chart of the Straits of Mackinac.

We recovered one of her wooden stock anchors in 1978 and donated it to Dossin Great Lakes Museum on Belle Isle in Detroit. It sits proudly on their lawn today.

Northwest anchor at Dossin Great Lakes Museum, Detroit
(Authors, 1980)

VESSEL FACTS	**Site #13**
NAME:	NORTHWEST
RIG:	Schooner
OFFICIAL NO.:	105241
GROSS TONS:	1,017
LENGTH:	223'
HULL:	Wood
BUILT:	1873, Bangor MI, by T. Boston
DATE LOST:	April 6, 1898
CAUSE OF LOSS:	Cut by ice
LIVES LOST:	None
CARGO:	Corn
BOUND FROM/TO:	Chicago/Buffalo
LAST ENROLLMENT:	July 31, 1893, Cleveland Custom House, #10
SURRENDERED:	April 13, 1898, Cleveland, "Loss of vessel"
CONFIGURATION:	1 Deck, 4 Masts, Square Stern, Plain Stem
DEPTH:	73'

WRECK LOCATION

In Lake Michigan, 6.2 miles, 273 degrees from Old Mackinac Point.

LORAN: 31270.2/48102.2   LAT/LON: 45 47 32/84 51 30

WRECK CONDITION AND FEATURES

The *Northwest* is upright but is broken up. She has a donkey steam engine and other machinery on her. The transom is broken out and lies on the bottom. The wreck is collapsed to the port side. The *Northwest* is an interesting dive and is at a comfortable depth. The fact that it has fallen apart has created a disarray of wreckage that makes it difficult for the inexperienced wreck diver to understand the layout of the vessel.

PESHTIGO *(Propeller)*

Peshtigo (propeller)
(Courtesy Ralph Roberts Collection)

Not to be confused with the schooner *Peshtigo*, The propeller *Peshtigo* was, however, originally built as a two-masted schooner.[1] She was converted to a propeller at the Wyandotte Boat Works in late 1895, using an old, secondhand, 1869 steeple compound steam engine and a used 1893 fire box boiler.[2] As a propeller, she was put into the lumber trade. In October 1898, she suffered severe damages in a collision with the propeller *George W. Roby* on Lake Huron, 12 miles north of Thunder Bay Island.[3]

The *Peshtigo* stranded during a strong northeast gale on Mission Point on Mackinac Island, and was abandoned.[4] A rudder recovered from this wreck has been on display at the Marine Museum of the Mackinac Island State Park Commission in Mackinaw City. For years the wreckage of the *Peshtigo* lay about 300 feet offshore from Mackinac Island. In time, she was broken up by the ice and most of the remains were pushed up onto the shore. Finally, during a landfill project, her keel and rib structure was covered over with rocks.

Scattered pieces of the wreck can be found between Red Buoy #2 and the shoreline.

VESSEL FACTS   Site #26

NAME:	PESHTIGO
RIG:	Propeller
OFFICIAL NO.:	54218
GROSS TONS:	817
LENGTH:	203'
HULL:	Wood
BUILT:	1869, Trenton MI, by Alvin A. Turner
DATE LOST:	October 23, 1908
CAUSE OF LOSS:	Stranded
LIVES LOST:	None
CARGO:	Lumber
BOUND FROM/TO:	Unknown
LAST ENROLLMENT:	May 16, 1906, Marquette Custom House, #9
SURRENDERED:	March 31, 1909, Marquette, "Vessel lost"
CONFIGURATION:	1 Deck, 2 Masts, Round Stern, Plain Stem
DEPTH:	10'–13'

WRECK LOCATION

Two thousand feet northeast of the end of the east breakwall at Mackinac Island Harbor.

LORAN: 31176.8/48108.8   LAT/LON: 45 51 09/84 35 99

WRECK CONDITION AND FEATURES

The small amount of wreckage that remains in the water is completely broken up. The keel and rib structure is buried in a landfill slightly northeast of Mission Point. The *Peshtigo* provides little of interest to the diver.

RICHARD WINSLOW

Richard Winslow at Port Arthur, Ontario, c.1885
(Courtesy Patrick Labadie and the Thunder Bay Historical Museum Society, Ontario)

As one of the "Big Boys," the schooner *Richard Winslow* was, for a time, the largest sailing craft to navigate the Great Lakes.[1] When launched from the Detroit Springwells shipyards of master builder James M. Jones on May 6, 1871, the *Winslow* became the first full-rigged, four-masted schooner on the Lakes as well as the largest at 885.2 gross tons.[2] By full-rigged is meant a vessel with the full complement of sails for schooner rigs, including gaff-topsails.[3] Only two years later she was relegated to second largest with the launching of the schooner *John Martin*, which slid off her ways in Cleveland in 1873 at 937 tons and a length of 220.2 feet.

On her first trip, she carried 1,550 tons of coal from Cleveland to the Gas Works in Chicago.[4] This was a record tonnage for a sailing vessel. On July 5, 1871, she made her first appearance in Buffalo carrying 59,156 bushels of corn from Chicago. Again, this was a sailing vessel record. With this load, her draft was so great that she was unable to enter the river and had to unload her cargo outside the harbor.[5] For the next several years, the *Richard Winslow* continued in the Winslow fleet carrying coal from Cleveland to Chicago and grain to Buffalo on the return trip. In 1890, she was sold to commercial interests in Buffalo and cut down to a tow barge.[6]

Mangled remains of *Winslow's* iron wheel
(Photo by Dave DeNike, 1981)

On Saturday, September 3, 1898, the *Winslow* left Escanaba carrying 1,600 tons of iron ore to be delivered at the Oglebay, Norton and Company docks in Cleveland.[7] She was in the tow of the propeller *Inter Ocean* commanded by Captain Peter Wex of Buffalo. He was a native born German who had 30 years experience as a Lakes captain and had commanded the *Inter Ocean* since 1892.[8] The

Winslow was in command of Captain Dennis Galligan who was a part owner of the vessel.

As the *Winslow* approached the Straits Sunday evening, September 4, a strong southwest gale was blowing. By eleven o'clock that night, the gale had proved too much for this 27-year-old vessel. To their horror, the crew discovered that the water was rising rapidly in her hold and she soon became unmanageable. Captain Galligan decided to abandon ship. In response to the *Winslow's* distress signals, Captain Wex brought the *Inter Ocean* alongside and, with a big sea running, engaged in taking off the crew. This life or death task was accomplished with great difficulty, but in due time all hands made it to safety. The *Inter Ocean* stood by in the area for approximately two hours as the *Winslow* slowly settled to the bottom.[9]

Two days after her sinking, she was located near the buoy on White Shoals with her masts sticking out of the water.[10] A lighted black spar buoy was placed in 33 feet of water about 300 feet north of the sunken *Winslow*.[11] This buoy had been set by the U.S. Lake Survey of the Corps of Engineers, and in the September 27, 1898, issue of the *Detroit Free Press*, they published a *Notice to Mariners* that gave a detailed description of her exact location.[12] Because she was a hazard to navigation, the wreck position was marked on a 1902 chart of the Straits of Mackinac. Finally, in 1902, the wreck was dynamited by the Corps of Engineers such that a depth of 24-1/2 feet was possible over the wreck.[13]

The wreck of the *Winslow* remained untouched until May 1981, when Ray Dickerson and his crewmembers Joe Ault and Jerry McRoberts from Indianapolis relocated her. They shared the location of the wreck with many divers. Unfortunately, their openness led to disappointment, as less than three weeks later the wreck had been stripped of her most prized possessions — two giant wooden stock schooner anchors. In August 1981, a diver from Alpena was arrested and later convicted of receiving and concealing stolen property with a value over $100 — a felony in the State of Michigan since the passing of Public Act 184 on July 2, 1980.

VESSEL FACTS **Site #5**

NAME:	RICHARD WINSLOW
RIG:	Schooner
OFFICIAL NO.:	110003
GROSS TONS:	885
LENGTH:	216'
HULL:	Wood
BUILT:	1871, Detroit MI, by James M. Jones
DATE LOST:	September 5, 1898
CAUSE OF LOSS:	Foundered
LIVES LOST:	None
CARGO:	Iron Ore
BOUND FROM/TO:	Escanaba/Cleveland
LAST ENROLLMENT:	February 2, 1893, Buffalo Custom House, #34
SURRENDERED:	December 28, 1898, Buffalo, "Vessel lost"
CONFIGURATION:	1 Deck, 4 Masts, Square Stern, Plain Stem
DEPTH:	32'

WRECK LOCATION

In Lake Michigan, 1.4 miles, 287 degrees from White Shoals Light.

LORAN: 31356.4/48026.4   LAT/LON: 45 50 45/85 09 48

WRECK CONDITION AND FEATURES

The *Richard Winslow* is completely broken up due to dynamiting by the Corps of Engineers. The wreckage is scattered over a very wide area. Components of the vessel machinery and other construction factors are easily accessible by novice divers. A dive on this wreck is not worth the long boat ride from port, however, you may wish to visit the *Winslow* as a second dive to the schooner *Colonel Ellsworth* or the propeller *Cayuga*.

ST. ANDREW

Good luck was something that all nineteenth century Great Lakes sailors sought — and for good reason. A variety of talismanic items were placed aboard the old sailing vessels. An upside-down horseshoe nailed to a mast was sure to help when a vessel was in distress. When vessels were being built, the owners would sometimes place a coin in a mast step before the mast was put in place. The date of the coin was always the same as the year the vessel was launched. Such coins were commonly called "stepping coins" and were meant to bring good luck.

Frequently when a sailing vessel sank, the masts would be pulled out of their step in the keel and float away rather than break off at

Stepping coin from the *St. Andrew*
(Courtesy Jerrie Hayden, 1990)

the deck level. This leaves the mast step open to inspection by the knowledgeable diver in search of a stepping coin. Retrieving one is not as easy as it sounds. Most often the hold of a 100-year-old shipwreck is filled with three or four feet of silt that has to be removed before you can even find the step in the keel. This is a difficult task underwater. For one thing, the stirred up silt creates a dense cloud in the water that makes it impossible to see for more than a few inches. This is compounded by the fact that the diver is usually in a confined closed space between the deck and the vessel's bottom. It is a scary feeling to be caught in a silt cloud and not be able to find your way out of the bowels of a sunken vessel.

These factors did not deter Jerri Hayden, her father Brownie (Leonard) Brown and diver Roy Enos of Baldwin, Michigan, from recovering the stepping coin from the wreck of the schooner *St. Andrew* in 1972. The coin (see photo) is an American Flying Eagle one-cent piece that was minted from 1856 to 1858.[1] The date on the coin clearly reads 1857, the year the *St. Andrew* was built.

The *St. Andrew* sank at night after colliding with the schooner *Peshtigo* about five miles west of Cheboygan.[2] When they struck, the *St. Andrew* fell over on the *Peshtigo*, taking out both her foremast and mainmast. Two of her crew jumped on the *Peshtigo* near the bow. They heard Captain Peter Lynch of the *Peshtigo* say to his second mate, "John, you done a bad job. Why didn't you call me?"[3]

Jeri Feltner measures windlass on the *St. Andrew*
(Authors, 1981)

The *Peshtigo's* crew was ordered to lower the boat. A deckhand and John Boyle, the second mate who was at the wheel when the accident occurred, went below for their clothes. Boyle was not seen again and apparently went down with the vessel. By this time, the *Peshtigo* was going down fast, stem first, and her stern was high in the air. The deckhand lowered himself to the water on the davit falls,

181

but drowned before the yawl could reach him. All the crew of the *St. Andrew* got away safely in their yawl boat. Two hours later, both crews were picked up by the schooner *S. V. R. Watson*.[4]

For some reason, the *St. Andrew's* last Certificate of Enrollment was not surrendered until almost nine years later. Her Captain was Edward L. Fitzgerald, whose father, Edmond Fitzgerald, was the owner of the *St. Andrew*.[5] He was part of the Fitzgerald family that produced the namesake for the well-known propeller *Edmund Fitzgerald* that sank on Lake Superior in 1975. Perhaps he refused to abandon the wreck of the *St. Andrew* in hopes that he might raise her.

The identity of this wreck as the *St. Andrew* has never been proven conclusively. However, the date of the stepping coin matches her build date, and our measurements of the wreck are virtually identical with those of the *St. Andrew*. The location is consistent with several newspaper reports, although inconsistent with others. Her configuration matches that on her original Certificate of Enrollment except that the figurehead has been removed. All of this evidence, although circumstantial, has led us to conclude that the wreck is, in fact, the schooner *St. Andrew*. For many years she was mistakenly called the brig *Henry Clay* that sank nearby. The *Clay* was 45 feet shorter and sank in 1851, well before the date of the stepping coin.

Given that this wreck is the *St. Andrew*, where then is the wreck of the schooner *Peshtigo*? For years, many divers claimed to have dived on another wreck in the early 1970s within a half-mile of the *St. Andrew*. Today, no one has been able to relocate this second wreck. Its whereabouts remain a mystery.

VESSEL FACTS	Site #31
NAME:	ST. ANDREW
RIG:	Schooner
OFFICIAL NO.:	22416
GROSS TONS:	425
LENGTH:	135'
HULL:	Wood
BUILT:	1857, Milan OH, by Merry & Gay
DATE LOST:	June 26, 1878
CAUSE OF LOSS:	Collision
LIVES LOST:	None
CARGO:	Corn
BOUND FROM/TO:	Chicago/Buffalo
LAST ENROLLMENT:	May 13, 1878, Chicago Custom House, #25
SURRENDERED:	March 31, 1887, Chicago, "Sank June 26, 1878"
CONFIGURATION:	1 Deck, 3 Masts, Square Stern, Eagle Head
DEPTH:	61'

WRECK LOCATION

In Lake Huron, 11.4 miles, 124 degrees from Old Mackinac Point.

LORAN: 31180.2/48195.1   LAT/LON: 45 42 07/84 31 46

WRECK CONDITION AND FEATURES

The *St. Andrew* is upright and mostly intact. The bow area is in good condition, while the stern section is broken up. Her centerboard is intact and is representative of construction methods of the period. The windlass is particularly interesting as it uses a crude pawl and chock system for locking the position of the windlass barrel. This wreck is an extremely easy dive with little current and usually no silt. She is an excellent wreck for beginning divers.

SANDUSKY

Brig similar to the *Sandusky*
(Courtesy Loudon G. Wilson)

Although fore-and-aft schooners were by far the favored rig for Great Lakes sailing vessels in the nineteenth century, many vessels carried the brig rigging in the period before 1860. Such vessels, although very fast on the open seas, were less maneuverable in the confined waters of the Great Lakes. They eventually gave way to the more responsive fore-and-aft schooner rig. Brig-style rigging disappeared completely on the Great Lakes with the sinking of the *Robert Burns* in the Straits of Mackinac on November 16, 1869.[1] She was the last full-rigged American brig ever to sail the Lakes.[2]

The Straits of Mackinac, often called the *crossroads of the Great Lakes*, presented many special hazards to the brigs that passed through. The Straits are guarded at both the east and west ends by many shoals and reefs. Once inside these, the early navigator was forced to steer a tight course to avoid stranding on one of the many islands or on the shoreline of the constricted Straits passage. In severe storms, strong gales or darkness, a Straits passage on a brig was indeed a real challenge. One such brig that accepted this challenge and lost was the *Sandusky*. This vessel and all her crew were lost in a violent storm in the Straits of Mackinac in 1856.[3]

Throughout her lifetime, the *Sandusky* changed hands several times. On September 11, 1856, she was acquired by a new set of owners.[4] Apparently the demands of the new owners caused disgruntlement among the crew, as two men, Samuel McQue and Charles O'Shea, deserted the vessel. They were arrested by the Chicago gendarmes and placed in jail. Later they were released in custody of Captain Thomas H. Smith of the *Sandusky* and forced to board the vessel and sail on her to Buffalo.[5] Unknown to McQue and O'Shea, this action was tantamount to signing their death certificates, for the *Sandusky* was destined to shortly become yet another victim of the deadly Straits of Mackinac.

According to the Vessel Passages section of the *Chicago Tribune*, the *Sandusky* left the Chicago Harbor on September 16, 1856.[6] On September 18, a violent gale sprang up on the northern end of Lake Michigan, wreaking death and destruction on those who sailed on her waters. One of the first public signs of disaster appeared in the *Milwaukee Sentinel* on September 23, 1856, which noted that "There is a report that a brig has foundered in the Straits with all hands

185

lost."[7] The brig *Columbia*, under the command of Captain Wells, saw the *Sandusky* sink with men clinging to her masts but was unable to render assistance.[8]

According to the *Detroit Advertiser and Tribune*, a downbound sailing vessel came into Mackinac and reported a vessel sunk with several men clinging to a spar. The side-wheeler *Queen City*, bound for Chicago, set out from Mackinac to the aid of the distressed sailors.[9] When Captain Watts of the *Queen City* arrived on the scene,

Sandusky nameboard
(Photo provided by anonymous source)

only three sailors were still clinging to the spar of the sunken vessel. In the face of gale-force seas, try as he may, Captain Watts could not maneuver his vessel into a position to save the three crewmen. They were left to find a watery grave.

Although the identity of the sunken vessel was never proven, the propeller *Oriental* issued a report that they had sighted the vessel near Beaver Island in a dismasted condition.[10] On October 1, 1856, the *Milwaukee Sentinel* stated that there was little doubt that "the brig sunk in the gale near Mackinac was the *Sandusky* bound for Buffalo from Chicago with a cargo of grain." The *Sentinel* further noted that "a bottle is said to have been picked up at Grand River containing a paper with some almost illegible writing but which is believed to have been written on the *Sandusky* in a sinking condition."[11] Seven

Gemini II crewmembers Tony Gramer, Ben Cline, Captain Chuck Feltner and crewmember Chuck Muller *(Authors, 1981)*

sailors lost their lives making this one of the worst disasters to occur in the Straits of Mackinac.

On May 2, 1981, we located the wreckage of the brig *Sandusky*. On board our boat, the *Gemini II*, were crewmembers Ben Cline, Tony Gramer and Chuck Muller. During the 1981 dive season, we made

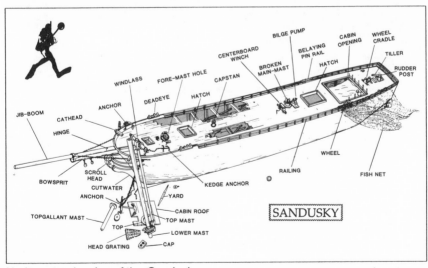

Underwater drawing of the *Sandusky*
(Copyright © 1981 Chuck & Jeri Feltner)

about 50 dives on the wreck doing archaeological survey work and shooting documentary film and still photographs. The accompanying drawing shows the condition of the wreck when we first found it. Of all the wrecks we had dived in the Great Lakes, the *Sandusky* was by far the most magnificent. The bow is a captivating sight for the wreck has a scroll figurehead, cutwater bow, bowsprit and jib-boom. Blocks, belaying pins, deadeyes, anchors, nameboards, crew belongings and other artifacts adorned the wreck. We left the wreck intact and did not reveal its location.

Jeri Feltner at the *Sandusky's* wheel
(Photo by Stan Stock, 1982)

In the summer of 1985, a group of divers located the wreck and made its position public. In the ensuing years, hundreds of divers have visited this wreck. It has become the premier dive site in the Straits of Mackinac. Unfortunately most of the artifacts have now disappeared, including a nameboard. In 1988, the figurehead became loose and was removed for safekeeping by local Mackinaw City divers Fred Leete and Janet Provost, and turned over to the State of Michigan for preservation. A replica of the original figurehead was made by a group of people from the Detroit-area including Bill

Covington, Franz Estereicher, Tony Gramer and Mike Kohut, and placed on the wreck in the summer of 1989. Irrespective of these problems, the wreck of the *Sandusky* is still a magnificent sight.

VESSEL FACTS	**Site #14**
NAME:	SANDUSKY
RIG:	Brig
OFFICIAL NO.:	None
GROSS TONS:	225 (BOM)
LENGTH:	110'
HULL:	Wood
BUILT:	1848, Sandusky OH, by Dan Dibble
DATE LOST:	September 20, 1856
CAUSE OF LOSS:	Foundered
LIVES LOST:	7
CARGO:	Grain
BOUND FROM/TO:	Chicago/Buffalo
LAST ENROLLMENT:	September 11,1856, Chicago Custom House, #102
SURRENDERED:	Unknown (probably Chicago)
CONFIGURATION:	1 Deck, 2 Masts, Square Stern, Scroll Stem
DEPTH:	83'

WRECK LOCATION

In Lake Michigan, 5.2 miles, 280 degrees from Old Mackinac Point.

LORAN: 31261.8/48100.9   LAT/LON: 45 48 09/84 50 06

WRECK CONDITION AND FEATURES

The *Sandusky* is upright and intact. Exciting things to see include a scroll figurehead and a completely intact bowsprit and jib-boom. Both wood stock anchors are still on the wreck. The steering mechanism is of considerable interest. As of July 1991, divers have destroyed the wheel and taken away much of the unique steering gear mechanism. Some dead eyes have survived the wreck strippers and are still present adjacent to the forward mast. This is an outstanding wreck for the sport diver. It is exemplary of an early Great Lakes sailing vessel.

ZEN AND THE DIVING OF THE *SANDUSKY*

Chuck Feltner, September 8, 1981

Each time I backrolled off the boat and broke through the surface of the water it was like entering a time machine. The sensations I felt in passing through the sharp thermocline and losing the daylight were tantamount to being propelled into some sort of twilight zone. As the pressure of depth squeezed ever harder on my body and the biting cold of the 40 degree water of early May numbed my bones, I began to wonder why I voluntarily do this. Very quickly the answer appeared in the form of a ship's deck rail barely visible through greenish-murky water. In a moment I landed on the deck and after the first puff of silt had blown off I realized the time warp was complete. Here I was in this holy place again. Exploring the wreck was like going through an ancient European Cathedral except there were no crowds for I was alone...completely alone. The presence of another diver would have been a desecration of this sacred rite. Slowly I moved from one display to another – first a row of deadeyes, then a windlass and next a bowsprit – each one a virgin to the eyes. The experience was enhanced by careful control of my buoyancy so that I was forever suspended in a weightless state. A slow and lazy swim kick was sufficient to drive me forward along the halls of this underwater museum. It seemed almost sinful to touch anything for by now the religious dimension of the dive had taken me over completely.

As always, the one thing that constantly reminded me that I was alone was the sound of my breathing. The only other sensation was the usual slight squeeze of my dry suit which acted like the arm band of a giant blood pressure measuring device covering my whole body and making me feel my pulse everywhere. In this state it took little effort to create a picture in my mind's eye of the *Sandusky's* sailors frantically working the bilge pump in front of the broken main-mast trying to clear the hold of water while each crashing wave opened the seams of the hull still further. Realizing it was a losing effort, they ran down the deck to the fore-mast and climbed the ratlines to the upper reaches of the mast and held on for dear life as the *Sandusky* slowly settled beneath the surface. No doubt they stared in fright as the water began to rise quickly up the mast — all the time wondering how deep the water *really* was. And then, with a slight bump, the hull struck bottom leaving them momentarily safe in their precarious perch. In the distance they probably could see the side-wheeler *Queen City* fighting her way towards them through the roaring gale. But her progress was agonizingly slow and in the interim, Sam McQue, Charlie O'Shea and two others were swept away by the violent seas. The three who remained must have prayed to God with all the force of their souls for the arrival of the *Queen City*. I could only imagine their sense of resignation to death when a beam sea turned their rescue ship away. Most likely they knew they would be gone before she could circle back.

The picture of the drama of the *Sandusky* on the video screen of my mind was interrupted by the trained response to check my air supply. A glance at my pressure gage indicated that the doors to this great Cathedral would soon be closing. The anchor line took me out of the vestibule and back through the time warp with its attendant thermal and pressure change sensations. Breaking surface I knew I was back in my intended world and time frame.

It has always been a strange feeling to swim along the side of our boat after surfacing from a solo dive and look up into my wife Jeri's face and see an expression that looks as though she has been attending a wake for the gravely endangered. This expression changes quickly as soon as I flash her the "A-Okay" sign. The reunion with the non-aquations of the boat is completed when they eagerly accept the pieces of gear I hand them as I climb out of the water onto the swim platform. In the cockpit I strip the tank, weight belt and hood. Next comes the ritual of verbal intercourse with my diving companions who are eager to share vicariously in my experience. They engulf me with questions. What did you see? How was it down there? What did you see? Was there a current? What did you see? How was the visibility? What did you see? How — ? What — ? The whole thing takes on a primordial spirit like that associated with the return of the single-combat warrior.

When the gear is stored and things become settled, I reflect upon the practice of this religion. What has it meant? In short, I feel physically awakened and emotionally cleansed — for this has been an experience on one of the upper ledges of the Ziggurat of the Brotherhood of Scuba. Very simply, diving the *Sandusky* is my Zen.

SEA GULL

Sea Gull
(Courtesy Patrick Labadie)

Around 1888, the tug *Sea Gull* came to the Great Lakes from the New England area.[1] She was owned by Captain James Reid, the famous wreck salvor (see *Cayuga*, page 82) who was mayor of St. Ignace in the period 1888 to 1892. Reid had salvaged scores of wrecks. The *Sea Gull* was one of the few cases where he was on the wrong end of a disaster.

On a Sunday evening in late April 1893, the *Sea Gull* left Detour, Michigan, with the propeller *Ohio* in tow for Chicago.[2] Captain Murdock, who commanded the *Sea Gull*, had finished his supper and gone on deck when he saw a sudden puff of smoke emitted from a gangway. Hurriedly he proceeded to investigate the cause. When he looked down the forward hatch, a sea of flames greeted him. The fire had gained such headway that Captain Murdock knew that it was impossible to fight. He gave the order to abandon ship.

Quickly the yawl boat was lowered and the crew of 13 got into it and made for their tow, the *Ohio*. For over two hours, Captain Murdock and his crew watched the tug burn. On Mackinac Island, the captain of the propeller *Charles West* saw the light from the burning tug and went to their rescue. He succeeded in putting out the fire and towing the hull onto the beach of Bois Blanc Island.[3]

None of the crew saved any of their effects. Fortunately the night was calm, for if it had been rough some of them probably would have been lost. The *Sea Gull* was valued at $40,000 and insured for $28,255.

Sea Gull's capstan cover
(Photo by Marty Jahn)

A representative of the insurance companies was on board and was glad to escape with his life. He had been inspecting the propeller *Ohio*. The next day, Captain Murdock hired a harbor tug in Cheboygan and visited what remained of the tug. He noted that nothing but the shell of her hull was left, and her machinery was so badly damaged by the fire as to be worthless.[4]

Later in the week Captain James Reid showed up to survey his loss. Jokingly, the *Cheboygan Tribune* reported that "Capt. James Reid, owner of the *Sea Gull*, which burned last Sunday night, has been in the city this week. This forenoon he chartered the tug *Clayt* to visit the remains of the *Sea Gull*. He took City Treasurer Clune along as commissary and John H. Clery, observer of the Weather Bureau, to look after the weather."[5]

Marty D. Jahn of Chicago located the wreck in the early 1970s. Marty owns the decomissioned Bois Blanc Island Lighthouse and discovered the wreck while snorkeling. One of his more interesting finds was the capstan cover with the tug's name on it (see photo), leaving little doubt about the wreck's identity.

VESSEL FACTS	Site #38
NAME:	SEA GULL
RIG:	Propeller
OFFICIAL NO.:	22098
GROSS TONS:	521
LENGTH:	160'
HULL:	Wood
BUILT:	1863, Mystic CT
DATE LOST:	April 30, 1893
CAUSE OF LOSS:	Burned and beached
LIVES LOST:	None
CARGO:	None
BOUND FROM/TO:	Detour/Chicago
LAST ENROLLMENT:	May 20, 1891, Detroit Custom House, #89
SURRENDERED:	June 30, 1893, Detroit, "Vessel lost"
CONFIGURATION:	2 Decks, 1 Mast, Round Stern, Plain Stem
DEPTH:	15'

WRECK LOCATION

In Lake Huron, about 1/2 mile south of the Bois Blanc Island Light.
LORAN: 31123.7/48158.4   LAT/LON: 45 48 41/84 24 65

WRECK CONDITION AND FEATURES

What remains of the *Sea Gull* is completely broken up and scattered over a large area. There is not much for divers to see. The wreck can be reached from shore.

UGANDA

Uganda
(Courtesy Great Lakes Marine Collection, Milwaukee Public Library)

In early spring at the beginning of the navigation season, ice was always a danger to vessels plying the Lakes. People from warmer climes than Michigan marvel at the fact that the upper Lakes freeze solid during an average winter. In January, cars and trucks regularly travel across the ice from St. Ignace to Mackinac Island to deliver goods to the year-round Island residents.

The clearing of the ice in the Straits of Mackinac occurs around April 20. In the latter half of the nineteenth century, the passage of the first vessel through the Straits of Mackinac was considered to be the time at which general navigation on the Lakes opened. From 1854 onward, this date was recorded regularly.[1] Before 1900, the earliest Straits passage was April 2, 1871, and the latest was May 5, 1885. Those vessels who dared a passage in April were courting danger. With shifting winds, ice floes could quickly close in on a vessel and

> ### Mackinac Straits May Be Open Today
> ### Boats are Making Slow Progress Through Ice
>
> *Mackinaw City, Michigan.* – April 19 – Steamers are making slow progress through the Straits. Those that passed up yesterday morning are in the ice eight miles west of this point. The downbound fleet is near Waugoshance. A north wind is driving the ice to the south and it looks now as through the entire fleet would be able to get through today.
>
> The railroad car ferry *Chief Wawatam* stuck in a heavy floe of ice at 2 o'clock this morning and at 10 a.m. had been unable to free herself. The vessel is being carried by the ice slowly to the eastward, but is in no danger.

Detroit News April 19, 1913

cut her hull open. The propeller *Uganda* was one such vessel. Others include the *Eber Ward*, the *Minneapolis,* and the *Northwest*.

Bound for Buffalo with a full cargo of grain, the *Uganda* passed White Shoals Light on Saturday evening, April 19, 1913, and headed eastward through the Straits. Soon after passing the Light, the ice crowded in around the vessel and cut through her hull. Captain Crockett started all the bilge pumps but they could not keep up with the rising water. Realizing the vessel was doomed, he began to blow distress signals. Fortunately, the propeller *John A. Donaldson* was close behind the *Uganda* and came to her aid. The *Donaldson* saved all 22 crew members just before the *Uganda* sank, stern first, about four miles east of White Shoals Light. The forward

Gage panel on the *Uganda*
(Photo by Ben Cline)

195

ICE SENDS BOAT TO BOTTOM; CREW OF 22 MEN SAVED

UGANDA CUT THROUGH AND GOES DOWN IN MACKINAC STRAITS.

STEAMER DONALDSON RESPONDS TO DISTRESS SIGNALS AND RESCUES ALL.

Vessel Was Laden With 100,000 Bushels of Corn; Ice Imprisons Big Fleets Elsewhere.

PORT HURON, Mich. — April 20 — The steamer John A. Donaldson, Capt. Heggs, arrived here this morning with the crew of the steamer Uganda, which was sunk by the ice in the Straits at 8 p.m. Saturday.

Capt. Crockett, of the Uganda, reports that the Uganda cleared from Milwaukee with 100,000 bushels of corn for Buffalo and everything went all right until they got to the heaviest part of the ice off of White Shoals, which cut through the planking and the boat started to leak. The captain stopped and started all pumps. But the water gained and the boat began to settle fast. He blew distress signals and the Donaldson, which was close behind the Uganda, worked her way up through the ice alongside and took the crew of 22 men off.

After backing away, the Uganda started to settle aft and finally sank stern first, about four miles east of White Shoal lightship.

When the Uganda went down, the forward part of the boat was blown off. She was owned by Edward Mehl of Erie, and was uninsured.

The Uganda was a wooden vessel, 291 feet in length and was built in 1892.

Detroit News April 21, 1913

cabins were blown off and drifted away on ice floes when the vessel sank.[2]

With Stan Stock of Gaylord, Michigan, we found this wreck in the summer of 1983. It is almost exactly where you would expect it to be based on newspaper accounts of her sinking, i.e., 4.3 miles east of White Shoals Light within 100 feet of the designated steamer lane. The wreck sits in a trough that is about one-third mile wide and 220 feet deep at its center. This trough has steep sidewalls that rise to a depth of about 120 feet. It runs east-west down through the Straits and is the ancient river bed of the western reaches of the St. Lawrence River. Downstream, the wreck of the *Eber Ward* sits about 100 feet from the edge of this trough. It appears that the *Uganda* initially settled on the upper edge of the trough and then slid down the sidewalls to the bottom. The highest point of the wreck is at 185 feet, making it a difficult and dangerous dive.

VESSEL FACTS **Site #7**

NAME:	UGANDA
RIG:	Propeller
OFFICIAL NO.:	25289
GROSS TONS:	2,298
LENGTH:	291'
HULL:	Wood
BUILT:	1892, West Bay City MI, by F. W. Wheeler & Co.
DATE LOST:	April 19, 1913
CAUSE OF LOSS:	Cut by ice
LIVES LOST:	None
CARGO:	Corn
BOUND FROM/TO:	Milwaukee/Buffalo
LAST ENROLLMENT:	April 8, 1905, Erie Custom House, #13
SURRENDERED:	April 24, 1913, Erie, "Sunk - Abandoned"
CONFIGURATION:	1 Deck, 2 Masts, Round Stern, Plain Stem
DEPTH:	207'

WRECK LOCATION

In Lake Michigan, 4.3 miles, 90 degrees from White Shoals Light.
LORAN: 31321.7/48047.2   LAT/LON: 45 50 30/85 03 49

WRECK CONDITION AND FEATURES

The *Uganda* is upright and intact. The cabins are gone except for a very interesting center cabin (see vessel photo, page 194) that is still present. Anchors and mechanical equipment are still on the wreck. Engines and boilers are interesting. At the time of this writing, the *Uganda* was a virgin wreck. Since she sits nearly in the bottom of the deep channel, there is often a strong current. This factor, combined with her extreme depth, makes this wreck very dangerous for divers.

WILLIAM H. BARNUM

William H. Barnum in 1873, drawing by Samuel Ward Stanton c.1895[1]
(Courtesy Detroit Public Library)

Over the years, the condition of the propeller *William H. Barnum* had deteriorated and it was reflected in her insurance ratings and valuation. Upon launching in 1873, the Board of Lake Underwriters gave her an A-1 rating and an $80,000 valuation.[2] By 1875, her valuation had dropped to $60,000.[3] In 1893, she was down to $35,000 and an A-2 rating which was being seriously questioned by the insurance underwriters.[4] By the winter of 1893-94, her condition was poor and the Inland Lloyds' inspector, Captain Daniel McLeod, refused to give her a rating or valuation until prescribed repairs were made.[5]

The underwriters claimed the vessel was not seaworthy, and after much argument and negotiation, a compromise was reached.

The underwriters agreed to insure the vessel for $22,000 for a single trip, departing April 1, 1894, for Port Huron.[6] Once there, and upon promise of the owners, she would be repaired and brought up to Inland Lloyds' A-2 rating. The records don't indicate the insurance premiums paid for this high-risk, one-trip venture, but they were undoubtedly large.

Finally, at noon Sunday, April 1, 1894, the underwriters officially declared the shipping season open in Chicago. The *Barnum*, along with 18 other boats, left the Chicago River Harbor with the propeller *E. M. Peck* in the lead. [7] In this same group of boats was the propeller *Minneapolis*, whose loss is described previously in this book.

Laden with 55,000 bushels of corn shipped by Irwin Green and Company of Chicago for export via Port Huron, the *Barnum* pushed her way northward on Lake Michigan. She was under the command of 29-year-old Captain William Smith of Marine City, Michigan.[8] He was on his first trip as master of the *Barnum*. Little did he know it would be his last. Without barges to tow, she reached the Straits of Mackinac well ahead of the rest of the fleet only to encounter heavy weather and extensive ice floes. As she rounded the turn at White Shoals and headed down the Straits, the heavy weather and grinding ice proved too much for her. Water began to pour into the hold as her seams opened.

Barnum rudder at St. Ignace waterfront park *(Authors, 1980)*

199

Frantic efforts were made by Captain Smith and the crew to stem the inflow of water by putting canvas over the holes. But, with the poor condition of the vessel, the battering of the ice and heavy seas took their toll. The pumps fell behind and, in a final cry for help, the *Barnum* sounded the distress call on her steam whistle as she passed below Mackinaw City. The tug *Crusader* which happened to be in the area, came to her aid.

An attempt was made to tow the *Barnum* into shallow water and beach her. Unfortunately, the ice extended in a solid mass far out from shore and blocked the way. The *Crusader* then turned her loose and started for Cheboygan to get steam pumps. Scarcely had the *Crusader* gotten away than the *Barnum* sounded the distress call on her whistle again. The *Crusader* returned, took the crew off the *Barnum*, and stood by and watched as she sank at six o'clock in the morning on April 3, 1894.[9] The insurance underwriters had lost their one-shot gamble.

Only one day after she sank, a wrecking crew out of St. Ignace headed by Captain Fred Ryerse, found the wreck of the *Barnum* off Freedom, Michigan, about five and one-half miles east-southeast of Mackinaw

Barnum artifiacts, Ken Teysen (left), Mr. & Mrs. Ike Brigham *(Photo by Fred Leete, 1966)*

> **Wanted More Of The Barnum's Cargo.**
> Mackinaw City. May 23.—(Special.)—Mr. Schmidten, representing the Brantford, Ont., starch works, which bought the corn in the steamer W. H. Barnum when she sank a year ago, is here to see if any more of the cargo can be saved. Diver John Dodd went down and examined the wreck this afternoon. He found the boat covered with moss and the corn badly decomposed. The best samples he could obtain were soft and so sticky that slight pressure reduced them to paste. Probably this will be the last attempt to save the rest of the cargo.

Detroit Free Press May 24, 1895

City.[10] Captain Ryerse made several dives on the *Barnum*, and finding her to be in good condition, felt the vessel could be raised and salvaged. Additionally, he arranged with the underwriters to salvage the cargo of corn and sell it to the Brantford (Ontario) Starch Works.[11] However, he never did salvage the cargo. Captain Ryerse, the first diver on the *Barnum*, was part of a pioneer family in St. Ignace.

The *Barnum* rested quietly in her watery grave for almost 70 years. Then, in the summer of 1963, a merry band of innovative

The *Penmanta* crew c.1963
Includes Fred Leete (front center), Norm McCready (right center), Jim Sawtelle (far left), Chum LaWay (far right), and Dick Charboneau (left, in wet suit), and Nancy Sawtelle (third from left)
(Courtesy Underwater Diving Technology)

201

wreck searchers, led by Norm McCready of Indianapolis, found the wreck while searching for her with Norm's 35-foot boat, the *Penmanta*.[12] Among this group was Ike Brigham, founder of Ikelite Corporation, maker of underwater lighting systems. One of the crewmembers, Ken Teysen, owner of Teysen's Restaurant in Mackinaw City, salvaged the brass engine maker's plate. It is on display in the marine museum in his restaurant. In raised letters, it reads, "Frontier Iron Works – Detroit – No. 6 – *Barnum*." Later, in July 1969, a group of divers from St. Ignace, recovered the rudder from the *Barnum* and placed it on permanent display in the St. Ignace marine park near the State Marina.[13] Ironically, in this group was Jim Ryerse, the great-grandson of Captain Fred Ryerse, who had first dived on the *Barnum* 75 years earlier.

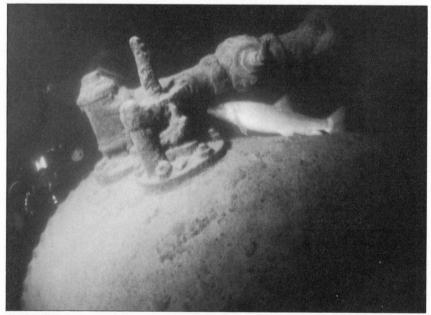

A whitefish inspects the boiler of the *Barnum*
(Photo by Mark Gammage, 1980)

VESSEL FACTS	Site #27
NAME:	WILLIAM H. BARNUM
RIG:	Propeller
OFFICIAL NO.:	80342
GROSS TONS:	1,212
LENGTH:	218'
HULL:	Wood
BUILT:	1873, Detroit MI, by James M. Jones
DATE LOST:	April 3, 1894
CAUSE OF LOSS:	Foundered
LIVES LOST:	None
CARGO:	Corn
BOUND FROM/TO:	Chicago/Port Huron
LAST ENROLLMENT:	April 17, 1893, Detroit Custom House, #73
SURRENDERED:	May 22, 1894, Detroit, "Vessel lost"
CONFIGURATION:	2 Decks, 2 Masts, Round Stern, Plain Stem
DEPTH:	74'

WRECK LOCATION

In Lake Huron, 5.6 miles, 122 degrees from Old Mackinac Point.

LORAN: 31205.5/48153.3   LAT/LON: 45 44 42/84 37 53

WRECK CONDITION AND FEATURES

The *Barnum* is upright and mostly intact. Divers with a mechanical bent will enjoy seeing the engines, boilers, windlass and other machinery on the wreck. The stern section was destroyed when she was dynamited to remove the rudder. Portions of the main deck have collapsed. Nevertheless, being double-decked, the wreck offers many opportunities for penetration. In the summertime, when the thermoclines are at their greatest depth, many fish can be seen patrolling the grave of the *Barnum*. This is one of the most popular dive sites in the Straits of Mackinac.

WILLIAM STONE

The first sawmill in the Straits area was built circa 1790 at Mill Creek three miles southeast of Mackinaw City. It supplied lumber to Fort Mackinac on Mackinac Island and today is a State Park. Later, in the latter half of the nineteenth century, the lumber industry around Mackinac flourished. In 1878, the Callam Lumber Company built a sawmill and dock at Cecil Bay, six miles west of Mackinaw City, on Lake Michigan.[1] The dock (see photo on page 206) was completely exposed to storms blowing from northerly directions.

In 1901, the small schooner *William Stone* was caught at the Cecil Bay Callam Lumber Company dock during a northwest gale and blown ashore. She broke up and went to pieces.[2] The wreckage lies near the remains of the sawmill dock. The remains of the old dock are underwater and are approximately 1,000 feet west of the mouth of the Carp Lake River.

Windlass from the *William Stone* c.1964
(Photo by William C. Duman)

VESSEL FACTS	Site #16
NAME:	WILLIAM STONE
RIG:	Schooner
OFFICIAL NO.:	81548
GROSS TONS:	185
LENGTH:	108'
HULL:	Wood
BUILT:	1896, Vermilion OH, by Bellford Crosier
DATE LOST:	October 13, 1901
CAUSE OF LOSS:	Stranded
LIVES LOST:	None
CARGO:	Lumber
BOUND FROM/TO:	Callam Lumber Company dock at Cecil Bay
LAST ENROLLMENT:	April 18, 1900, Detroit Custom House, #50
SURRENDERED:	January 18, 1902, Detroit, "Vessel lost"
CONFIGURATION:	1 Deck, 2 Masts, Square Stern, Figurehead
DEPTH:	10'

WRECK LOCATION

In Cecil Bay on Lake Michigan, 1,200 feet west of Carp Lake River and 800 feet offshore

LORAN: 31270.7/48128.2   LAT/LON: 45 44 90/84 50 05

WRECK CONDITION AND FEATURES

The *William Stone* is completely broken up. The small amount of wreckage remaining holds little of interest to divers. However, if you visit the wreck, be sure and dive the remains of the Callam Lumber Company dock.

Callam Lumber Company dock in Cecil Bay c. 1900
(Reprinted from "Memories of Mackinaw," courtesy Nancy Campbell)

DISCOVERED BUT NOT IDENTIFIED WRECKS

We are aware of six wrecks in the Straits that have been discovered whose identity is unknown or highly uncertain. Three of these wrecks are in shallow water, and are so badly broken up and scavenged, that it is virtually impossible to identify them using standard underwater archaeological techniques. The other three, *Chuck's Barge*, *Mackinac Island Harbor Wreck* and *Spectacle Reef Wreck*, are of such a nature that we have not been able to identify them. The following descriptions of the *discovered but not identified* wrecks are presented in increasing order of Site Number, which is essentially west to east.

George's Wreck – Site #17

This wreck sits offshore from a cottage owned by George Dunkelberg and Rose Armstrong, long-time Straits divers. Although completely broken up, it is clearly at least a two-masted sailing vessel of greater than 100 feet in length. The remains include a significant portion of the keel and some rib structures. No centerboard box is evident. Based on this information and the location of the wreck, we would guess, by a process of elimination, that its most probable identity is the brig *Odd Fellow* (see page 260). The wreck is located in Trails End Bay, Lake Michigan, 5.85 miles, 226 degrees from the south tower of the Mackinac Bridge. It lies in 12 feet of water about 1,100 feet offshore. (LORAN: 31265.2/48127.3)

Headlands Wreck – Site #18

At the far east end of Trails End Bay on McGulpin Point, sits a magnificent building on a section of land known as the Headlands. This site is a private training school for American-Indian children, and is supported by the McCormick Foundation. Directly offshore rests the wreckage of a propeller-driven vessel. It is over 100 feet long with a portion of the propeller shaft still there. In the early 1960s, Ken Teysen removed the rudder from this wreck. According to Ken, the wreck was an abandoned vessel that was used as a work barge during the construction of the State Ferry dock in Mackinaw City in 1923. After completion of the dock, the vessel was towed to its current location and scuttled. It was locally known under the name *Aching Heart*. We have not been able to find a vessel registered under this name. The wreck lies in seven to 15 feet of water about 500 feet offshore. (LORAN: 31252.3/48119.0)

Chuck's Barge – Site #20

Found by the Authors in the summer of 1982, this barge has become a popular dive site for novice divers. The wreck is a barge used for holding dredge material that was subsequently dumped. These vessels were commonly called dump scows. The bottom consists of two large openings with two hinged doors covering each opening. The hinged doors are equipped with restraining chain mechanisms to hold the doors closed. Presumably, once on site, the chains could be released causing the doors to swing open and the barge contents to be dropped through the bottom into the Lake. Lore has it that the barge was lost in the 1940s by Durocher Dock and Dredge Company of Cheboygan. It is located in Lake Michigan one mile from St. Helena Island Light on a heading of 118 degrees. The barge is about 60 feet long, is intact, and lies upside down in 43 feet of water. (LORAN: 31255.8/48074.3)

Mackinac Island Harbor Wreck – Site #25

Just inside the east breakwall of the Mackinac Island Harbor, lies the upside down remains of a partly-buried wooden wreck with a centerboard mounted in her hull. The wreck measures approximately 100 feet long and 22 feet wide and the hull protrudes a few feet above the silt and mud with essentially no opportunity for penetration. As a consequence of the centerboard and the absence of a propeller shaft, we have concluded that this wreck is a sailing vessel. However, we are not aware of any sailing vessel that sank in this proximity to Mackinac Island Harbor. The wreck lies in 52 feet of water about 150 feet inside the east breakwall of the Mackinac Island Harbor. (LORAN: 31180.1/48110.1)

Spectacle Reef Wreck – Site #39

As noted in the next section on *undiscovered wrecks*, at least four vessels were known to have been wrecked on Spectacle Reef. Diver Steve Kroll from Rogers City, Michigan, has "sledded" this area. This time-proven search method usually involves using a small wooden sled that is weighted and upon which a diver rides while being towed by a slow moving boat. The diver is pulled back and forth over the area of interest and attempts visually to spot any wreckage. Today, self-propelled underwater scooters are available that accomplish the same task but with the diver having more direct control. While sledding off the northwest corner of Spectacle Reef, Steve and his companions found the wreckage of an old sailing vessel. The wreck is completely broken up and lies on a slope ranging in depth from 45 to 70 feet with the main section of the wreckage at 70 feet. The wreckage is probably from one of the four vessels lost on the reef, i.e., the *Augustus Handy, Kate Hayes, Nightingale* or *R. G. Winslow.* (LORAN: 31038.1/48210.5)

Hammond Bay Harbor Wreck – Site #41

Approximately 1.5 miles along the shoreline southeast of Hammond Bay harbor of refuge in Lake Huron, lies the wreckage of a sailing vessel. The wreck is about 100 yards offshore in 10 to 12 feet of water and is completely broken up. Judging from the location, there is a strong possibility that this is the wreck of the schooner *John Jewett.* The wreck was found several years ago by Steve Kroll. No LORAN numbers are available.

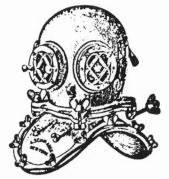

Polk's Marine Directory, 1884

PART IV

UNDISCOVERED WRECKS

INTRODUCTION TO UNDISCOVERED WRECKS

There are 43 wrecks that supposedly have not been *discovered*. Data on these *undiscovered* wrecks is summarized in the *List by Vessel Name* on page 216, and they have a site number that designates their approximate position on the associated wreck chart. Note that there is a possibility that all but three of the six *discovered-but-not-identified* wrecks are a match with the identity of wrecks on the *undiscovered* list. The exceptions are *Chuck's Barge*, the *Headlands Wreck* and the *Mackinac Island Harbor Wreck* for which there are no comparable wrecks on this list.

A high percentage of the *undiscovered* wrecks were sail powered (69%). Additionally, 60% of the *undiscovered* wrecks were lost before 1870 with 62% having been lost due to stranding. Most of the stranded wrecks on the *undiscovered* list were lost in open-water locations, i.e., Skillagalee Reef, Grays Reef, White Shoals and Spectacle Reef. These wrecks would have been pounded to pieces by the Lakes' storms. This factor, combined with their age, would lead to the conclusion that little is left of these wrecks to find today. Others might be easier to find.

One wreck, the schooner *D. N. Barney*, was shown on the 1854 U.S. Lake Survey chart of the Straits of Mackinac. Three others, the schooners *Lawrence* and *Lucy J. Clark*, and the brig *Robert Burns* were located and dived on by hard-hat divers some time after they had sunk. Comparison of the *Discovered* and *Undiscovered Wreck Maps* shows that most of the deep water wrecks close to Mackinaw City have been discovered. Not surprising, as deep water wrecks are the best preserved, and those close to the docks are the wrecks most sought after by modern-day wreck hunters.

To the authors' knowledge, the last wreck discovered in the Straits was the propeller *Canisteo* in 1988. Some of the more fascinating wrecks yet to be discovered include the schooners *Gertrude*, *Lawrence*, *Newell A. Eddy*, and *Peshtigo*, the propellers *Challenge*, *Colonist*, and *Henry J. Johnson*, and the brig *Robert Burns*. Who will rise to the challenge of finding these wrecks? Perhaps the information contained in the following stories will inspire a new generation of wreck hunters to locate some of the Straits of Mackinac's *undiscovered* shipwrecks. Good Luck!

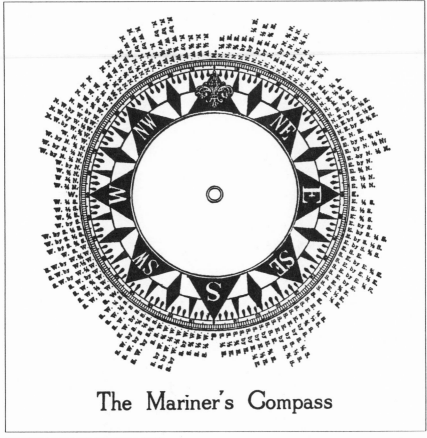

The Mariner's Compass

Trimble's Lake Pilot's Handbook, 1907

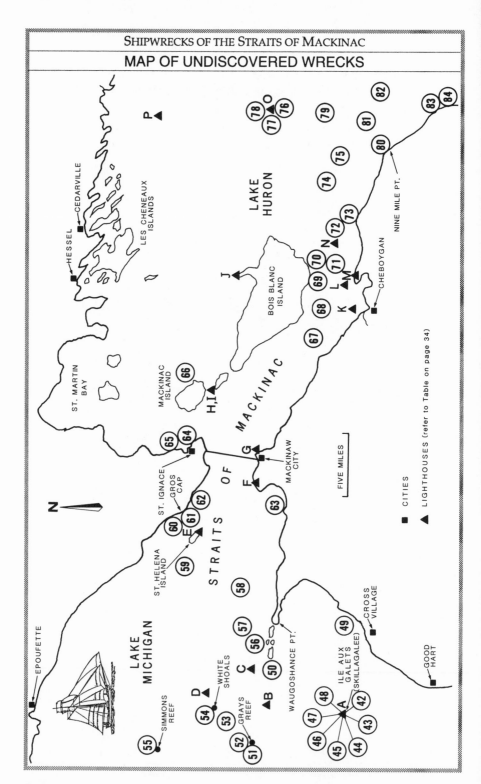

SHIPWRECKS OF THE STRAITS OF MACKINAC

MAP OF UNDISCOVERED WRECKS

LIGHTHOUSES (refer to Table on page 34)

FIVE MILES

■ CITIES

▲ LIGHTHOUSES

UNDISCOVERED – BY SITE NUMBER (43 Total)

42	A. D. Patchin
43	Clarion
44	Condor
45	Julia Dean
46	Oriental
47	Wellington
48	White Swan
49	Lucy J. Clark
50	Island Queen
51	Free State
52	Walrus
53	Francis Palms
54	W. S. Lyons
55	Marold II
56	Thomas Kingsford
57	Dolphin
58	Gertrude
59	Lawrence
60	Leander
61	J. E. Shaw
62	Oliver Lee
63	Odd Fellow
64	Remora
65	Favorite
66	Elva
67	Peshtigo (schooner)
68	Perseverance
69	Bonnie Doon
70	Flight
71	Challenge
72	Robert Burns
73	Anna Smith
74	Newell A. Eddy
75	Colonist
76	Augustus Handy
77	Kate Hayes
78	R. G. Winslow
79	Nightingale
80	John Jewett
81	Henry J. Johnson
82	J. C. Liken
83	Glad Tidings
84	D. N. Barney

See **BY VESSEL NAME** list on following page for detailed information.

UNDISCOVERED – BY VESSEL NAME
(43 Total Undiscovered)

NAME	SITE	RIG	LENGTH	TONS	BUILT	LOST	CAUSE/WHERE
A. D. Patchin	42	sws	225	873	1846	1850	Stranded/Skillagalee Reef
Anna Smith	73	prop	178	939	1873	1889	Stranded/Cordwood Pt
Augustus Handy	76	sch	126	338	1855	1861	Stranded/Spectacle Reef
Bonnie Doon	69	sch	133	255	1855	1867	Stranded/Bois Blanc Is
Challenge	71	prop	197	665	1853	1853	Exploded/15m below Mac Is
Clarion	43	brig	108	236	1844	1860	Stranded/Skillagalee Reef
Colonist	75	prop	134	341	1854	1869	Foundered/Cheboygan
Condor	44	sch	112	237	1857	1862	Stranded/Skillagalee Reef
D. N. Barney	84	sch	110	149	1845	1849	Stranded/7m se of 9 Mile Pt
Dolphin	57	sch	119	233	1862	1869	Collision/Waugoshance Pt
Elva	66	barge	95	83	1889	1954	Scuttled/Mackinac Island
Favorite	65	prop	139	409	1864	1907	Burned/St. Ignace Harbor
Flight	70	sch	114	177	1857	1865	Stranded/Bois Blanc Is
Francis Palms	53	sch	172	560	1868	1889	Stranded/3m nw Grays Reef
Free State	51	prop	195	949	1856	1871	Stranded/Grays Reef
Gertrude	58	sch	135	267	1855	1868	Cut by ice/deep water
Glad Tidings	83	sch	113	183	1866	1898	Stranded/9 Mile Pt
Henry J. Johnson	81	prop	260	1997	1888	1902	Collision/9 Mile Pt
Island Queen	50	sch	115	257	1854	1859	Stranded/Waugoshance Pt
J. C. Liken	82	prop	90	78	1873	1890	Foundered/Spectacle Reef
J. E. Shaw	61	sch	118	293	1854	1856	Stranded/Gros Cap
John Jewett	80	sch	91	103	1866	1898	Stranded/9 Mile Pt
Julia Dean	45	brig	150	498	1854	1855	Stranded/Skillagalee Reef
Kate Hayes	77	sch	130	349	1856	1856	Stranded/Spectacle Reef
Lawrence	59	sch	120	284	1847	1850	Cut by ice/St. Helena Is
Leander	60	sch	84	145	1838	1857	Stranded/Gros Cap
Lucy J. Clark	49	sch	137	308	1863	1883	Capsized/2m ne of Cross Vil
Marold II	55	prop	122	283	1911	1937	Exploded/Simmons Reef
Newell A. Eddy	74	sch	242	1270	1890	1893	Foundered/Bois Blanc Is
Nightingale	79	sch	138	272	1856	1869	Stranded/Spectacle Reef
Odd Fellow	63	brig	107	234	1845	1854	Stranded/8m w of Old Mac Pt
Oliver Lee	62	bark	169	433	1844	1857	Stranded/Gros Cap
Oriental	46	prop	222	950	1854	1859	Stranded/Skillagalee Reef
Perseverance	68	sch	121	294	1855	1864	Collision/off Cheboygan
Peshtigo	67	sch	161	384	1863	1878	Collision/5m w of Cheboygan
R. G. Winslow	78	bark	148	389	1857	1867	Stranded/Spectacle Reef
Remora	64	prop	100	184	1883	1892	Burned/St. Ignace dock
Robert Burns	72	brig	127	277	1848	1869	Foundered/Bois Blanc Is
Thomas Kingsford	56	sch	136	263	1856	1871	Cut by ice/Waugoshance Lt
W. S. Lyons	54	sch	136	258	1866	1871	Stranded/White Shoals
Walrus	52	sch	134	264	1857	1868	Stranded/Grays Reef
Wellington	47	sch	127	225	1855	1867	Stranded/Skillagalee Reef
White Swan	48	prop	81	99	1922	1956	Stranded/Skillagalee Reef

A. D. PATCHIN

A. D. Patchin painting by Loudon Wilson
(Courtesy Ralph Roberts Collection)

The side-wheel steamer *A. D. Patchin* was built in Truago, Michigan (Truago was later renamed Trenton, now a suburb of Detroit). In the spring of 1850, she had the engine from the steamer *Missouri*, wrecked in 1848 on Lake Huron, put into her.[1] The May 21, 1850, issue of the *Milwaukee Sentinel* noted that "She is in tip-top order throughout, is commanded by a thorough-going seaman, and carries with her an excellent cotillion band. She leaves Milwaukee for Buffalo every alternate Tuesday." On one of these trips in late September 1850, the *Patchin* stranded on Skillagalee Reef in Lake Michigan.[2]

Several attempts were made to free her. The first of these was by the side-wheel steamer *Keystone State* on October 2.[3] When this attempt failed, the U. S. iron-hull steamer *Michigan* was called in. The *Michigan* met with a succession of storms and was forced to lay up in Mackinac for two days. From that place she set out for the wreck, having taken on board a number of laborers and a detachment of 25 soldiers from Fort Mackinac.

217

Upon arriving at the wreck, it was so rough nothing could be done. After laying there all day and night, and the wind not abating, she went to Beaver Island, where she stayed for five days waiting for the wind to go down. Eventually the *Michigan* gave up and returned to Detroit.[4] The final attempt to free the *Patchin* was made by the propeller *Lexington* in early December. However, the *Lexington* was damaged when she stranded on her way to the wreck and had to return to port.[5] In mid-December, after two and one-half months on Skillagalee Reef, the *A. D. Patchin* was abandoned and shortly afterwards she broke up and went to pieces.[6]

The *Patchin* was owned and commanded by Captain Harry Whittaker whose nephew, Albert E. Goodrich, founded the famous Goodrich Transit Company popularly known as the Red-Stack Line. The first job held by Albert Goodrich on a Great Lakes vessel was as a clerk aboard the *A. D. Patchin* in 1847.[7]

VESSEL FACTS	Site #42
NAME:	A. D. PATCHIN
RIG:	Side-wheel steamer
OFFICIAL NO.:	None
GROSS TONS:	873 (BOM)
LENGTH:	225'
HULL:	Wood
BUILT:	1846, Truago MI, by J. M. Keating
DATE LOST:	September 27, 1850
CAUSE OF LOSS:	Stranded
WHERE LOST:	Skillagalee Reef in Lake Michigan
LIVES LOST:	None
CARGO:	Merchandise
BOUND FROM/TO:	Milwaukee/Buffalo
LAST ENROLLMENT:	March 22, 1849, Buffalo Custom House, #6
SURRENDERED:	Buffalo, "Wrecked in 1850"
CONFIGURATION:	2 Decks, 1 Mast, Scroll Stem

ANNA SMITH

Anna Smith burning off Cordwood Point in 1889
(Courtesy Ralph Roberts Collection)

In 1889, a fierce November gale swept the Great Lakes and was promptly pronounced by old and experienced mariners as the worst storm they had ever seen. The propeller *Anna Smith*, upbound with the schooner *Red Wing* in tow, was hit by this storm off Thunder Bay in Lake Huron. When abreast of Presque Isle, the towline parted and the *Smith* sprang a serious leak. Captain Timese LeMay opened the *Smith's* throttle wide and managed to beach her eight miles below Cheboygan near Cordwood Point in Lake Huron.[1]

The crew of the *Anna Smith* spent a cold night aboard their vessel during which heavy seas washed over her. The next day she looked like an iceberg, the water having frozen on her decks and cabins. With no rescue in sight, Henry Roeme, second mate and a nephew of the captain, was drowned in a daring attempt to get to the shore about 400 feet away. He threw a hatch overboard, jumped onto it, and tried to swim ashore. He was washed off by the heavy seas, and all attempts by the crew to save him with lines thrown in the water failed.[2]

After another lonely night on the stricken vessel, the tug *Clayt* from Cheboygan arrived and rescued the crew.[3] To keep from freezing to death during the previous night, the crew started a fire

219

in the vessel's coal bunker. The fire was left burning and eventually consumed the portion of the vessel that stood above the waterline. Later the tug *George W. Cuyler* stripped all the equipment of value from the wreck.[4] The captain of the *Anna Smith*, Timese LeMay, was later captain of the *Eber Ward*, which sank in the Straits in 1909. He holds the ignominious distinction of being the only captain to have lost two vessels in the Straits.

VESSEL FACTS	Site #73
NAME	ANNA SMITH
RIG:	Propeller
OFFICIAL NO.:	105276
GROSS TONS:	939
LENGTH:	178'
HULL:	Wood
BUILT:	1873, Algonac MI, by James Navagh
DATE LOST:	November 27, 1889
CAUSE OF LOSS:	Sprang leak/beached/burned
WHERE LOST:	Cordwood Point in Lake Huron
LIVES LOST:	1
CARGO:	Coal
BOUND FROM/TO:	Toledo/Milwaukee
LAST ENROLLMENT:	April 20, 1886, Detroit Custom House, #43
SURRENDERED:	January 24, 1890, Detroit, "Vessel lost"
CONFIGURATION:	1 Deck, 3 Masts, Round Stern, Plain Stem

AUGUSTUS HANDY

Of all the dangers encountered by Great Lakes vessels, being hit by lightning during a storm was the one cause of shipwreck that was determined by pure chance. The *Augustus Handy's* number came up on September 1, 1855, during her first year of service. She was upbound for Chicago on Lake Huron about 40 miles north of Port Huron when she was hit by lightning.[1] The bolt split both her fore and mainmast into pieces, with her spars, sails and rigging being lost overboard. Her jib-boom and bowsprit were also splintered and fell in the water. Although severely stunned, Captain Gale and his crew survived. The vessel lay dead in the water. Fortunately the *Handy* was spotted by the steamer *Sam Ward* who towed her to safety in Port Huron.[2]

In May 1861, the *Augustus Handy* left Chicago with 16,000 bushels of wheat bound for Buffalo. This time she was not so lucky. During a strong gale, she stranded on Spectacle Reef in Lake Huron. The crew was rescued by the propeller *Cleveland* and taken to Detroit.[3] By the end of the year, the *Handy* had broken up and disappeared beneath the waves.

VESSEL FACTS	**Site #76**
NAME:	AUGUSTUS HANDY
RIG:	Schooner
OFFICIAL NO.:	None
GROSS TONS:	338 (BOM)
LENGTH:	126′
HULL:	Wood
BUILT:	1855, Cleveland OH, by Quayle & Martin
DATE LOST:	May 5, 1861
CAUSE OF LOSS:	Stranded
WHERE LOST:	Spectacle Reef in Lake Huron
LIVES LOST:	None
CARGO:	Wheat
BOUND FROM/TO:	Chicago/Buffalo
LAST ENROLLMENT:	September 16, 1859, Cleveland Custom House, #78
SURRENDERED:	No endorsement
CONFIGURATION:	1 Deck, 2 Masts, Square Stern, Figurehead

BONNIE DOON

The schooner *Bonnie Doon* stranded at the foot of Bois Blanc Island (the southeast corner) in Lake Huron in the late fall of 1867.[1] Ironically, she had stranded at the same spot four years earlier in August 1863.[2] This time she could not be removed and was left on the beach for the winter. When visited in April 1868 by the steamer *Magnet*, she was found to be broken in two. Her cargo of lumber was removed and the wreck was stripped of masts and gear.[3]

Several rumors circulated in the newspapers regarding possible salvage of the *Bonnie Doon*. None were apparently true and she was left abandoned on the beach.[4] We have not been able to determine that her enrollment papers were ever surrendered. In fact, she was listed in the Board of Lake Underwriters *Vessel Register* through 1870[5] and *Merchant Vessels of the United States* through 1876.[6]

On launching, the *Bonnie Doon* was valued at $11,000[7] and upon sinking, her valuation was $6,500. In between her valuation dropped steadily, e.g, $9,400 in 1860, $8,500 in 1863 and $7,000 in 1866.[8] She was a fast vessel, and in 1856 she sailed from Chicago to Detroit in 56 hours — a record that stood until 1873.[9]

VESSEL FACTS	Site #69
NAME:	BONNIE DOON
RIG:	Schooner
OFFICIAL NO.:	2136
GROSS TONS:	255
LENGTH:	133'
HULL:	Wood
BUILT:	1855, Huron OH, by William Shupe
DATE LOST:	November 6, 1867
CAUSE OF LOSS:	Stranded
WHERE LOST:	Foot of Bois Blanc Island in Lake Huron
LIVES LOST:	None
CARGO:	Lumber
BOUND FROM/TO:	Upbound
LAST ENROLLMENT:	April 18, 1865, Chicago Custom House, #218
SURRENDERED:	No endorsement
CONFIGURATION:	1 Deck, 2 Masts, Square Stern, Plain Stem

CHALLENGE

The boiler on the *Challenge* exploded and she sank in deep water in Lake Huron.[1] Enroute to Buffalo from Chicago, she had stopped at Mackinac Island to pick up mail and then proceeded onward. The propeller *Northerner* passed some of her floating wreckage about 15 miles below Mackinac Island.[2] It is not clear from the reports on her loss whether she took the North or South Passage downbound from Mackinac Island.

We would guess that she took the South Passage. Prior to the construction of Round Island Light in 1895, vessels passing through the Straits did not normally use the North Passage, as the channel between Mackinac Island and Round Island was undredged and contained many dangerous shoals.[3]

The propeller *Challenge* was a brand new vessel and was valued by the underwriters at $30,000.[4] She was launched on April 11, 1853,[5] and sank on June 22 of the same year. From launch to loss she survived a mere 73 days.

VESSEL FACTS	Site #71
NAME:	CHALLENGE
RIG:	Propeller
OFFICIAL NO.:	None
GROSS TONS:	665 (BOM)
LENGTH:	197'
HULL:	Wood
BUILT:	1853, Newport MI, by J. E. Dixon
DATE LOST:	June 22, 1853
CAUSE OF LOSS:	Boiler exploded
WHERE LOST:	15 miles below Mackinac Island in Lake Huron
LIVES LOST:	5
CARGO:	Oats and pork
BOUND FROM/TO:	Chicago/Buffalo
LAST ENROLLMENT:	April 16, 1853, Detroit Custom House, #42
SURRENDERED:	No endorsement
CONFIGURATION:	1 Deck, Round Stern, Plain Stem

CLARION

Prior to 1850, square-rigged vessels such as brigs were very popular on the Great Lakes. This type of rig had been widely used on the open oceans, and its design, predating the schooner, was one of the first brought to the Great Lakes. The brig *Clarion* was exemplary of this model.

Enroute to Chicago in 1851, the *Clarion* lost two locomotives off her deck in a storm near Grand River on Lake Erie.[1] She was rebuilt in 1857 at Milan, Ohio, by Merry and Gay.[2] Downbound from Milwaukee in May 1860, she lost her fore and main-top mast on Lake Michigan.[3] In October 1860, the *Clarion* stranded on Skillagalee Reef during a storm.[4] She was stripped of her gear and abandoned. Within two weeks she had completely broken up and disappeared beneath the waves.[5]

An interesting challenge for wreck hunters would be to find the locomotives lost off Grand River. They would make a great recreational dive site.

VESSEL FACTS	Site #43
NAME:	CLARION
RIG:	Brig
OFFICIAL NO.	None
GROSS TONS:	236 (BOM)
LENGTH:	108'
HULL:	Wood
BUILT:	1844, Presque Isle PA, by John Richards
DATE LOST:	October 30, 1860
CAUSE OF LOSS:	Stranded
WHERE LOST:	Skillagalee Reef in Lake Michigan
LIVES LOST:	None
CARGO:	Grain
BOUND FROM/TO:	Chicago/Buffalo
LAST ENROLLMENT:	October 18, 1858, Sandusky Custom House, #29
SURRENDERED:	No endorsement
CONFIGURATION:	1 Deck, 2 Masts, Square Stern, Plain Stem

COLONIST

Built in Sarnia, Ontario,[1] the home port of the propeller *Colonist* was Montreal.[2] She underwent large repairs in 1863, and consequently her value increased from $12,900 in 1860 to $14,000 in 1863.[3] She suffered several minor casualties,[4] including springing a bad leak on Lake Michigan in September 1863, a collision with the schooner *Wanderer* on Lake Ontario in May 1869, and running ashore in the St. Lawrence River in October 1869.

The *Colonist* foundered in a November 1869 gale on Lake Huron.[5] Just prior to sinking, she made an emergency stop in Manitowoc, Wisconsin, on or about November 21, 1869, due to bad weather and leaking steam pipes. One of her firemen was badly scalded about the arms and lower part of the body and was not expected to live.[6] She was reported to have carried a "valuable cargo."[7]

VESSEL FACTS	**Site #75**
NAME:	COLONIST
RIG:	Propeller
OFFICIAL NO.:	33481 (Canadian)
GROSS TONS:	341 (BOM)
LENGTH:	134'
HULL:	Wood
BUILT:	1854, Port Sarnia ON, by Robert Steed
DATE LOST:	November 25, 1869
CAUSE OF LOSS:	Foundered
WHERE LOST:	Near Cheboygan in Lake Huron
LIVES LOST:	None
CARGO:	Wheat and flour
BOUND FROM/TO:	Chicago/Montreal
LAST ENROLLMENT:	October 24, 1854, Montreal Custom House, #22
SURRENDERED:	April 30, 1870, Montreal, "Vessel wrecked"
CONFIGURATION:	1 Deck, 1 Mast, Round Stern, Plain Stem

CONDOR

The *Condor* was one of the many small schooners built at Milan, Ohio, in the period 1841 to 1869.[1] She had a flat or scow bottom which allowed her to run in extremely shallow water.[2] In 1861, the *Condor* was in a near-fatal collision with the schooner *J. M. Jones* off Manitowoc, Wisconsin, in Lake Michigan.[3] The *Jones* sank immediately, having been cut in two. The *Condor* lost her bowsprit, mainmast and all her sails and rigging. The crew of the *Jones* saved themselves by jumping onto the *Condor* before the two vessels separated after the collision occurred. The *Condor* rolled about at the mercy of the waves for 24 hours before she was picked up and towed to Milwaukee by the propeller *F. W. Backus*.

In 1862, the *Condor* stranded on Skillagalee Reef in Lake Michigan and went to pieces.[4] The wrecking tug *Leviathan* salvaged her sails, rigging and other equipment.[5]

VESSEL FACTS	Site #44
NAME:	CONDOR
RIG:	Schooner
OFFICIAL NO.:	None
GROSS TONS:	237 (BOM)
LENGTH:	112'
HULL:	Wood
BUILT:	1857, Milan OH, by Merry & Gay
DATE LOST:	November 16, 1862
CAUSE OF LOSS:	Stranded
WHERE LOST:	Skillagalee Reef in Lake Michigan
LIVES LOST:	None
CARGO:	Unknown
BOUND FROM/TO:	Unknown
LAST ENROLLMENT:	March 22, 1862, Cleveland Custom House, #4
SURRENDERED:	No endorsement
CONFIGURATION:	1 Deck, 2 Masts, Round Stern, Scroll Stem

D. N. BARNEY

In 1825 there were only about 60 American sail craft registered on the Lakes. By 1832, when the lightship *Louis McLane* was placed on station at Waugoshance Point, this number had increased to about 100.[1] Very few of these ventured west of Detroit. In the 1840s, side-wheel steamers carried the majority of passengers and freight to the rapidly growing towns on the shores of Lake Michigan.[2] During this period, navigation aids improved and the westward traffic of sailing vessels increased.

With this increased traffic came an increase in the number of wreck incidents. One of the earliest wrecks in the Straits was the loss of the schooner *D. N. Barney*. She stranded in May 1849 about seven miles below Nine Mile Point in Lake Huron.[3] With no help available, the *Barney* was abandoned and remained intact for some time. The Corps of Topological Engineers of the U.S. Lake Survey recorded the position of the wreck of the *Barney* on their first chart of the Straits of Mackinac produced around 1854.[4]

VESSEL FACTS	Site #84
NAME:	D. N. BARNEY
RIG:	Schooner
OFFICIAL NO.:	None
GROSS TONS:	149 (BOM)
LENGTH:	110'
HULL:	Wood
BUILT:	1845, Clayton NY, by J. Oades
DATE LOST:	May 31, 1849
CAUSE OF LOSS:	Stranded
WHERE LOST:	7 miles southeast of Nine Mile Pt. in Lake Huron
LIVES LOST:	None
CARGO:	Potter's clay
BOUND FROM/TO:	Upbound
LAST ENROLLMENT:	April 4, 1846, French Creek, #7
SURRENDERED:	Unknown
CONFIGURATION:	1 Deck, 2 Masts, Square Stern, Plain Stem

DOLPHIN

Dolphin with tug *Margaret* at Racine
(Courtesy Ralph Roberts Collection)

In the period that the schooner *Dolphin* of Racine, Wisconsin, ran on the Lakes, two other schooners of the same name were in operation. One of these was based in Chicago,[1] with the other having its home port in Detroit.[2] The situation was so confusing that the newspapers of the day referred to them as the *Dolphin No. 1*, the

Dolphin No. 2, etc. Researching these three vessels was also a confusing task. The schooner *Dolphin* lost in the Straits carried Official No. 6205 with her home port being Racine.[3]

The *Dolphin* sank in a collision with the bark *Badger State* near Waugoshance Point on July 6, 1869.[4] She was struck forward of the cathead and damaged so severely that she remained afloat only about 20 minutes. The *Badger State* had her bobstays and cutwater carried away. The crew of the lost vessel was taken off and landed at Mackinac Island. From there, they were transferred to Milwaukee by the propeller *Fountain City*. The only thing the crew managed to save was their clothes.

VESSEL FACTS	**Site #57**
NAME:	DOLPHIN
RIG:	Schooner
OFFICIAL NO.:	6205
GROSS TONS:	233
LENGTH:	119'
HULL:	Wood
BUILT:	1862, Milwaukee WI, by Allen & McLelland
DATE LOST:	July 6, 1869
CAUSE OF LOSS:	Collision
WHERE LOST:	Near Waugoshance Point in Lake Michigan
LIVES LOST:	None
CARGO:	Coal
BOUND FROM/TO:	Upbound
LAST ENROLLMENT:	April 29, 1867, Milwaukee Custom House, #108
SURRENDERED:	No endorsement
CONFIGURATION:	1 Deck, 2 Masts, Square Stern, Scorpion Head

ELVA

Elva as the Gospel Ship Glad Tidings in 1889
(Courtesy Institute for Great Lakes Research, Bowling Green State University)

The Elva was originally built for evangelist Henry Bundy as the propeller Glad Tidings.[1] She was a "Gospel Ship" and Captain Bundy travelled from port to port spreading his message to all who would listen. In 1896, she was sold and her name changed to Elva, in honor of the wife of the new owner, James F. Keightley.[2] She became one of the Arnold Transit Co. ferry boats in the Straits in 1898. The Elva was lengthened 20 feet in 1904-05 by J. B. Lund in Cheboygan.[3] Up until 1922, she made a regular run from Cheboygan to Mackinac Island stopping at Point Aux Pins (Bois Blanc Island), Point Nipigon (a now-defunct dock at Point Nipigon Resort founded in 1914), and Mackinaw City, with a return to Cheboygan via the same ports.

The Elva was used by various owners as a passenger ship in the Straits until 1939. She was reduced to a flat deck barge in 1944 and abandoned in 1952. In May 1954, she was set afire about a mile east of Arch Rock off Mackinac Island as a spectacle to celebrate the ground breaking for the Mackinac Bridge.[4] Thus died the Lakes unique Gospel Ship.

Elva as an Arnold Transit Co. ferry boat in 1898
(Courtesy Institute for Great Lakes Research, Bowling Green State University)

Elva shortly before she was scuttled c.1954
(Courtesy Institute for Great Lakes Research, Bowling Green State University)

Elva burning off Mackinac Island in 1954
(Courtesy Institute for Great Lakes Research, Bowling Green State University)

VESSEL FACTS Site #66

NAME:	ELVA
RIG:	Barge
OFFICIAL NO.:	86059
GROSS TONS:	83
LENGTH:	95'
HULL:	Wood
BUILT:	1889, Chicago IL, by Thomas Miller
DATE LOST:	May 16, 1954
CAUSE OF LOSS:	Scuttled
WHERE LOST:	Off Mackinac Island
LIVES LOST:	None
CARGO:	None
BOUND FROM/TO:	Scuttled
LAST ENROLLMENT:	January 17, 1951, Sault Ste. Marie #34
SURRENDERED:	May 14, 1954, Sault Ste. Marie, "Abandoned"
CONFIGURATION:	1 Deck, No Masts, Straight Stem, Round Stern

FAVORITE

Favorite
(Courtesy Institute for Great Lakes Research, Bowling Green State University)

In the late 1800s as newer and larger bulk freighters were introduced, the need for more powerful tugs equipped for salvage work became acute. In recognition of this, the Swain Wrecking Company purchased the passenger vessel *Favorite,* and over the winter of 1889-90 had her converted by the Milwaukee Ship Yard Company to a first-rate wrecking and salvage tug.[1] She was stationed at Cheboygan, Michigan, and became immediate competition for the tug *Leviathan,* which one year later caught fire and burned at the Cheboygan docks. The fate of the *Leviathan* is described earlier in this book. Thus, in 1892, the *Favorite* replaced the *Leviathan* as the best wrecking tug on the Lakes.

The inadequacy of harbor tug service had also become a major problem. This business was fragmented and service was provided by many independent operators and small companies scattered around the Lakes ports. Their tugs were generally of limited power and were designed to handle schooners and older vintage steamers. Rates were confusing and the competition was fierce. Rival operators developed agreements to take turns in towing vessels in a particular port, often resulting in delays while the company whose turn it was found an available tug. More often than not, this tug was not matched in terms of power or other equipment to the task at hand. Out of this tangled picture came the formation of the Great Lakes Towing Company.[2]

Favorite towing the damaged and sinking *Joseph L. Hurd* into Harbor Springs, Michigan, after collision with the *Cayuga* in 1895
(Courtesy Institute for Great Lakes Research, Bowling Green State University)

Vessel owners had become increasingly frustrated with the unreliable tug service available. After reviewing several ideas, a group of them decided to form a company that would purchase as much of the then existing equipment as made sense. The new company would redistribute the resulting fleet according to the needs of each port. In time, new tugs would be built to meet the growing needs. The Great Lakes Towing Company was formed on July 7, 1899, and is still in business today. It was designed to be a benevolent monopoly, and over the years it greatly improved both harbor and salvage tug service. The U.S. Government initiated an antitrust suit against the Great Lakes Towing Company in 1914, which was settled in 1917 with the result that the Towing Company was forced to publish standard rates.[3]

In 1902, the Great Lakes Towing Company purchased the tug *Favorite* from A. A. and B. W. Parker of Detroit who operated the Parker and Swain Wrecking Company. Although a very old wooden steamer, she commanded a purchase price of $40,000 because of her dominance in the wrecking business.[4] She was actually owned by the Union Towing and Wrecking Company, a wholly-owned subsidiary of the Great Lakes Towing Company. The *Favorite* was used around the Lakes to handle the toughest salvage operations. During the winter of 1906-07 she was laid up in winter quarters at St. Ignace. While there, she mysteriously caught fire on January 9, 1907, and was destroyed.[5]

The dock used by the *Favorite* while she was based in St. Ignace still exists today. It is used by the Arnold Transit Company ferry boats and is named the "Favorite Dock."

VESSEL FACTS	Site #65
NAME:	FAVORITE
RIG:	Propeller
OFFICIAL NO:	9201
GROSS TONS:	409
LENGTH:	139'
HULL:	Wood
BUILT:	1864, Fort Howard WI, by William H. Wolf
DATE LOST:	January 9, 1907
CAUSE OF LOSS:	Burned
WHERE LOST:	St. Ignace Harbor
LIVES LOST:	None
CARGO:	None
BOUND FROM/TO:	At the dock
LAST ENROLLMENT:	February 7, 1902, Duluth Custom House, #17
SURRENDERED:	March 26, 1908, Duluth, "Total loss"
CONFIGURATION:	1 Deck, 2 Masts, Round Stern, Plain Head

FLIGHT

The schooner *Flight* was built in Cleveland in 1857 for Valentine Swain and Reuben Becker.[1] She ran in the grain trade between Chicago and Buffalo. The 1860 list of vessels laid up for the winter in Cleveland included the *Flight*.[2] She was damaged in the amount of $1,700 in a gale on Lake Huron in May 1863,[3] and lost a man overboard in November of the same year during a storm on Lake Erie.[4] She was sold to L. Silverman of Chicago for $10,000 on September 15, 1863.[5]

In November 1865, the *Flight* was caught in a storm and stranded on Bois Blanc Island. She was abandoned for the winter.[6] The June 1, 1866, *Detroit Free Press* reported "We are informed by Long John Miller that the schooner *Flight*, which he had contracted to get off the beach at Bois Blanc Island, was set on fire and entirely consumed a few days before his arrival there. He declares it an act of vandalism, and says the hull was in such excellent condition that he would have had it in safe harbor within two days after beginning operations." She was insured by the Home Insurance Company for $7,000.[7]

VESSEL FACTS	Site #70
NAME:	FLIGHT
RIG:	Schooner
OFFICIAL NO.:	None
GROSS TONS:	177
LENGTH:	114'
HULL:	Wood
BUILT:	1857, Cleveland OH, by Roderick Calkins
DATE LOST:	November 6, 1865
CAUSE OF LOSS:	Stranded
WHERE LOST:	Bois Blanc Island in Lake Huron
LIVES LOST:	None
CARGO:	Unknown
BOUND FROM/TO:	Unknown
LAST ENROLLMENT:	March 13, 1865, Chicago Custom House, #9
SURRENDERED:	No endorsement
CONFIGURATION:	1 Deck, 2 Masts, Raking Stern, Serpent Head

FRANCIS PALMS

Built in Marine City, Michigan, in 1868, the bark *Francis Palms* was named after a respected Detroit citizen.[1] In 1871, she was converted from a bark rigging to a three-masted schooner.[2] She was badly damaged in 1872 when she ran ashore outside the Duluth Harbor.[3] During 1879, the *Francis Palms* carried coal from Black River to Milwaukee for one dollar per ton.[4]

Coming down from Escanaba with a load of iron ore in November 1889, she stranded on the north side of Grays Reef in Lake Michigan.[5] Although late in the shipping season, traffic was still heavy in the Straits, as 38 vessel passages were reported the day the *Palms* stranded.[6] The tug *Gladiator* rescued the crew but could not free the stranded vessel.[7] A strong westerly gale delayed further salvage attempts.[8] On November 5, Captain Fitzgerald of the propeller *John Rugee* reported the *Palms* sunk two miles northeast of Grays Reef near White Shoals.[9] She apparently was washed off Grays Reef into deep water. Nothing but the tops of her three masts could be seen above the water.[10]

VESSEL FACTS	Site #53
NAME:	FRANCIS PALMS
RIG:	Schooner
OFFICIAL NO.:	9749
GROSS TONS:	560
LENGTH:	172′
HULL:	Wood
BUILT:	1868, Marine City MI, by Thomas Arnold
DATE LOST:	November 2, 1889
CAUSE OF LOSS:	Stranded
WHERE LOST:	3 miles northwest of Grays Reef in Lake Michigan
LIVES LOST:	None
CARGO:	Iron Ore
BOUND FROM/TO:	Escanaba/Cleveland
LAST ENROLLMENT:	March 12, 1889, Detroit Custom House, #43
SURRENDERED:	December 9, 1889, Detroit, "Total loss"
CONFIGURATION:	3 Masts, 1 Deck, Square Stern, Plain Stem

FREE STATE

Not long after the railway systems had extended their lines to the Great Lakes region, they expanded their control of the transportation system by acquiring numerous steamers and sailing vessels. The steamers were fast propellers and were known as package freighters, as they carried freight that could be shipped in package form by rail from the eastern seaboard. The New York Central Railroad started its Lake fleet with the incorporation of the Western Transit Company in 1855.[1] By June 1856, they had put into service the propeller *Free State* which ran a regular schedule between Buffalo and Chicago.[2]

On one run from Chicago in 1859, the *Free State* rescued the crews of the propeller *Milwaukee* and the schooner *J. H. Tiffany* after they collided and sank northwest of Skillagalee Reef.[3] In September 1871, the *Free State* ran aground on Grays Reef in Lake Michigan only five miles from the site of the *Milwaukee–Tiffany* collision.[4]

The *Free State* cleared Chicago on September 27, 1871. Two days later she stranded on Grays Reef in a thick fog.[5] The tug *Magnet* worked for several days to free her but met with no success.[6] By early November not a vestige of the wreck was visible.[7]

VESSEL FACTS	Site #51
NAME:	FREE STATE
RIG:	Propeller
OFFICIAL NO.:	9157
GROSS TONS:	949
LENGTH:	195'
HULL:	Wood
BUILT:	1856, Buffalo NY, by Bidwell & Banta
DATE LOST:	September 29, 1871
CAUSE OF LOSS:	Stranded
WHERE LOST:	Grays Reef in Lake Michigan
LIVES LOST:	None
CARGO:	Flour and Grain
BOUND FROM/TO:	Chicago/Buffalo
LAST ENROLLMENT:	April 29, 1865, Buffalo Custom House, #87
SURRENDERED:	September 30, 1874, Buffalo, "Vessel wrecked"
CONFIGURATION:	2 Decks, 1 Mast, Round Stern, Plain Stem

GERTRUDE

For the Charles Mears Company of Chicago, April 1868 was a disaster. They lost two vessels in quick succession. First was the loss of the schooner *E. M. Peck*, which foundered during a severe storm on Lake Michigan.[1] She was found floating bottom up on April 10, about seven miles off Kenosha, Wisconsin. Her entire crew of eight people was lost.[2]

A day after the hull of the *Peck* was towed into the Chicago Harbor, another Mears' vessel, the schooner *Gertrude*, departed with a cargo of 19,500 bushels of corn to be delivered in Buffalo.[3] The Mears Company was still mourning its lost crew. Although the ice had largely cleared from the Straits, some heavy floes were still drifting about.

As she passed through the Straits on the night of April 21, 1868, the *Gertrude* collided with a large ice floe and reportedly sank in deep water.[4] This time the crew survived. They managed to get into the yawl boat before their vessel sank and row to shore. We have not been able to ascertain approximately where in the Straits the *Gertrude* sank.

VESSEL FACTS	Site #58
NAME:	GERTRUDE
RIG:	Schooner
OFFICIAL NO.:	10203
GROSS TONS:	267
LENGTH:	135'
HULL:	Wood
BUILT:	1855, Cleveland OH, by William Jones
DATE LOST:	April 21, 1868
CAUSE OF LOSS:	Cut by ice
WHERE LOST:	Deep water in the Straits
LIVES LOST:	None
CARGO:	Corn
BOUND FROM/TO:	Chicago/Buffalo
LAST ENROLLMENT:	March 27, 1868, Chicago Custom House, #249
SURRENDERED:	No endorsement
CONFIGURATION:	1 Deck, 2 Masts, Square Stern, Eagle Head

GLAD TIDINGS

Glad Tidings
(Courtesy Great Lakes Historical Society)

In contrast to her name, the schooner *Glad Tidings* brought lots of bad news to her owners over her lifetime. In September 1868, she ran ashore near Rondeau, Ontario, on Lake Erie and badly damaged her hull.[1] Only two months later, she was caught in a gale, again on Lake Erie, and lost her sails and ground tackle.[2] Near Buffalo in 1870, she became waterlogged and had to be towed to port for repairs.[3]

On Lake Michigan during an 1873 gale, she lost a main boom and much of her rigging.[4] In 1877, she was in two collisions on Lake Michigan.[5] She arrived in Frankfort, Michigan, in September 1879, with her rudder badly twisted.[6] In July 1894, three crewmen lost their lives when she was sunk in the Detroit River in a collision with the propeller *Pathfinder.*[7]

All of this bad news culminated for the *Glad Tidings* during a gale in 1898. In an attempt to ride out the storm, she dragged her anchors and was driven ashore six miles west-northwest of Hammond Bay Life Saving Station below the Straits South Passage.[8] She was abandoned as a total wreck. Two days later the Life Saving crew assisted in stripping the *Glad Tidings* of her anchors, masts and rigging.

VESSEL FACTS	Site #83
NAME:	GLAD TIDINGS
RIG:	Schooner
OFFICIAL NO.:	10238
GROSS TONS:	183
LENGTH:	113'
HULL:	Wood
BUILT:	1866, Detroit MI, by James M. Jones
DATE LOST:	April 19, 1898
CAUSE OF LOSS:	Stranded
WHERE LOST:	Below Nine Mile Point in Lake Huron
LIVES LOST:	None
CARGO:	Unknown
BOUND FROM/TO:	Unknown
LAST ENROLLMENT:	May 19, 1897, Detroit Custom House, #73
SURRENDERED:	June 2, 1898, Detroit, "Vessel lost"
CONFIGURATION:	1 Deck, 3 Masts, Square Stern, Eagle Head

HENRY J. JOHNSON

Henry J. Johnson towing schooner *Helvetia*
(Courtesy Great Lakes Marine Collection, Milwaukee Public Library)

Iron ore was first discovered in the Upper Peninsula (a.k.a. the UP) of Michigan in 1844 near Negaunee.[1] Growth of mining was limited until the canal connecting Lake Superior with the lower Lakes was completed at Sault Ste. Marie in 1855.[2] Entrepreneurs of the time decided that, in addition to shipping raw ore, they would smelt the ore at the point of mining. Thus, in the period 1848 to 1898, a robust iron-making industry flourished in the UP.[3]

To make money, the raw ore and the finished pig iron had to be shipped to the ports on Lake Erie that fed the growing iron and steel making business centered in Pennsylvania. The port cities of Cleveland and Ashtabula became the major receptors.[4] At that time, the shipping season on Lake Superior was limited to the months of May through October because of the ice. To extend the shipping season, a 63-mile-long railroad from Negaunee to Escanaba on Lake Michigan was constructed in 1865.[5] Thus, Escanaba became a major iron-shipping port and over the next 15 years, three large ore docks were built.

The establishment of Escanaba as a major port caused a significant increase in vessel traffic through the Straits of Mackinac with a concomitant increase in shipwrecks whose cargo was iron ore. In fact, eight of the shipwrecks in the Straits were carrying iron ore, all bound from Escanaba to Cleveland. One of these was the propeller *Henry J. Johnson.*

The *Johnson* collided with the upbound propeller *Fred Pabst* in a dense fog off Nine Mile Point, ten miles southeast of Poe Reef in Lake Huron. The *Johnson* was struck by the *Pabst* ten feet aft of the bow, and she sank almost immediately in 150 feet of water.[6] All the crew succeeded in getting into the lifeboats before the *Johnson* sank. After being adrift for several hours, they were picked up by the tug *Parker* and taken to Cheboygan. The *Pabst* did not stop after the collision, and made no effort to rescue the crew from the *Johnson.* Later the same day, the *Pabst* was sighted passing Mackinaw City with a canvas patch over her bow with her consort, the schooner *Armenia,* in tow.[7]

VESSEL FACTS	Site #81
NAME:	HENRY J. JOHNSON
RIG:	Propeller
OFFICIAL NO.:	95950
GROSS TONS:	1,997
LENGTH:	260′
HULL:	Wood
BUILT:	1888, Cleveland OH, by Cleveland Dry Dock Co.
DATE LOST:	July 24, 1902
CAUSE OF LOSS:	Collision
WHERE LOST:	Off Nine Mile Point in Lake Huron
LIVES LOST:	None
CARGO:	Iron Ore
BOUND FROM/TO:	Escanaba/Cleveland
LAST ENROLLMENT:	April 19,1900, Sandusky Ohio, Custom House,#22
SURRENDERED:	March 31, 1903, Sandusky, "Lost by collision"
CONFIGURATION:	1 Deck, 2 Masts, Round Stern, Plain Stem

ISLAND QUEEN

The dangers of shipwreck in the Straits of Mackinac were so great that it was not uncommon for a vessel that regularly passed that way to be involved in more than one major accident. The schooner *Island Queen* was an example. In the summer of 1858, she loaded 100,000 board feet of lumber at Port Huron. It was being shipped to Chicago, which at that time was undergoing enormous expansion and had an insatiable appetite for lumber. Enroute to Chicago, she ran ashore on Bois Blanc Island and filled with water.[1] It took the tug *Oswego* several days to free the *Island Queen*. Fortunately, it was late July, a period in which the Straits usually has very calm weather. Repairs to her hull amounted to more than $1,500.[2]

The next year, in her second encounter, she was not so lucky. This time she was downbound from Chicago with a load of wheat. During a September gale, the *Island Queen* was blown off course and struck on Skillagalee Reef in Lake Michigan. To prevent her sinking, she was beached on Waugoshance Point where she later broke up and became a total wreck.[3] The newspapers of the time reported her as being ashore at "Wobbleshanks," a widely-used slang term for Waugoshance.[4]

VESSEL FACTS	Site #50
NAME:	ISLAND QUEEN
RIG:	Schooner
OFFICIAL NO.:	None
GROSS TONS:	257 (BOM)
LENGTH:	115'
HULL:	Wood
BUILT:	1854, Orleans NY
DATE LOST:	September 17, 1859
CAUSE OF LOSS:	Holed and beached
WHERE LOST:	Waugoshance Point in Lake Michigan
LIVES LOST:	None
CARGO:	Wheat
BOUND FROM/TO:	Chicago/Unknown
LAST ENROLLMENT:	March 19, 1857, Ogdensburgh Custom House, #2
SURRENDERED:	No endorsement
CONFIGURATION:	1 Deck, 2 Masts, Plain Head

J. C. LIKEN

The small propeller *J. C. Liken* left Cheboygan on a Saturday evening bound for Toledo where she was to run as an excursion boat. To help pay the expenses of taking her down, the captain took on a cargo of lath. Sometime after leaving, she encountered a strong northeaster abreast of Spectacle Reef in Lake Huron, and the sea became so heavy that she completely buried herself with each successive wave. She sprang a serious leak and decided to put about for Cheboygan. The engineer, George Amy, said he kept four pumps going but could not keep her afloat. She sank stern first, 15 miles off Spectacle Reef in 100 feet of water.[1] The crew escaped in a small boat, rowed to shore at Hammond Bay, and walked 35 miles back to Cheboygan.[2]

The *Liken* was built in 1873, at Sebewaing on Saginaw Bay,[3] for John C. Liken, after whom she was named, and for several years ran between that port and Bay City. She then went into the excursion business, running between Bay City and the resorts on the beach at the mouth of the Saginaw River.[4]

VESSEL FACTS	Site #82
NAME:	J. C. LIKEN
RIG:	Propeller
OFFICIAL NO.:	75507
GROSS TONS:	78
LENGTH:	90'
HULL:	Wood
BUILT:	1873, Sebewaing MI, by Carpenter
DATE LOST:	May 5, 1890
CAUSE OF LOSS:	Foundered
WHERE LOST:	Below Spectacle Reef in Lake Huron
LIVES LOST:	None
CARGO:	Lath wood
BOUND FROM/TO:	Cheboygan/Toledo
LAST ENROLLMENT:	April 12, 1890, Cleveland Custom House, #83
SURRENDERED:	May 15, 1890, Cleveland, "Vessel lost"
CONFIGURATION:	1 Deck, No Masts, Plain Head, Round Stern

J. E. SHAW

The first appearance in port of a new sailing vessel generally caused a stir amongst the marine reporters. They regularly wrote glowing descriptions of these white-winged craft. Following is the account in the *Detroit Free Press*[1] when the *J. E. Shaw* first sailed into Detroit on September 27, 1854: "Schooner *J. E. Shaw* — She is a beautiful model of construction and sits in the water like a duck. Her hull is made entirely of oak, is double-arched and well put together. Her steering apparatus is of most approved design and is patented and manufactured in Boston. We understand there are only a few like it on the Lakes. Her cabin is large, airy, and pleasant and she is a fast sailer. Coming down the Lake she distanced the bark *Sovereign-of-the-Lakes* by six miles in 24 hours."

Caught in a severe gale in September 1856, the *J. E. Shaw* stranded near Gros Cap on the north shore of the Straits in Lake Michigan. She was carrying 15,000 bushels of wheat bound for Oswego. The *Shaw* broke up and disappeared within three to four days.[2] She sank in the same storm as the brig *Sandusky*, about six miles away.

VESSEL FACTS	Site #61
NAME:	J. E. SHAW
RIG:	Schooner
OFFICIAL NO.:	None
GROSS TONS:	293 (BOM)
LENGTH:	118'
HULL:	Wood
BUILT:	1854, Milan OH, by James Stebbins
DATE LOST:	September 22, 1856
CAUSE OF LOSS:	Stranded
WHERE LOST:	Gros Cap in Lake Michigan
LIVES LOST:	None
CARGO:	Wheat
BOUND FROM/TO:	Milwaukee/Oswego
LAST ENROLLMENT:	September 23, 1854, Oswego Custom House, #49
SURRENDERED:	No endorsement
CONFIGURATION:	1 Deck, 2 Masts, Square Stern, Scroll Stem

JOHN JEWETT

The small schooner *John Jewett* was built in 1866 and sailed the Lakes for 32 years. By some standards this made her an old vessel. However, many others lived longer, with one of the longest-lived being the schooner *William Aldrich*, which survived 60 years.[1] During her life, the *Jewett* suffered several mishaps including being sunk by collision on Lake St. Clair in November 1870[2] and loss of her centerboard on Lake Michigan in November 1871.[3] In 1886, she was rebuilt, but by 1891 her value had dropped to only $1,800.[4]

On October 7, 1898, the *John Jewett* stranded at Grace Harbor at Isle Royale in Lake Superior.[5] She got off only to meet her final end 11 days later when she stranded eight miles northwest of Hammond Bay near Nine Mile Point in Lake Huron and went to pieces.[6]

VESSEL FACTS	Site #80
NAME:	JOHN JEWETT
RIG:	Schooner
OFFICIAL NO.:	75090
GROSS TONS:	103
LENGTH:	91'
HULL:	Wood
BUILT:	1866, Vermilion OH, by H. Lutz
DATE LOST:	October 18, 1898
CAUSE OF LOSS:	Stranded
WHERE LOST:	Nine Mile Point in Lake Huron
LIVES LOST:	None
CARGO:	Unknown
BOUND FROM/TO:	Unknown
LAST ENROLLMENT:	June 19, 1897, Detroit Custom House, #81
SURRENDERED:	October 26, 1898, Detroit, "Vessel lost"
CONFIGURATION:	1 Deck, 2 Masts, Square Stern, Plain Stem

JULIA DEAN

Ile Aux Galets (Island of Pebbles) is a small island in Lake Michigan surrounded by a reef due east of Beaver Island and about eight miles southwest of Waugoshance Point. After the British displaced the French on the Lakes, it became known as Skillagalee which was a bastardization of the French name. Being a hazard to navigation, a lighthouse was established there in 1851.[1] At that time, the Mormons, led by James Jesse Strang, controlled Beaver Island with Strang representing the region in the Michigan State Legislature.[2] He had considerable influence on the appointment of the light keeper on Skillagalee. Vessel captains regularly complained that the Mormon keeper would turn off the main light and display false lights to lure ships onto the reef so that they might be pirated.

In October 1855, the brig *Julia Dean* stranded on Skillagalee Reef and became a total loss.[3] Captain E. S. Wilson of the *Dean*, claimed that he was lured onto the reef with a false light. This was vigorously denied by the Mormons in the March 13, 1856, edition of their newspaper, *The Northern Islander*.[4] In July 1856, the Mormons were driven from Beaver Island by Gentile fisherman who launched their attack from St. Helena Island in the Straits.[5]

VESSEL FACTS	Site #45
NAME:	JULIA DEAN
RIG:	Brig
OFFICIAL NO.:	None
GROSS TONS:	498 (BOM)
LENGTH:	150'
HULL:	Wood
BUILT:	1854, Cleveland OH, Peck & Masters
DATE LOST:	October 6, 1855
CAUSE OF LOSS:	Stranded
WHERE LOST:	Skillagalee Reef in Lake Michigan
LIVES LOST:	None
CARGO:	Unknown
BOUND FROM/TO:	Unknown
LAST ENROLLMENT:	May 12, 1854, Chicago Custom House, #51
SURRENDERED:	No endorsement
CONFIGURATION:	1 Deck, 2 Masts, Square Stern, Figurehead

KATE HAYES

Bound from Milwaukee to Oswego with 15,000 bushels of wheat, the schooner *Kate Hayes* stranded on Spectacle Reef in Lake Huron on a clear calm night.[1] In July 1856, the tug *Rescue* made several attempts to free her including the use of two Palmer steam pumps. When these failed, she was abandoned and broke up and went to pieces.[2] The *Kate Hayes* was a brand new vessel and survived only two and one-half months before being wrecked. She was owned by the Lake Navigation Company of Buffalo.

The captain claimed an error in his charts caused him to run on the reef.[3] We investigated his claim by studying a copy of the only Straits chart available in 1856. Our examination shows he was correct that the chart was in error, as the longitude lines were off by about five minutes or a distance of over four miles. Clearly this was a serious error if he were using celestial navigation. However, he may have used the chart error as simply an excuse, since dead reckoning and coastal navigation were the usual navigation methods employed on the Lakes. To our knowledge, celestial navigation with a sextant was rarely utilized.

VESSEL FACTS	Site #77
NAME:	KATE HAYES
RIG:	Schooner
OFFICIAL NO.:	None
GROSS TONS:	349 (BOM)
LENGTH:	130′
HULL:	Wood
BUILT:	1856, Buffalo NY, by E. K. Bruce
DATE LOST:	July 14, 1856
CAUSE OF LOSS:	Stranded
WHERE LOST:	Spectacle Reef in Lake Huron
LIVES LOST:	None
CARGO:	Wheat
BOUND FROM/TO:	Milwaukee/Oswego
LAST ENROLLMENT:	May 16, 1856, Buffalo Custom House, #96
SURRENDERED:	No endorsement
CONFIGURATION:	1 Deck, 2 Masts, Square Stern, Plain Stem

LAWRENCE

The schooner *Lawrence* was cut by ice in April 1850, and sank about one mile westward of St. Helena Island reportedly in eight fathoms of water.[1] She was carrying 11,000 bushels of wheat. Captain Stone of the side-wheel steamer *Keystone State* reported seeing her masts sticking out of the water.

In 1882, John Dodd, a hard-hat diver from Cheboygan, dove the wreck.[2] He stated that it was deeply imbedded in mud in 42 feet of water. Three anchors, 600 feet of chain and the steering gear were recovered aboard the tug *Bennett*. The wheel was an old style "rope barrel" wheel. Throughout 1882 and 1883 there was much talk about raising the hull of the *Lawrence*.[3] We cannot find any evidence that this was ever done.

During the summer of 1982, we searched for this wreck but could not find it. Our efforts included walking on the bottom and probing large mounds of sand and mud with steel rods. In the process of searching for the schooner *Lawrence*, we found the unidentified dump barge *(Chuck's Barge)* off the southeast tip of St. Helena Island.

VESSEL FACTS	Site #59
NAME:	LAWRENCE
RIG:	Schooner
OFFICIAL NO.:	None
GROSS TONS:	284 (BOM)
LENGTH:	120'
HULL:	Wood
BUILT:	1847, Milwaukee WI, by D. Merrill & Co.
DATE LOST:	April 10, 1850
CAUSE OF LOSS:	Cut by ice
WHERE LOST:	1 mile west of St. Helena Island in Lake Michigan
LIVES LOST:	None
CARGO:	Wheat
BOUND FROM/TO:	Milwaukee/Buffalo
LAST ENROLLMENT:	November 15, 1849, Chicago Custom House, #55
SURRENDERED:	No endorsement
CONFIGURATION:	1 Deck, 2 Masts, Scroll Head

LEANDER

The little schooner *Leander* is the oldest vessel described in this book, having been built in 1838.[1] She stranded in November 1857 along with the bark *Oliver Lee*, the schooner *Enterprise*, and two other schooners at Gros Cap on the north shore of the Straits in Lake Michigan.[2] She was abandoned and went to pieces. The *Enterprise* was gotten off and towed to Mackinac Island. The fate of the *Oliver Lee* is described elsewhere in this book.

VESSEL FACTS	Site #60
NAME:	LEANDER
RIG:	Schooner
OFFICIAL NO.:	None
GROSS TONS:	145 (BOM)
LENGTH:	84'
HULL:	Wood
BUILT:	1838, Marblehead OH, by E. Bates
DATE LOST:	November 17, 1857
CAUSE OF LOSS:	Stranded
WHERE LOST:	Gros Cap in Lake Michigan
LIVES LOST:	None
CARGO:	Unknown
BOUND FROM/TO:	Unknown
LAST ENROLLMENT:	May 9, 1854, Detroit Custom House, #45
SURRENDERED:	No Endorsement
CONFIGURATION:	1 Deck, 2 Masts, Scroll Stem

LUCY J. CLARK

Originally built as a brig, the *Lucy J. Clark* was rerigged as a schooner in 1879.[1] While loading cord wood at the Cross Village, Michigan, lumber dock, she was blown on shore. The tug *S. S. Coe* from Milwaukee succeeded in getting her off and started to tow her to Sturgeon Bay in Lake Michigan. However, her steering gear was broken and she was unmanageable. The *Coe* turned back to the Cross Village dock, but a severe northwest gale came up and she had to cut the *Clark* loose.[2]

The *Clark* dropped her anchors and held fast. Captain Johnson, his crew of six and a steam pump engineer from the *Coe*, got into the yawl boat and headed for shore. Almost immediately after leaving her, the *Clark* capsized and sank. About 125 yards from shore, the yawl boat capsized and three of the crew drowned. The wreck, about two miles northeast of Cross Village in Lake Michigan, was later visited by a hard-hat diver who tried to recover the steam pump lost in the sinking.[3]

VESSEL FACTS	Site #49
NAME:	LUCY J. CLARK
RIG:	Schooner
OFFICIAL NO.:	14713
GROSS TONS:	308
LENGTH:	137'
HULL:	Wood
BUILT:	1863, Port Huron MI, by James Pickering
DATE LOST:	November 11, 1883
CAUSE OF LOSS:	Capsized
WHERE LOST:	2 miles northeast of Cross Village in L. Michigan
LIVES LOST:	3
CARGO:	Cord wood
BOUND FROM/TO:	Cross Village/Chicago
LAST ENROLLMENT:	May 23, 1879, Chicago Custom House, #88
SURRENDERED:	December 21, 1883, Chicago, "Vessel lost"
CONFIGURATION:	1 Deck, 2 Masts, Square Stern, Plain Stem

Cross Village lumber dock c.1888
(Courtesy Mary Belle Shurtleff)

MAROLD II

Marold II
(Courtesy Institute for Great Lakes Research, Bowling Green State University)

On November 11, 1936, the tanker *J. Oswald Boyd* got off course in a blinding snowstorm and grounded on Simmons Reef about five miles northwest of White Shoals Light in Lake Michigan.[1] She was outbound from Whiting, Indiana, with 900,000 gallons of gasoline in her holds. The *Boyd* was abandoned by her owners when they were unable to free her from the reef. Many small vessels from surrounding ports made trips to the wreck to salvage the precious, but dangerous, gasoline cargo. One of these, the *Marold II*, exploded and sank while removing some of the cargo on New Year's Day, 1937. All five of her crew members were killed.[2]

Despite the *Marold II* accident, the boat trips to the *Boyd* continued until the Lake froze. By February, fisherman from Brevort, in the Upper Peninsula of Michigan, had laid out a twisting, 15-mile "road" on the ice from the north shore of the Lake to the stranded vessel. The fisherman secretly carried on their salvage work. Then word of the ice road to the *Boyd* got out.[3]

Residents from miles around swarmed to the wreck for free gasoline (see photo). One of these, Grant Brooks from Cedarville, Michigan, drowned when his truck, laden with three tons of gasoline broke through the ice and sank.[4] This accident caused the Mackinac

254

County Sheriff to appeal to officials at Selfridge Air National Guard Base in Mt. Clemens, Michigan, to send planes to bomb the wreck to stop the rush of salvors in their trucks and cars. Nothing came of this appeal, and in the spring, when the ice melted, the wreck of the *Boyd* was pulled off the reef and towed to Detour, Michigan.

The *Marold II* was originally built in 1911 as a luxury motor yacht named *La Belle*.[5] Her owner, Alexander Winton, was the pioneer builder of the Winton automobile. She was sold in 1919 to Harold Wills, then part owner of the Wills-St. Clair Car Company and formerly longtime partner and chief engineer for Henry Ford.[6] He renamed her *Marold II*, which was a combination of his wife's name Mary, and his name, Harold.

J. Oswald Boyd on Simmons Reef in 1937
(Courtesy Institute for Great Lakes Research, Bowling Green State University)

In 1921, the *Marold II* burned and sank at her dock in Marysville, Michigan, on the St. Clair River. She was raised and rebuilt in 1925 as a combination passenger and package freight vessel. The Beaver Island Transit Company purchased her in 1935, and she ran as a ferry boat between Beaver Island and Charlevoix until she met her fate on Simmons Reef in Lake Michigan.[7]

When the *Marold II* exploded, her main deck and most of her superstructure were blown onto the deck of the *J. Oswald Boyd*. Since there were no survivors, the exact cause of the explosion was never determined. The wreck was later reported to be in 22 feet of water at the southeast corner of the reef.[8]

VESSEL FACTS   Site #55

NAME:	MAROLD II
RIG:	Propeller
OFFICIAL NO.:	208565
GROSS TONS:	283
LENGTH:	122'
HULL:	Steel
BUILT:	1911, Camden NJ, by J. H. Dialogue & Son
DATE LOST:	January 1, 1937
CAUSE OF LOSS:	Explosion
WHERE LOST:	Simmons Reef in Lake Michigan
LIVES LOST:	5
CARGO:	None
BOUND FROM/TO:	Beaver Island/Simmons Reef
LAST ENROLLMENT:	October 21, 1935, Milwaukee, #27
SURRENDERED:	February 18, 1937, Milwaukee, "Explosion"
CONFIGURATION:	1 Deck, No Masts, Plain Head, Round Stern

WILSON & HOY,
Submarine Divers
And Wreckers,

Will attend to all calls promptly from any and all parts of the Union or Canada.

OFFICE,

Foot of Second St.

Residence, 16 CHASE STREET,

DETROIT, MICH.

Polk's Marine Directory, 1884

NEWELL A. EDDY

Severe gales are not common during April in the Straits of Mackinac. This was little consolation to Captain W. R. Barton and the crew of the schooner *Newell A. Eddy* in April 1893. Under tow of the propeller *Charles Eddy*, she was caught in a southeast gale while passing downbound in the Straits. About ten miles below Cheboygan Light in Lake Huron, her towline parted, and she was last seen drifting in the direction of Bois Blanc Island apparently helpless, as no canvas was set.[1]

The *Charles Eddy* kept the drifting schooner in sight for some time, but the steering gear on the propeller broke and no help could be rendered. Marine men of the day surmised that the *Newell Eddy's* rigging was probably frozen, and before sail could be made, she capsized.[2] The entire crew of nine men was never seen again. When the storm subsided, the tug *Clayt* made a thorough search for the lost vessel in the vicinity of Bois Blanc Island, but could not find her. A few days later, the tug *George W. Cuyler* found the entire stern section, with the name on it, washed ashore near the Bois Blanc Island Light.[3]

VESSEL FACTS	Site #74
NAME:	NEWELL A. EDDY
RIG:	Schooner
OFFICIAL NO.:	130467
GROSS TONS:	1,270
LENGTH:	242'
HULL:	Wood
BUILT:	1890, West Bay City MI, by F. W. Wheeler & Co.
DATE LOST:	April 20, 1893
CAUSE OF LOSS:	Foundered
WHERE LOST:	Near east end of Bois Blanc Island in Lake Huron
LIVES LOST:	9
CARGO:	Corn
BOUND FROM/TO:	Chicago/ Buffalo
LAST ENROLLMENT:	May 8, 1890, Port Huron Custom House, #140
SURRENDERED:	June 30, 1893, Port Huron, "Vessel wrecked"
CONFIGURATION:	1 Deck, 3 Masts, Eagle Head, Square Stern

NIGHTINGALE

BROWER'S UNION SALT DOCKS
CHARLES. H. BROWER
CHICAGO

Nightingale (far right)
(Courtesy Burton Historical Collection, Detroit Public Library)

Spectacle Reef is a pair of shoals in Lake Huron about ten miles east of Bois Blanc Island and ten miles offshore from Nine Mile Point.[1] Over the years, scores of vessels stranded on this shallow water reef. In 1871, construction was begun on an 86-foot tall lighthouse which was completed in 1874.[2] Because of the isolated location, the requirement for an underwater foundation, and the severe weather, this project was a major engineering feat. The schooner *Nightingale* added to the difficulty.

In September 1869, the *Nightingale* stranded on Spectacle Reef. Efforts to free her failed and she was abandoned.[3] Oddly enough, the wreckage, including the iron ore cargo, lay in the exact spot on the reef where the Spectacle Reef Lighthouse was to be built.[4] The owners of the wrecking tug *Magnet* were hired to remove the cargo and wreckage. A dredging machine was used to remove the 500 tons of iron ore. The hull was broken into pieces, towed to deep water, and scuttled.[5] The Lighthouse's Second Order Fresnel Lens, installed in 1874, was replaced in 1982 and is now on display at the Great Lakes Historical Society Museum in Vermilion, Ohio.[6]

VESSEL FACTS	**Site #79**
NAME:	NIGHTINGALE
RIG:	Schooner
OFFICIAL NO.:	18123
GROSS TONS:	272
LENGTH:	138'
HULL:	Wood
BUILT:	1856, Conneaut OH, by Shaler
DATE LOST:	September 11, 1869
CAUSE OF LOSS:	Stranded
WHERE LOST:	Spectacle Reef in Lake Huron
LIVES LOST:	None
CARGO:	Iron Ore
BOUND FROM/TO:	Marquette/Cleveland
LAST ENROLLMENT:	October 29, 1866, Erie Custom House, #138
SURRENDERED:	June 30, 1872, Erie, "Vessel lost"
CONFIGURATION:	1 Deck, 2 Masts, Square Stern, Scroll Stem

Frank Rann,
SUB-MARINE DIVER
AND CONTRACTOR
For all kinds of Sub-Marine Work.
25 E. Kinzie St.,   CHICAGO. ILL.
TELEPHONE 3248.

Beeson's Marine Directory, 1887

259

ODD FELLOW

Before the railroads arrived in the early 1850s, the only way to move substantial amounts of goods westward in the Great Lakes region was by water transportation. The flow of goods can be traced through the vessel arrivals listed in the old newspapers. For example, the *Milwaukee Sentinel* on October 10, 1851, noted "Arrived – Brig *Odd Fellow*, Buffalo, 40 packages of merchandise, 120 kegs of powder, 1,543 flagging;" and on November 13 "Arrived – Brig *Odd Fellow*, Buffalo, 1,900 barrels of apples."[1] Grain was usually the cargo on the return trip to the lower Lakes.

On one such return trip, the *Odd Fellow*, under the command of Captain Harper, stranded about eight miles west of Old Mackinac Point in Lake Michigan. Shortly afterwards, the brig *Belle* salvaged her anchors, chain, and rigging and took it to Milwaukee. The *Odd Fellow* broke up and went to pieces.[2] This wreck, and the unidentified *George's Wreck* (Site #17), may be the same.

VESSEL FACTS	Site #63
NAME:	ODD FELLOW
RIG:	Brig
OFFICIAL NO.:	None
GROSS TONS:	234 (BOM)
LENGTH:	107'
HULL:	Wood
BUILT:	1845, Cleveland OH, by Turner
DATE LOST:	November 30, 1854
CAUSE OF LOSS:	Stranded
WHERE LOST:	8 miles west of Old Mackinac Pt. in Lake Michigan
LIVES LOST:	None
CARGO:	Wheat
BOUND FROM/TO:	Kenosha/Buffalo
LAST ENROLLMENT:	September 13, 1854, Buffalo Custom House,#185
SURRENDERED:	Buffalo, "Vessel lost"
CONFIGURATION:	1 Deck, 2 Masts, Square Stern, Scroll Stem

OLIVER LEE

Sailing vessels on the Great Lakes frequently had their rigging changed. Not so common was a change in the basic vessel power, i.e., from sail to steam or vice versa. Three vessels amongst the wrecks of the Straits of Mackinac had their power changed, including the *Peshtigo* (schooner to propeller), the *Genesee Chief* (propeller to schooner) and the *Oliver Lee* (side-wheel steamer to bark).[1]

The *Oliver Lee* was originally built in 1844 as the Canadian side-wheel steamer *London* in Chippewa, Ontario.[2] She was part of the North Shore Line begun in 1842 as an express route between Detroit and Buffalo along the north shore of Lake Erie.[3] In August 1845, she collided with her running mate, the steamer *Kent* off Point Pelee in Lake Erie. The *Kent* sank with the loss of several lives.[4] The *Oliver Lee* was converted to a sailing vessel in 1856.[5] In November of the next year, she stranded near Gros Cap in Lake Michigan. The tug *Salvor* tried to get her off but failed and she went to pieces.[6] In June 1858, the wrecking schooner *G. L. Marshall* salvaged her windlass, anchors, and chain.[7]

VESSEL FACTS	Site #62
NAME:	OLIVER LEE
RIG:	Bark
OFFICIAL NO.:	None
GROSS TONS:	433 (BOM)
LENGTH:	169'
HULL:	Wood
BUILT:	1844, Chippewa ON, Niagara Harbor & Dock Co.
DATE LOST:	November 17, 1857
CAUSE OF LOSS:	Stranded
WHERE LOST:	Gros Cap in Lake Michigan
LIVES LOST:	None
CARGO:	Oats
BOUND FROM/TO:	Downbound
LAST ENROLLMENT:	October 2, 1856, Cleveland Custom House, #93
SURRENDERED:	No endorsement
CONFIGURATION:	1 Deck, 3 Masts

ORIENTAL

The propeller *Oriental* was a package freighter and was part of the fleet of the American Transportation Company of Buffalo. She usually ran between Buffalo and Chicago.[1] In 1856, she ran into and sank the brig *Nebraska* on Lake Michigan.[2]

In October 1859, the *Oriental* stranded on Skillagalee Reef in Lake Michigan with a cargo of 316 barrels of flour, 3,500 barrels of beef and 1,000 hides. Shortly afterwards the propeller *Cuyahoga* attached a hawser to her but could not pull her off.[3] The propeller *Potomac* came alongside and removed some of her cargo to lighten her. Later, the wrecking tug *Leviathan* came from Mackinac and put two steam pumps on her. Before the pumps could make any headway, the vessel broke up and went to pieces.[4] Both steam pumps were lost in the process.[5]

VESSEL FACTS	Site #46
NAME:	ORIENTAL
RIG:	Propeller
OFFICIAL NO.:	None
GROSS TONS:	950 (BOM)
LENGTH:	222'
HULL:	Wood
BUILT:	1854, Buffalo NY, by Bidwell & Banta
DATE LOST:	October 14, 1859
CAUSE OF LOSS:	Stranded
WHERE LOST:	Skillagalee Reef in Lake Michigan
LIVES LOST:	None
CARGO:	Flour, beef and hides
BOUND FROM/TO:	Unknown
LAST ENROLLMENT:	May 7, 1855, Buffalo Custom House, #45
SURRENDERED:	No endorsement
CONFIGURATION:	1 Deck, 1 Mast, Square Stern, Plain Stem

PERSEVERANCE

With the heavy vessel traffic on the Great Lakes, damage or sinking by collision was an ever-present danger. Fourteen of the 78 vessels described in this book were lost by collision. As the following account shows, the schooner *Perseverance* seemingly possessed a concupiscence to end her days by colliding with another vessel.

On her maiden voyage four days after her launch on May 7, 1855,[1] she collided with the bark *Mechanic* off Point Aux Barques in Lake Huron. The damage was relatively minor, amounting to $2,000.[2] Two years later in October 1857, she was in another collision, this time with the schooner *Oneida Chief* off Lexington, Michigan, in Lake Huron only about 50 miles south of her previous accident. She was towed to Port Huron and the damage was assessed at $600.[3]

In November 1864, she collided with the schooner *Grey Eagle* and sank in the Straits reportedly off Cheboygan.[4] The crew were all saved by getting on board the *Grey Eagle* and later were taken to Detroit by the propeller *Winslow*.

VESSEL FACTS	**Site #68**
NAME:	PERSEVERANCE
RIG:	Schooner
OFFICIAL NO.:	None
GROSS TONS:	294 (BOM)
LENGTH:	121'
HULL:	Wood
BUILT:	1855, Buffalo NY, by F. N. Jones
DATE LOST:	November 24, 1864
CAUSE OF LOSS:	Collision
WHERE LOST:	Off Cheboygan in Lake Huron
LIVES LOST:	None
CARGO:	Wheat
BOUND FROM/TO:	Chicago/Ogdensburg
LAST ENROLLMENT:	April 16, 1863, Cleveland Custom House, #44
SURRENDERED:	No endorsement
CONFIGURATION:	1 Deck, 2 Masts, Square Stern, Scroll Head

THOS. J. REYNOLDS,
Ship Builder

AND

Submarine Diver

Estimates Given on Application.

Correspondence Solicited.

34 YEARS' EXPERIENCE.

REFERENCES:

Reid Towing and Wrecking Co.,
Milwaukee Bridge and Iron Co.,
and others along the Lakes.

ADDRESS:

West Bay City, - Mich.

Beeson's Marine Directory, 1888

PESHTIGO *(Schooner)*

The schooner *Peshtigo* was originally built as a bark and subsequently changed to a schooner rig in 1876.[1] In June 1878, she collided with the schooner *St. Andrew* about five miles west of Cheboygan and sank. The complete description of this disaster is recounted in the story of the *St. Andrew* on page 180. When the collision occurred, the captain of the *Peshtigo* yelled at his mate "John, you done a bad job."[2] Two of her crew members were lost in the sinking.

The masts of the *Peshtigo* stuck out of the water for some time after her sinking. There was some controversy over the location of her sinking, with at least one account stating that the accident happened between Beaver Island and Skillagalee Light.[3]

Although the *St. Andrew* was found, the whereabouts of the *Peshtigo* remains a mystery. In the early 1970s, several divers reported diving on a wreck within a half mile of the *St. Andrew* that may have been the *Peshtigo*. However, no one has been able to relocate this mystery wreck.

VESSEL FACTS	Site #67
NAME:	PESHTIGO
RIG:	Schooner
OFFICIAL NO.:	19663
GROSS TONS:	384
LENGTH:	161'
HULL:	Wood
BUILT:	1863, Peshtigo WI, by Thomas Spears
DATE LOST:	June 25, 1878
CAUSE OF LOSS:	Collision
WHERE LOST:	5 miles west of Cheboygan in Lake Huron
LIVES LOST:	2
CARGO:	Coal
BOUND FROM/TO:	Erie/Chicago
LAST ENROLLMENT:	April 12, 1876, Chicago Custom House, #66
SURRENDERED:	June 26, 1878, Chicago, "Vessel lost"
CONFIGURATION:	1 Deck, 3 Masts, Square Stern, Plain Stem

R. G. WINSLOW

In a gale or severe storm, a common practice of vessels on the Great Lakes was to find a sheltered spot in the lee of the wind, drop anchor, and wait out the rough weather. This practice is still in use today. During a storm in December 1860, the bark *R. G. Winslow* was caught in the open along the south shore of Lake Erie, abreast of Dunkirk, New York. When her canvas was all blown away, she had no alternative but to drop her anchors and ride out the storm on the open Lake. She narrowly escaped disaster only to repeat the process a year later off Point Pelee near the western end of Lake Erie.[1]

In November 1867, the *Winslow* was caught in the same storm on Lake Huron that sank the schooners *Albemarle* and *Bonnie Doon* in the Straits. This time she was not so fortunate. She stranded on Spectacle Reef near the schooner *Annie Vought*.[2] The next spring, the *Vought* was pulled off but the *Winslow* had broken up and disappeared beneath the waves.[3]

VESSEL FACTS	Site #78
NAME:	R. G. WINSLOW
RIG:	Bark
OFFICIAL NO.:	21139
GROSS TONS:	389
LENGTH:	148'
HULL:	Wood
BUILT:	1857, Cleveland OH, by Quayle & Martin
DATE LOST:	November 6, 1867
CAUSE OF LOSS:	Stranded
WHERE LOST:	Spectacle Reef in Lake Huron
LIVES LOST:	None
CARGO:	Unknown
BOUND FROM/TO:	Chicago/Buffalo
LAST ENROLLMENT:	May 12, 1866, Buffalo Custom House, #114
SURRENDERED:	Buffalo, "Copy in place lost document"
CONFIGURATION:	1 Deck, 3 Masts, Square Stern, Plain Stem

REMORA

Remora leaving Put-In-Bay
(Courtesy Great Lakes Marine Collection, Milwaukee Public Library)

Owned throughout her lifetime by the S. H. Davis Company of Detroit, the propeller *Remora* operated as a passenger vessel. For a while, she ran from Detroit to Put-In-Bay on South Bass Island in Lake Erie. On one of these runs, a child was lost overboard.[1] In 1888, she was rebuilt in Algonac, Michigan, with a second deck added.[2] In her last few seasons, she ran as a passenger and freight vessel between St. Ignace and Naubinway along the north shore of Lake Michigan.[3]

The *Remora* burned and sank at the St. Ignace dock on August 3, 1892. Her machinery and equipment were removed and sold at public auction by her owners. The hulk of the wreck was left to rot in six feet of water in the St. Ignace Harbor.[4]

VESSEL FACTS Site #64

NAME:	REMORA
RIG:	Propeller
OFFICIAL NO.:	110573
GROSS TONS:	184
LENGTH:	100'
HULL:	Wood
BUILT:	1883, Detroit MI, by Cooper
DATE LOST:	August 3, 1892
CAUSE OF LOSS:	Burned
WHERE LOST:	At St. Ignace dock
LIVES LOST:	None
CARGO:	None
BOUND FROM/TO:	Unknown
LAST ENROLLMENT:	April 14, 1888, Detroit Custom House, #68
SURRENDERED:	August 16, 1892, Detroit, "Total loss"
CONFIGURATION:	2 Decks, No Masts, Round Stern, Plain Stem

Augustus Siebe's diving suit c.1885

ROBERT BURNS

During a severe November gale in 1869, the brig *Robert Burns* foundered east of Bois Blanc Island in Lake Huron with the loss of her entire crew.[1] She was located by the salvor Captain Peter Falcon in the spring of 1870 in 40 feet of water three miles east of Bois Blanc Island. Her masts stuck out of the water and several vessels reported her position.[2] In June 1870, Falcon sent a letter to the *Chicago Tribune* describing his exploration of the wreck. We have reproduced the contents of this letter on the following page.[3]

Peter Falcon raised the wreck of the *Robert Burns*, but she sank again while under tow. Although she is generally recognized as the last operating brig on the Great Lakes, this was probably not true. The *Lucy J. Clark*, for example, operated as a brig until 1879 before she was converted to a schooner. The *Robert Burns* was an old vessel and was frequently in the marine news.[4]

VESSEL FACTS	Site #72
NAME:	ROBERT BURNS
RIG:	Brig
OFFICIAL NO.:	21177
GROSS TONS:	277
LENGTH:	127'
HULL:	Wood
BUILT:	1848, Port Huron MI, by Zadoc Pangborn
DATE LOST:	November 17, 1869
CAUSE OF LOSS:	Foundered
WHERE LOST:	East of Bois Blanc Island in Lake Huron
LIVES LOST:	10
CARGO:	Wheat
BOUND FROM/TO:	Chicago/Buffalo
LAST ENROLLMENT:	April 17, 1867, Chicago Custom House, #317
SURRENDERED:	No endorsement
CONFIGURATION:	1 Deck, 2 Masts, Scroll Stem, Square Stern

MARINE INTELLIGENCE

BRIG ROBERT BURNS

(From *Chicago Tribune.*)

We have been favored with the following letter which explains itself:

Mackinac, June 13, 1870.

To the President of the Republic Insurance Co.:

Dear Sir, — I found the wreck of the Brig Robert Burns, three miles east of Bois Blanc Island, in forty feet of water. I went down to examine her and found both her masts gone, the foremast flush with the deck, and nothing remaining of the main mast. Her anchors and chains are not to be found within a circle of three cable's lengths of the wreck, excepting seventeen fathom of the port chain, the end of which was on deck, and weather bitted, the out board end has been dragged over a rocky bottom some distance and it is bright still. The broken link which came up on the end shows the vessel had been riding, and parted and drifted until she brought up where she now lies. But the greatest mystery is that a kedge has been let go from the port side, and forty fathoms of a five inch line bent and paid over but not made fast. Going aft I found the bulwarks nearly all gone, running and standing rigging tangled on deck, and over both sides, hatches all aboard and battered down.

Her cabin, or house, is gone, slipping over starboard quarter to look at the stern I find half her quick work on the bottom; then climbing up I find she has been run into, which I think knocked rudder and wheel out of her but they may be found under the fragments of her stern. This damage can be repaired with not much expense as it is all light work, but large enough to row a yawl boat through, and would have caused her to sink in a minute. All I could find worth saving I took and landed at this place. There is no cargo to be found on deck, and the grain is so swollen that entrance to the hole is impossible till the grain is removed.

Yours,

P . E. Falcon.

Submarine Diver.

Peter Falcon's letter to the *Chicago Tribune* June 23, 1870

THOMAS KINGSFORD

Another victim of an early spring attempt to get through the Straits, the schooner *Thomas Kingsford* became jammed in the ice 100 feet off Waugoshance Light in April 1871.[1] Subsequently, the ice pushed her eastward and she sank one-half mile from Waugoshance Light in 26 feet of water.[2]

In June 1871, Captain Michael Buffel of the sloop *D. M. Norton* recovered the anchors, 90 fathoms of chain and a portion of the blocks and rigging of the *Kingsford*. He was salvaging the wreck for the Western Insurance Company of Buffalo. He reported that she was split in two from stem to stern and was not worth recovering.[3]

We searched for this wreck from the air at the same time we found the propeller *Canisteo* but could not find it.

VESSEL FACTS	Site #56
NAME:	THOMAS KINGSFORD
RIG:	Schooner
OFFICIAL NO.:	24143
GROSS TONS:	263
LENGTH:	136'
HULL:	Wood
BUILT:	1856, Oswego NY, by George Rogers
DATE LOST:	April 8, 1871
CAUSE OF LOSS:	Cut by ice
WHERE LOST:	East of Waugoshance Light in Lake Michigan
LIVES LOST:	None
CARGO:	Corn
BOUND FROM/TO:	Chicago/Buffalo
LAST ENROLLMENT:	March 23, 1871, Chicago Custom House, #103
SURRENDERED:	Date and place unknown, "Vessel lost"
CONFIGURATION:	1 Deck, 2 Masts, Square Stern, Plain Stem

W. S. LYONS

Coming down from Escanaba with a load of iron ore, the schooner *W. S. Lyons* stranded on White Shoals in Lake Michigan in October 1871.[1] The wrecking tug *Magnet* desperately tried to free her but to no avail. Unable to free the *Lyons*, Captain Gotham of the *Magnet* stripped her masts and gear.[2] The *Lyons* was abandoned. Two weeks later she broke up and went to pieces in a severe gale.[3] The propeller *Free State* had stranded nearby on Grays Reef and disappeared about the same time as the *Lyons*.

VESSEL FACTS	Site #54
NAME:	W. S. LYONS
RIG:	Schooner
OFFICIAL NO.:	26236
GROSS TONS:	258
LENGTH:	136'
HULL:	Wood
BUILT:	1866, Black River OH, by William S. Lyons
DATE LOST:	October 11, 1871
CAUSE OF LOSS:	Stranded
WHERE LOST:	White Shoals in Lake Michigan
LIVES LOST:	None
CARGO:	Iron Ore
BOUND FROM/TO:	Escanaba/Cleveland
LAST ENROLLMENT:	February 23,1870, Cleveland Custom House,#12
SURRENDERED:	August 2, 1875, Cleveland, "Vessel lost"
CONFIGURATION:	1 Deck, 2 Masts, Square Stern, Plain Stem

WALRUS

Vessel technology was developing rapidly when the schooner *Walrus* was launched in 1857. She had been fitted with a new steering gear that attracted much attention. According to the *Detroit Daily Advertiser*, "She has a new wheel (Robertson's patent) never before tried on our Lakes. It has a lever purchase with two separate screws and works smooth and sweet. The lever is very powerful and the screws are double. To prevent heating, the boxes in which the screws work are all brass. Two and a half turns puts the helm hard up or hard down, which is less than the Reed patent wheel takes."[1]

Under the command of Captain Everett, the schooner *Walrus* departed Chicago in early November 1868, with a cargo of 18,560 bushels of barley. On November 7, she stranded on Grays Reef in Lake Michigan in a heavy fog.[2] Two days later, during a strong southwest gale, she broke up and went to pieces.[3] She was owned by the Halsted and Jacobs Company of Chicago and was valued by the underwriters at $12,000.

VESSEL FACTS	Site #52
NAME:	WALRUS
RIG:	Schooner
OFFICIAL NO.:	26225
GROSS TONS:	264
LENGTH:	134'
HULL:	Wood
BUILT:	1857, Cleveland OH, by Lafrinier & Stevenson
DATE LOST:	November 7, 1868
CAUSE OF LOSS:	Stranded
WHERE LOST:	Grays Reef in Lake Michigan
LIVES LOST:	None
CARGO:	Barley
BOUND FROM/TO:	Chicago/Buffalo
LAST ENROLLMENT:	March 15, 1866, Chicago Custom House, #612
SURRENDERED:	December 2, 1868, Chicago, "Vessel lost"
CONFIGURATION:	1 Deck, 2 Masts, Square Stern, Plain Stem

WELLINGTON

When the schooner *Wellington* was launched in 1855, there were 1,196 sail and steam vessels operating on the Great Lakes. By the time she was wrecked in 1867, the number had grown to over 2,500, with more than 1,800 of these being sailing vessels.[1] In this crowd, a small and patently common sailing vessel could go largely unnoticed for most of her life, especially if she stayed out of trouble. Such was the case for the *Wellington*. Probably the most noteworthy thing about her was the fact that she was owned for the first ten years of her life by Captain Alva Bradley of Vermilion, Ohio, who was well-known in marine circles on the Lakes. The schooner *Alva Bradley*, sunk off the south end of North Manitou Island, was named after him.[2]

In September 1867, just as she had lived, the *Wellington* passed quietly out when she stranded on Skillagalee Reef in Lake Michigan and went to pieces.[3]

VESSEL FACTS	Site #47
NAME:	WELLINGTON
RIG:	Schooner
OFFICIAL NO.:	26224
GROSS TONS:	225
LENGTH:	127'
HULL:	Wood
BUILT:	1855, Vermilion OH, by Isaac W. Nicholas
DATE LOST:	September 15, 1867
CAUSE OF LOSS:	Stranded
WHERE LOST:	Skillagalee Reef in Lake Michigan
LIVES LOST:	None
CARGO:	Wheat
BOUND FROM/TO:	Chicago/Goderich
LAST ENROLLMENT:	April 27, 1867, Chicago Custom House, #361
SURRENDERED:	December 28, 1867, Chicago, "Vessel lost"
CONFIGURATION:	1 Deck, 2 Masts, Square Stern, Plain Stem

WHITE SWAN

White Swan
(Courtesy Ralph Roberts Collection)

The little freighter *White Swan* stranded November 29, 1956, on Skillagalee Reef. She was carrying a cargo of logs from Lime Island in the St. Mary's River. Captain Gustav Linell and his two crewmen were saved but they could not salvage the cargo. The U.S. Coast Guard stood by for several days in hopes of freeing the vessel, although it appeared her hull had been punctured badly. During a storm on an early December night, the *White Swan* disappeared.[1]

The vessel was operated by Ernest Manthei of Petoskey, Michigan, who, with his brother, ran a veneer mill in that city. He stated that he intended to salvage the log cargo and some equipment from the wreck in the following spring.[2]

The *White Swan* frequently carried supplies and mail to Beaver Island. In 1949, she was the first boat of the season to arrive in St. James Harbor after a long winter of isolation. Cheery Islanders lined the shore to watch her unload.[3]

VESSEL FACTS   **Site #48**

NAME:	WHITE SWAN
RIG:	Propeller
OFFICIAL NO.:	222237
GROSS TONS:	99
LENGTH:	81'
HULL:	Wood
BUILT:	1922, Manitowoc WI, by Burger Boat Co.
DATE LOST:	November 30, 1956
CAUSE OF LOSS:	Stranded
WHERE LOST:	Skillagalee Reef in Lake Michigan
LIVES LOST:	None
CARGO:	Logs
BOUND FROM/TO:	Lime Island/Petoskey
LAST ENROLLMENT:	May 8, 1956, Sault Ste. Marie, #44
SURRENDERED:	December 28, 1956, Sault Ste. Marie, "Stranded"
CONFIGURATION:	1 Deck, 1 Mast, Plain Stem, Elliptical Stern

Steamboats
⇥COALED⇤
DAY · OR · NIGHT

With the Best Quality
**Massillon, Jackson, and the cel-
ebrated Sunday Creek
Hocking Ridge
Coal.**

———— · ● · ————

Dock, first one East of Detroit and Milwaukee
R. R. Elevator.

J. & T. HURLEY,
DETROIT, MICH.

OFFICE—CHAMBER OF COMMERCE BUILDING.
TELEPHONE, 707.

Beeson's Marine Directory, 1890

APPENDICES

Appendix A

TERMS USED IN VESSEL FACTS 278

Appendix B

STRAITS OF MACKINAC BOTTOMLAND PRESERVE 285

Appendix C

TERMS DESCRIBING WRECK CONDITION 290

Appendix A

TERMS USED IN VESSEL FACTS

In the *Vessel Facts* part of each shipwreck story, standard professional maritime history terms have been used wherever possible. However, when the usage of such terminology limits reader comprehension, we have opted for compromise language that makes the material presented more understandable. Following is an explanation of the terminology used in *Vessel Facts*.

VESSEL NAME

Vessel names are derived from a variety of sources, but namesakes were most frequently people.[1] The standard for alphabetizing these names comes from the U. S. Government publication *List of Merchant Vessels of the United States* first published in 1868 and commonly called *Merchant Vessels.*[2] This system alphabetizes the vessel names, first by the first initial of the name, and then by the first letter of the first name. Thus, *J. A. Smith* comes before *James R. Bentley.* This is the convention that we have used in this book.

There were no restrictions on how many vessels could carry the same name. For example, the reader will find that there are two vessels in this book that carry the name *Peshtigo.*

RIG

For sailing vessels, we have used the terminology employed by *Merchant Vessels.* These terms, e.g., schooner, brig, bark, etc., are defined in the *Glossary.* Vessels powered by steam-driven, side-mounted paddle wheels are simply called side-wheel steamers. Vessels driven by propellers, regardless of engine type, are called propellers. Although this convention violates the conventions used by *Merchant Vessels*, it is much simpler for the reader. Vessels that are not self-powered are called barges. The rig listed in *Vessel Facts* is the rig of the vessel at the time of its loss.

Schooner rig
(Reprinted from "Merchant Vessels of the United States")

OFFICIAL NUMBER

After the Civil War, the U.S. Congress passed the Act of July 28, 1866, which prescribed the Official Number System for vessels. In this system, each vessel was assigned an Official Number that, along with its tonnage, had to be inscribed on the main deck beam of the vessel no later than July 1, 1868. In tracking vessel lineage, those that passed out before July 28, 1866, did not have an Official Number, while those in commission after July 1, 1868, had such a number. These numbers were assigned in blocks to the Custom Houses and were then assigned alphabetically to vessels using the *Merchant Vessels'* convention. Official Numbers were introduced in Canada in 1855. For those vessels that had them, the Official Number serves as an unique identifier.

GROSS TONS

The gross tonnage of a vessel is a measure of its volumetric carrying capacity, not the vessel's weight. A brief history of the derivation of this term follows.[3]

In ancient times, wine and olive oil were shipped in amphoras. However, by medieval times the standard shipping container had become the so-called Bordeaux cask, or tonneaux, which was a wooden barrel. The English term for the Bordeaux cask was the word *ton*, a derivation of the Anglo Saxon *tunne* or Celtic *tun*.[4]

By an Act of Parliament passed in 1423 in England, a tunne, or barrel, of wine was officially defined as measuring 252 gallons being equivalent to two butts or four hogsheads, which were smaller barrels. The tunne, with its contents of wine, closely approximated the *long ton* weight of 2,240 pounds and it occupied a space of approximately 40 cubic feet.

The English *ton* came into wide use as a container for shipment of a variety of commodities. Prior to the sixteenth century, when someone spoke of a vessel as measuring 500 tons, they simply meant it was capable of carrying 500 barrels in its hold. Although numerous formulae were introduced to calculate tonnage, the basic meaning has not changed.[5] Thus, today the tonnage values given for modern vessels, such as the 1,000-foot *Stewart J. Cort*, are still essentially a measure of how many barrels, or tunnes, the vessel can carry in its hold.

During the nineteenth century, two different systems were in use for measuring the tonnage of American vessels.[6] The first of these was known as the builder's old measurement, or BOM, method of calculation. This was supplanted by the Moorsom System through the U.S. Congress Act of May 6, 1864. Under this Act, all vessels had to be remeasured using the new method prior to May 1867. Consequently, any vessel built before May 6, 1864, that remained in commission after May 1867, would have carried two different tonnage designations in its lifetime.

The convention we have used in this book is to list the tonnage of the vessel at the time it was lost. Tonnages for vessels lost before the introduction of the Moorsom System are listed with the abbreviation BOM following the tonnage value.

LENGTH

The exact conditions for the measurement of the length of vessels were prescribed by the tonnage measurement systems discussed in the previous section. Basically, the length was the distance along the main deck from the stem post to the stern post of the vessel. The vessel lengths reported in this book were obtained from the Custom House records and have been rounded off to the next lowest whole number of feet.

Many vessels were rebuilt one or more times during their life and often were lengthened or shortened. The vessel lengths listed are the length of the vessel at the time of its loss.

HULL MATERIAL

Most vessels built on the Lakes before 1900 had wooden hulls. The first American iron-hulled commercial vessel was the propeller *Merchant* built in Buffalo in 1862.[7] The propeller *Spokane*, built by the Globe Iron Works of Cleveland in 1886, was the first steel-hulled Lakes vessel.[8] In the transition from wood to steel, some vessels had composite hulls made of iron and wood.

WHEN, WHERE, AND BY WHOM BUILT

The date built is the year in which the vessel was actually launched. The place built is self-explanatory. Builder's names have usually been obtained from Custom House records or from insurance records. Shipbuilding on the Lakes was a major business in the nineteenth century. Today it has all but disappeared. One of the best histories of shipbuilding on the Great Lakes is the book *Freshwater Whales* by Richard J. Wright.[9]

DATE LOST

The date of loss of a vessel is the day of the original wreck incident. Often a stranded vessel might not become a total loss for several weeks after the original stranding.

CAUSE OF LOSS

Some terms used to describe the loss of a vessel are largely self-explanatory. Stranding, the largest cause of loss, means the vessel ran aground either on a reef or on shore. When a vessel takes on excessive water and sinks due to the weight, it is said to founder. Cut by ice means that the hull of the vessel was ripped open by the ice causing it to take on water and sink. Wooden-hull vessels were most susceptible to being cut by ice and often had the forward section of the hull sheathed in metal to protect it.

Collision means colliding with another vessel that opened the hull causing either or both vessels to take on water and sink. Very few vessels capsized, but when they did it was usually fatal. Boiler explosions could tear apart a vessel's hull causing it to sink. Sometimes fire would burn a vessel to the waterline and the remains would sink. Occasionally vessels were abandoned due to old age and left to rot at a dock. These derelicts were often towed to remote locations and scuttled.

WRECK LOCATION/WHERE LOST

In the case of wrecks that have been discovered, their location is given in terms of distance and bearing from some known position or landmark such as a lighthouse. All bearings are true headings. Distances are in statute miles. The location of wrecks that have not been discovered are similarly described but with approximate or best-guess data.

The exact location (within 100 feet) of the discovered wrecks is also given in Loran C coordinates (8970 Chain) and latitude and longitude. The last two digits of each latitude and longitude listed is in hundredths of minutes and not whole seconds.

LIVES LOST

If a person lost his/her life in any way connected with the sinking of the vessel, he/she was counted as a life lost.

CARGO

Cargos of grain, coal, iron ore and lumber were the most common. In many cases we have not been able to determine the cargo carried by some wrecks.

BOUND FROM/TO

It is common on the Lakes to describe the direction of travel of a vessel by the direction that the water flows in its journey to the sea. Water in Lake Michigan flows generally northward to the sea, while that on Lake Huron flows southward. This direction is said to be downbound. The opposite direction is upbound.

These directions also determine on which side of a channel red or green channel marker buoys are placed. Rules of navigation on the Lakes call for the red buoy to be placed on the right side of an upbound channel and green on the left.

In this book, if the departure port and the arrival port are known, they are listed. Often the only thing known about a vessel's course is whether it is upbound or downbound.

LAST ENROLLMENT

The U.S. Custom Service, formed in 1789, opened its first Custom Houses on the Great Lakes shortly after the War of 1812.[10] All vessels had to be documented by a Custom House and carry a valid *Certificate of Enrollment*.[11] The *Certificate of Enrollment* contained information on the type of vessel, the dimensions and tonnage, the owners, the captain, the home port, the official number, the date of enrollment, the date of surrender, and the cause of surrender. When the home port, owners, dimensions, etc., of a vessel changed, the *Certificate* was surrendered and a new *Certificate* issued. When a vessel was lost, the *Certificate* had to be surrendered and the date and cause of the loss reported.

Copies of the surrendered *Certificates* were kept on file along with a log book of *Certificates* issued and surrendered. These log books, kept at each Custom House, were called *Master Abstracts.*[12] The majority of these records are now held by the U.S. National Archives in Washington D.C. They are a treasure trove of primary historical data about vessels that operated on the Great Lakes and provide a wealth of information when tracing the lineage of a vessel. The last *Certificate of Enrollment* includes a complete set of information on a vessel at the time it was lost.

LAST ENROLLMENT SURRENDERED

The information on the surrender of the last *Certificate of Enrollment* serves as prima facie evidence of the loss of a vessel. Actual data usually includes the date and cause of loss, and the date and place of surrender. If the section on the original *Certificate of Enrollment* calling for an explanation is blank, then the term "no endorsement" has been used.

CONFIGURATION

Information on the number of decks and masts, the shape of the stern, such as square or round, and whether the vessel had any type of figurehead, was listed on the Custom House *Certificate of Enrollment*. The data listed in this book is always taken from the last *Certificate of Enrollment*.

DEPTH

The depth of discovered wrecks is given in feet and is measured from the 1985 mean water datum for Lakes Michigan and Huron published by the U.S. Army, Corps of Engineers.[13] In many cases, a wreck may lie on a sloping bottom and its depth will vary several feet over the length of the wreck. The value of depth listed in *Vessel Facts* is the average value from the deepest to most shallow portion of the wreck.

Appendix B

STRAITS OF MACKINAC BOTTOMLAND PRESERVE

On December 13, 1983, the State of Michigan approved the designation of the Straits of Mackinac as a Great Lakes State bottomland or underwater preserve. The map below shows the boundaries of this Preserve. Within these boundaries are 20 known shipwrecks (Wreck Sites #11 through #31 on the *Map of Discovered Wrecks*, but excluding the *Algomah*). The status of Underwater Preserve provides special protection for the shipwrecks lying on the bottomlands of the preserve. It recognizes shipwrecks as a non-renewable public resource and restricts the removal of artifacts from these wrecks.

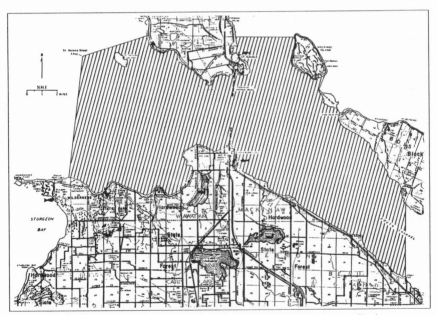

Straits of Mackinac Bottomland Preserve boundaries (148 square miles)
(Courtesy Michigan Department of Natural Resources)

285

The underwater preserve system was established by the passing of Public Act 184 on July 2, 1980.[1] This act was an amendment to Public Act 173 of 1929 entitled "An act to protect and preserve, and to regulate the taking of aboriginal records and antiquities within the State of Michigan, and to provide penalties for the violation of this act." Public Act 173 did not make it clear that it applied to the Lakes bottomlands that are owned by the State of Michigan. The Michigan Department of Natural Resources has published a booklet that describes the law and the permit process.[2]

Ownership of the bottomlands of the Great Lakes by the States surrounding the Lakes was established by the Northwest Territory Act of 1787.[3] Consequently, a portion of the border between Wisconsin and Michigan is actually in the middle of Lake Michigan. Similar borders exist with the States of Ohio, Indiana, Illinois and Minnesota as well as the province of Ontario. Michigan's 38,504 square miles of Great Lakes bottomlands are two-thirds the size of its normal 58,216 square miles of land mass. An estimated 1,500 shipwrecks rest on these bottomlands.[4]

Presently, nine Great Lakes State Bottomland Preserves have been designated in Michigan.[5] They total over 2,000 square miles — an area over 60% larger than the State of Rhode Island. Four are in Lake Superior: *Keweenaw* (243 square miles), *Marquette County* (made up of two non-contiguous areas: Marquette Unit: 74 square miles, Huron Islands Unit: 89 square miles), *Alger* (113 square miles), and *Whitefish Point* (376 square miles); three are in Lake Huron: *Thunder Bay* (288 square miles), *Thumb Area* (276 square miles), and *Sanilac Shores* (163 square miles); one is in Lake Michigan: *Manitou Passage* (282 square miles); and one lies partly in Lake Michigan and partly in Lake Huron: *Straits of Mackinac* (148 square miles). These preserves are extremely popular with scuba divers and serve as a national model for the preservation of underwater antiquities of historical and recreational value.

During the 1960s and 1970s, scuba divers who found shipwrecks largely practiced an ethic of *finders-keepers*. Divers took souvenirs and artifacts from shipwrecks like vultures after carrion. Furniture makers who specialized in nautical themes carted away large portions of deck and hull planking. In the late 1970s, it became increasingly clear that these practices were resulting in shipwrecks that were mere skeletons of their former appearance. Divers realized that soon there would be nothing left on which to dive.

Many of the artifacts, particularly those of historical significance, were being sold or taken outside the State of Michigan. This was especially distressing to the people in the Michigan Department of State who were responsible for museums, history and archaeology. Not only were our dive sites disappearing, but so was our maritime heritage.

This dual problem catalyzed a coalition between State officials and concerned divers that resulted in the passage of Public Act 184 and the subsequent creation of the Great Lakes State bottomland preserves. The authors of this book are proud to have been part of that process.

To administrate this new law, the State of Michigan formed the Underwater Salvage Committee composed of two members from the Department of State and two members from the Department of Natural Resources. The State of Michigan soon recognized that public participation on the Underwater Salvage Committee was needed.

On January 19, 1982, author Dr. Charles E. Feltner was selected by the State as the first Public Member-at-Large on the Underwater Salvage Committee with William Kenner chosen as Alternate Public Member-at-Large.[6] By that time two bottomland preserves had already been established — the Alger Preserve at Munising on Lake Superior and the Thunder Bay Preserve at Alpena on Lake Huron. We and others immediately began a campaign to get the Straits of Mackinac approved as a preserve.

This campaign took the form of a presentation to the Underwater Salvage Committee and the general public at a meeting in Mackinaw City on August 13, 1982.[7] In this presentation, the history and condition of the wrecks on the bottomlands of the Straits was reviewed and the initial boundaries for the Straits Preserve were proposed. On October 26, 1982, the Underwater Salvage Committee formally voted to proceed with the necessary rule making to establish the preserve.[8] We prepared the final technical description of the preserve boundaries and presented it to the Underwater Salvage

Committee on December 9, 1982.[9] They were approved and are reproduced as follows:

"That area of bottomlands of the Straits of Mackinac which connect Lake Michigan and Lake Huron, extending upward and including the surface of the water with a western boundary beginning at the longitude 84 degrees 56'22" W on the south shore, an official NOAA triangulation point located in Emmet county about 1/2 miles east of station point cabin on NOAA chart 14881, extending northward to St. Helena shoal buoy, 84 degrees 55'21" W and then generally northeastward to the north shore at a point where the dividing line between sections 5 and 8, T40N, R4W, of Mackinac county intersects the ordinary high-water mark. The eastern boundary shall be a line running directly north and south at longitude 84 degrees 30' W between Bois Blanc Island and the southern peninsula (Cheboygan county). The northern boundary shall begin at the place where the western boundary strikes the northern peninsula and extend generally eastward along the ordinary high-water mark to a point north of St. Ignace where the dividing line between sections 6 and 7, T40N, R4W, of Mackinac county intersects the ordinary high-water mark, approximately 45 degrees 52' 54" N latitude, and then directly true eastward to Mackinac Island. The boundary then moves generally south and eastward along the ordinary high-water mark of the south side of Mackinac Island until it reaches the southern tip of the east breakwall extending outward from Mission point on Mackinac Island. The northern boundary then extends in a southwesterly direction from the tip of the breakwall to the abandoned lighthouse on the west end of Round Island and then along the ordinary high-water mark of the southern shore of Round Island to the point of land at the southeastern tip of Round Island. The northern boundary extends from this point across to Lime Kiln Point on Bois Blanc Island and then along the ordinary high-water mark of the southern shore until it intersects the eastern boundary at 84 degrees 30' W longitude. The southern boundary shall start at the intersection of the western boundary with the southern peninsula, 84 degrees 56' 22" W longitude, and extends generally eastward along the ordinary high-water mark to appoint where the eastern boundary intersects the southern peninsula, 84 degrees 30' W longitude, Cheboygan, Emmet and Mackinac counties, Michigan, which area contains 148 square miles, more or less."

The Preserve proposal was submitted to the Joint Commission on Administrative Rules who authorized a public hearing to be held in Mackinaw City on April 19, 1983. At that hearing, we again reviewed the history and condition of the wrecks in the proposed Preserve boundaries.[10] The Joint Commission on Administrative Rules approved the Straits of Mackinac Bottomland Preserve on October 18, 1983, and it became law on December 13, 1983.

In 1988, Public Act 452 was passed. It cleared up ambiguities that had become obvious in the administration of Public Act 184 of 1980. At that time, the name of the Underwater Salvage Committee was changed to the Underwater Salvage and Preserve Committee. An excellent account of the evolution of the activities related to the development of Michigan Great Lakes State Bottomland Preserves has been authored by John R. Halsey, State Archaeologist of Michigan, in 1990.[11]

Since 1982, the Straits of Mackinac Underwater Preserve Committee, a volunteer organization comprised of interested divers and area businesses, has been promoting diving in the area. The Committee maintains buoys on several of the shipwrecks, and works with the community to develop shore-based dive access sites, and other projects related to making the Straits of Mackinac a safe and fun place to dive.

In 1989, the Straits Underwater Preserve Committee, Straits Diving Center, Ontario Ministry of Culture, Michigan Bureau of History, Michigan Sea Grant and several sport divers participated in an underwater archaeology course sponsored by Recreational Diving Systems of Royal Oak, Michigan. As part of this course, the participants conducted an underwater survey of a portion of East Moran Bay in St. Ignace, Michigan. Although far from complete, this survey was a good start in the exploration of the near-shore bottomland of one of Michigan's oldest settlements.[12]

Appendix C

TERMS DESCRIBING
WRECK CONDITION

It is common for people who dive shipwrecks to ask those who have previously dived a certain wreck to describe its condition. With this information they can better plan their dive. Besides interesting features on a wreck, such as anchors and the like, divers are mostly interested in the extent to which the wreck is intact. Often they are in very good condition, particularly if they are over 50 feet deep, thus escaping destruction by ice. The lack of Teredos, or ship worms, on the Lakes, the cold water (often never above about 50 degrees at over 100 feet), the reduced oxygen in the water at depth, and the near neutral pH, all contribute to only limited deterioration of wooden shipwreck hulls and their fittings.

To deal with questions from divers about wrecks we had discovered or frequently dived, we began in 1980 to make three-dimensional scale drawings of the wrecks and used these as illustrations in published articles and presentations about the wreck. Making these drawings to scale meant that they had to be measured in some detail. This can be an arduous task underwater and often can take well over 100 dives to obtain the appropriate information. Drawings of the wrecks of the *Cayuga, Cedarville, Eber Ward, Maitland* and *Sandusky* are the results of such efforts.

If an underwater drawing has not been made, verbal descriptions must suffice. However, since there are no precise definitions in use, considerable confusion or misunderstanding about the wreck condition often arises. To help alleviate this problem, a set of definitions describing the degree of intactness of a wreck have been developed. These definitions, although subjective, are based on four different criteria. The criteria include: the amount of the wreck that is standing erect and has not collapsed, the amount of imagination one must have to visualize what the wreck looked like, the extent to which various parts of the wreck are recognizable by people with varying amounts of knowledge about ship construction, and the degree of connectivity, or scatter, of the wreckage.

Using these criteria, four different levels of wreck intactness are defined and used consistently throughout this book.

INTACT

The hull is in one piece and the wreck could be raised, taken ashore, repaired, and put back in service. All parts of the hull are standing, no imagination is required to envision what the vessel looked like, most parts of the wreck are recognizable, even by those inexperienced in ship construction, and all of the wreckage is essentially connected. Examples include the *Eber Ward*, *Maitland* and *Sandusky*.

MOSTLY INTACT

It is not likely, without considerable effort, that the wreck could be repaired and put back in service. Large portions of the hull are standing, a minimum of imagination is required to visualize how the wreck originally appeared, many parts of the wreck are recognizable even by the inexperienced diver, and large portions of the wreck are still connected. Examples include the *Fred McBrier*, *M. Stalker* and *Minneapolis*.

BROKEN UP

The hull, for all practical purposes, is beyond repair. Very little, if any, of the hull is standing (other parts such as a centerboard may be standing), considerable imagination would be needed to envision the appearance of the original vessel, only a few parts of the wreck are recognizable by the inexperienced shipwreck diver, and the wreckage is loosely connected. The keel and a fair portion of the rib structure is still present. Examples include the *C. H. Johnson*, *Canisteo* and *Northwest*.

COMPLETELY BROKEN UP

This is an euphemism for the diver's term "a pile of boards," which is highly descriptive. Small portions of the hull may remain in the area with none of it standing. It is impossible to imagine what the original vessel looked like, although an experienced shipwreck diver would recognize some of the highly scattered parts in the wreckage. Examples include the *Henry Clay*, *Richard Winslow* and *Sea Gull*.

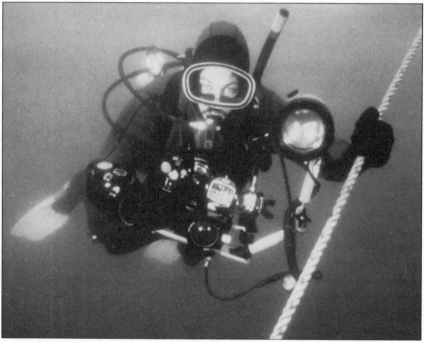

Stan Stock coming up the line after photographing a shipwreck in the Straits
(Authors, 1982)

GLOSSARY

Accurate maritime history inevitably employs a technical terminology specific to the geographic area being treated. Since this terminology may not be familiar to everyone, a *Glossary* of nautical terms used in this book has been provided. The definitions are derived from the nautical encyclopedias of McEwen & Lewis[1] and Kemp.[2] In most cases, substantial portions of the text is identical, or near identical, to that used by these authors. For simplicity, quotation marks have been left out where the material is identical to that in the references. For clarity, definitions have been shortened and tailored specifically to fit the Great Lakes maritime environment.

Aft deck: The deck at or towards the stern or after part of a vessel.

Aft of the bow: A position on the vessel that is after the bow.

Athwartship: At right angles to the fore-and-aft line.

Bateau: A flat-bottomed double-ended river boat, such as a *mackinaw*.

Barge: A freight boat with no motive power, and intended to be towed.

Bark (Barque): A three, four, or five-masted vessel having her mizzenmast for-and-aft rigged with the others being square rigged. Generally a three-masted vessel on the Great Lakes.

Barkentine: A three-masted vessel having her foremast square-rigged and her other masts for-and-aft rigged.

Belaying pins: Short lengths of wood or iron set up in racks in convenient places around which running rigging can be secured (or belayed).

Bent: A condition resulting from decompression sickness (the bends) wherein a diver's emergence from considerable depth of water is too rapid.

Bilge pump: A pump used to remove water from the bilges (the lowest portion of a vessel inside her hull).

Bitter end: Last link in a chain.

293

Block: A wooden or metal case in which one or more sheaves are fitted. It is a mechanical device for moving an object by means of a rope or chain leading over its contained sheaves.

Bobstay: A chain or heavy wire rigging running from the end of the bowsprit downward to the vessel's stem or cutwater.

Bow: The forward end of a vessel, i.e., the part where a vessel's sides trend inward to her stem.

Bowsprit: A large boom or spar projecting forward and slanting upward from a sailing vessel's stem. Its purpose is to furnish a stiffening support for the jib-boom and provide the means of staying a fore-topmast.

Brig: A two-masted vessel square-rigged on both fore and main masts.

Brigantine: A two-masted vessel, as a brig, but square-rigged on the foremast and fore-and-aft rigged on the mainmast.

Bulwark: The planking or woodwork, or steel plating in the case of steel vessels, along the sides of a vessel above her upper deck to prevent seas washing over her gunwales and also persons being washed overboard in rough weather.

Capstan: A vertical drum revolving on a spindle, used for exerting power required in heaving on a rope or on an anchor chain. Usually located on the center line of a vessel on the forecastle.

Capstan cover: Top cover for a capstan often made of brass and having the ship's name on it.

Cathead: A piece of timber projecting from each bow at forecastle deck and used as a crane for catting, or hoisting an anchor from water to bow.

Caulk: To drive oakum or other fiber into the seams of a vessel's wooden deck or sides to prevent water leakage, which operation is completed by paying the seams with pitch or some such water-resisting preparation.

Centerboard: A keel, housed in a water-tight box or centerboard box, that can be lowered or raised to reduce leeway.

Cut down: To reduce the size and class of a vessel by removing an upper deck.

Cutwater: A strengthening and protecting timber bolted to the fore side of a vessel's stem often shaped to provide a sleek forward curve to the stem.

Davit: A light, curved crane, fitted with hoisting and lowering equipment for lifting and lowering lifeboats or yawl boats.

Deadeye: A rounded block of hard wood, usually lignum vitae, pierced with smooth leading holes, through which a lanyard is rove often for the purpose of staying standing rigging.

Depth of hold: Distance from the top of the keel to the top of the upper deck beams measured at the middle of the length of the vessel.

Dismasted: State of having one or more masts carried away or lost usually due to force of wind or collision.

Donkey steam engine: A small auxiliary steam engine for heaving anchor, pumping water, handling cargo and other mechanical duties on board a vessel.

Double-decker: A vessel having two decks above the waterline.

Draft: The depth of water required to float a vessel.

Dry dock: A dock in which a vessel may lie entirely out of the water for repairs.

Fife rail: The circular or semi-circular rail around the base of a mast of a sailing vessel which holds the belaying pins to which the halyards of the sails are secured.

Figurehead: An ornamental carved figure erected on the continuation of the stem below the bowsprit generally expressing some aspect of the vessel's name or function.

Fire box: That part of a boiler containing the furnace.

Fire hole: The boiler room or stokehold.

Fore-and-aft: From stem to stern lengthwise and parallel, or nearly so, to the vessel's keel.

Fore-and-aft rig: General term for any sailing rig consisting of fore-and-aft sails only.

Forecastle (pronounced fokesel): The space beneath the raised deck at the bow of a vessel and forward of the foremast.

Foremast: That mast nearest the stem on a vessel with two or more masts.

Gaff: Spar which spreads the head of a fore-and-aft sail as that on a mainsail of a schooner.

Gafftopsail: A sail set above a gaff, its luff being stretched to the topmast.

Gangway: An alleyway or passage from one part of a vessel to another.

Go by the board: To be completely destroyed or carried away as a mast breaking off and falling overboard.

Ground tackle: A general term meaning all the gear including anchors, cables, windlass, capstan, etc., carried by a vessel to enable her to anchor or to moor.

Gunwales (pronounced gunnel): The upper edge of a vessel's side.

Halyard: A rope by which a sail is set or hoisted.

Hard up: Order to put vessel's tiller full way to weather side, thus turning the craft away from the wind.

Hard down: Order to put vessel's tiller full way to lee side, or opposite to hard up.

Hard to port: Order to helmsman to put his tiller to port, thus turning the vessel to starboard.

Hatch: An opening in the vessel's deck for ingress or egress of either cargo or persons.

Headgear: Rigging of bowsprit and jib-boom, jib-sheets, and other equipment forward of the foremast.

Helm: The apparatus by which a vessel is steered, usually including the steering wheel or tiller alone.

Hold: The entire cargo space below deck.

Hooker: Sailor's depreciative term for a clumsy, old-fashioned vessel.

Hove to (or heave to): To stop a sailing vessel's headway by lying to, as in bringing wind a little forward of the beam.

Hull planking: The planks on the sides of a vessel exclusive of deck-houses, all spars and rigging, boilers, machinery and other equipment.

Jib-boom: A spar, extending forward from, and attached to a bowsprit.

Jury rig: The contrivance of masts and sails to get a vessel underway after she has been disabled.

Kedge: A small anchor carried on board to move a vessel from one place to another.

Keel: Main structural member of a vessel, running longitudinally along the center line of the bottom.

Keelson: A re-enforcing structural member laid over the floors, parallel with, and through bolted to the keel.

Lanyard: Piece of small rope for fastening or temporarily holding an object.

Lighter: A dumb vessel, usually a barge or scow, used to convey cargo from ship to shore, or vice versa.

List: The inclining of a vessel from one side or the other due usually to a shift in cargo or the flooding of some part of the hull.

Littoral drift: Mass of matter, either floating or submerged, as loose rocks, sand or sunken objects, driven on a sea-shore or obstruction in the water (shipwreck) by action of waves or current.

Loran C: An electronic hyperbolic navigation system, the name derived from the initial letters of LOng RAnge Navigation.

Luff: The forward edge of a fore-and-aft sail.

Mackinaw boat: A large flat-bottomed square-sterned boat used by early explorers and traders on the upper Great Lakes, propelled by oars or sail, or both.

Main boom: Spar on which the foot of a fore-and-aft mainsail is extended.

Mainmast: The principal and heaviest mast in a vessel and second in order from the foremast.

Mainsail: The largest sail carried on a vessel and always set on the mainmast.

Mast doubler: The structure used to hold the doubling of masts together.

Mast step: The socket or strong box-like cavity that receives the heel, or lower end, of a mast on the keelson.

Mayday: An international distress signal made by voice on a standard radio frequency whose origin is the French *m'aidez*, help me.

Mizzenmast: Third mast from forward in a vessel having three or more masts.

Mushroom anchor: An anchor with a saucer-shaped head on a central shank, hence resembling a mushroom.

Oakum: Tarred hemp or manilla fibers made from old rope, used for caulking the seams of the decks and sides of a wooden ship in order to make them water tight.

Package freighter: Any vessel in which the cargo is put up in barrels, boxes, crates, etc., and usually excluding liquids in drums or casks.

Pawl: A short piece of wood or metal, pivoted at one end to allow it to drop into notches in a toothed wheel, to arrest motion, as in a windlass or capstan.

Pay: To allow to run out as to pay pitch in sealing the seams of a vessel.

Pillow block: A support for a propeller-shaft bearing.

Pilot house: Enclosed space on a vessel's bridge sheltering the helmsman and navigational instruments, and from which a vessel's course may be directed.

Port (-bow, -side, -stern): The left side of a vessel looking forward.

Porthole: Any opening in a vessel's side.

Quick work: In older shipbuilding parlance, certain planking in a vessel's upper works so termed because it can be quickly put in place.

Rib: One of the transverse frames in a vessel to which the outside planking is secured.

Rigging: Generally, the whole equipment of masts, spars, and cordage in any way connected therewith.

Rope barrel: In a vessel's steering apparatus, a cylinder on which the tiller ropes are wound.

Running rigging: All ropes and chains that are used in making or taking in sail.

Salvor: One who renders services in salving property or lives in distress.

Samson post: A bollard, bitt or post at the fore end of a vessel for making fast a tow rope.

Schooner: A vessel rigged with fore-and-aft sails on her two or more masts.

Scotch boiler: Marine fire tube type, having a cylindrical shell with internal circular-walled furnaces.

Scow: A beamy flat-bottomed vessel used for freighting or lighterage purposes.

Scroll head: Ornamental termination of the cutwater taking the place of a figurehead.

Scuba: The initial letters of self-contained underwater breathing apparatus.

Scuttle: Deliberately sinking a vessel by opening her sea cocks or by blowing holes in her bottom so that she fills with water and sinks.

Shrouds: Ropes constituting that part of a vessel's standing rigging which laterally supports a lower mast and a bowsprit, or serves as a means of climbing aloft.

Side-wheeler: A paddle-wheel steamboat with paddle wheels mounted on the sides of the vessel.

Sloop: One-masted fore-and-aft rigged vessel.

Spar: General term for a boom, mast, yard, etc.

Square rigged: Having some principal sails of square shape and spread on yards as on a brig or bark.

Standing rigging: The ropes, chains, turnbuckles, deadeyes, etc., with their lanyards that constitute the system of staying and supporting the masts, bowsprit and jib-boom.

Starboard: Pertaining to, or situated on, the right-hand side of a vessel, looking forward.

Staying: The act of securing or steadying a mast, bowsprit or jib-boom, usually with ropes or chains.

Steering gear: Arrangement of tackle, rods, chains, etc., by which a vessel's rudder is controlled.

Stem: The more or less upright continuation of the keel at the extreme forward end of the hull, i.e., a vessel's bow.

Stempost: The foremost timber forming the bow of a vessel joined at the bottom to the keel.

Stern: The extreme after end of a vessel.

Sternpost: The aftermost timber forming the stern of a vessel and joined to the keel.

Stringer: An inside longitudinal stiffener bridging the beams or frames in the transverse framing system.

Three-masted: Having three masts.

Topmast: Mast extending above a lower mast.

Topsail: Sail set on a topmast.

Tow-barge: An unpowered vessel designed to be towed.

Transom: The athwartship timbers bolted to the sternpost of a vessel to give her a flat stern.

Triple-expansion engine: A reciprocating engine in which steam is expanded successively in three cylinders.

Tug: Strongly built powered vessel of small tonnage specially designed for towing.

Twin-screw vessel: One driven by two propellers, or screws, one on each side of the fore-and-aft center.

Two-masted: Having two masts.

Waist: The widest part of the upper deck.

Waterlogged: A vessel saturated with water to the extent that she is kept afloat partly by the buoyancy of her cargo.

Ways: Timbers on which a vessel slides while being launched.

Weather rigging: Rigging, such as shrouds, on the windward side of vessel under sail.

Wheel: Hand-wheel used by the helmsman in steering a vessel. Also the propeller on a vessel.

Windlass: A winch or capstan of special design for heaving in an anchor.

Windrow: A row heaped up by the wind and waves, such as windrow ice.

Windward: In the direction from which the wind is blowing, i.e., the weather side or opposite the leeward side.

Wooden-stock anchor: A common anchor with a transverse wooden member or cross-piece at the upper end.

Yawl: A vessel's small working boat or lifeboat.

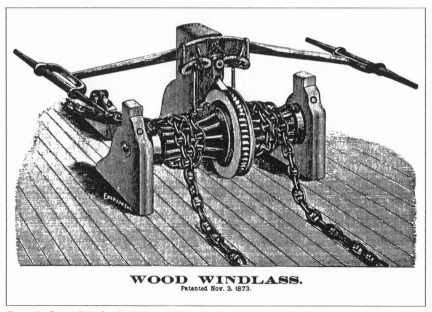

WOOD WINDLASS.
Patented Nov. 3, 1873.

Barnet's Coast Pilot for the Lakes, 1887

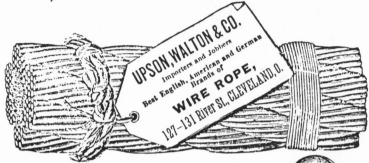

SHIP, RAILWAY & MINING SUPPLIES

UPSON, WALTON & CO.
Importers and Jobbers
Best English, American and German
Brands of
WIRE ROPE,
127–131 River St., CLEVELAND, O.

AGENTS FOR THE

Cleveland Block

Shells of Malleable Iron, Pins of
Best Steel, Hooks and
Straps of Best
Iron.

ALL METAL—UNEQUALED.

WRITE FOR PRICES.

MANILA ROPE,
WOODBERRY CANVAS,
AMERICAN WINDLASSES,
CHAINS, ANCHORS, Etc., Etc.

UPSON, WALTON & CO

Ship Chandlers, Sail Makers and Riggers

CLEVELAND, O.

Beeson's Marine Directory, 1890

SOURCES

The original set of candidate vessels for the Straits of Mackinac shipwreck list was derived from Wright[1] and Mansfield.[2] Various sources were used to confirm the wreck list, including such works as Lytle,[3] Mills,[4] Poole,[5] Runge,[6] Jensen,[7] and several shipwreck casualty lists, wreck charts, and vessel and marine directories listed in Feltner & Feltner.[8] Articles from newspapers of the day were extensively used. With the exception of newspapers and certain special notes, complete information for the references below is given in the *Bibliography*.

INTRODUCTION

[1]Mansfield (1) 1899:66
[2]Ibid:423-439

PART I — SKETCHES

INTRODUCTION

[1]Williams 1912
[2]Wood 1918

GEOLOGICAL FORMATION

[1]Hatcher 1944:26; Halsey 1990:9; Larsen 1987
[2]Mansfield (1) 1899:5

FRENCH DISCOVERY

[1]Mansfield (1) 1899:65
[2]Parkman 1895:113
[3]Thwaites 1896-1901
[4]Wood 1918:683
[5]Mansfield (1) 1899:73; Branstner 1989
[6]Wood 1918:683
[7]Ibid:686

[8]Anderson 1901; Hennepin 1698; Burton 1903; Marshall 1870
[9]MacLean 1974; Tappenden 1946:3

THREE FLAGS

[1]Havighurst 1966
[2]Wood 1918:687
[3]Ibid:688
[4]Havighurst 1966:48
[5]Henry 1809
[6]Burgtorf 1976
[7]Rogers 1765
[8]Wood 1918:690; Mansfield (1) 1899:583
[9]Olson 1978; Wood 1918:690
[10]Mansfield (1) 1899:584
[11]Porter 1991
[12]Havighurst 1966:115
[13]Mansfield 1899:178

ISLANDS

[1]Davis 1947:20
[2]Charlevoix 1761
[3]Havighurst 1966:169
[4]Davis 1947:25, 27

[5]Cronyn 1958
[6]Davis 1947:35
[7]Ibid:34
[8]Ibid:40
[9]Ibid:42
[10]Porter 1991:8, Havinghurst 1966:108
[11]McKee 1981:171; Davis 1947:80
[12]Brehm 1991:229
[13]Davis 1947:85
[14]Williams 1987
[15]Van der Linden 1979:368

LIGHTHOUSES

[1]Mansfield (1) 1899:375; Hyde 1986:98
[2]Mansfield (1) 1899:613
[3]Ibid:371; Hyde 1986:103
[4]Putnam 1917:156; Snow 1955:230
[5]Mansfield (1) 1899:371
[6]*Detroit Free Press* 6 Nov 1886
[7]Brehm 1991:229
[8]Ratigan 1981:79
[9]*Cheboygan Democrat* 19 Apr 1883
[10]Hyde 1986:66
[11]Ibid

TRANSPORTATION

[1]Ranville & Campbell 1976:122
[2]Ibid:124, Hilton 1962:55
[3]Kloster 1989:105, Hilton 1962:55
[4]Van der Linden 1984:307, Hilton 1962:57
[5]Burgtorf 1976, Hilton 1962:61
[6]Van der Linden 1984:308, Hilton 1962:61
[7]Kloster 1989:106, Hilton 1962:63
[8]Rogers 1933:8
[9]Van der Linden 1979:32
[10]*Cheboygan Tribune* 2 Aug 1923
[11]Van der Linden 1984:196
[12]Ranville & Campbell 1976:131
[13]Van der Linden 1979:28
[14]Ranville & Campbell 1976:132
[15]Ibid:136
[16]Ibid
[17]Mackinac Bridge Authority

[18]Ibid 28 Mar 1934
[19]Cissel 1937:530
[20]Rubin 1958:9; McKee 1981:158
[21]Steinman 1957:11
[22]Ibid:202
[23]Mackinac Bridge Authority

PART II — OVERVIEW

INTRODUCTION

[1]Ranville & Campbell 1976:96
[2]Hemming 1981
[3]Bowen 1952:9
[4]Burton 1903; McKee 1981:125
[5]U.S. Customs Service *Wreck Report*, Sch *Jura* 16 Oct 1911
[6]*Detroit Free Press* 25 Sep 1895
[7]Bowen 1952:254
[8]Halsey 1991
[9]*St. Ignace Enterprise* 1 Oct 1914
[10]Lytle & Holdcamper 1952:262
[11]*Detroit Free Press* 16 Sep 1870; *Detroit Advertiser & Tribune* 18 Aug 1870; 5 Sep 1870; Dean 1945

PART III — DISCOVERED WRECKS

ALBEMARLE

[1]Mansfield (1) 1899:439
[2]Dowling 1975:68
[3]*Marine Casualties* Nov 1867
[4]*Milwaukee Sentinel* 27 Nov 1867
[5]*Detroit Free Press* 18 Aug 1868

ALGOMAH

[1]Ranville & Campbell 1976:124; Kloster 1989
[2]Koster 1989
[3]Ranville & Campbell 1976:125, 264
[4]Lacey 1986:24

ANGLO SAXON

[1]Ranville & Campbell 1976:44
[2]*Detroit Free Press* 10 Sep 1887

[3]Ranville & Campbell 1976:43
[4]*Cheboygan Democrat* 15 Sep 1887
[5]Board of Lake Underwriters 1866:7
[6]U.S. Customs Service *Certificates of Vessel Enrollments*; Public Archives of Canada

C. H. JOHNSON

[1]Davis 1947:20
[2]*Milwaukee Sentinel* 24 Sep 1895
[3]Coffman 1976:46
[4]*Detroit Free Press* 24 Sep 1895

CANISTEO

[1]Hyde 1986
[2]McDonald 1947
[3]Dowling 1946
[4]Elliott 1967:78
[5]*Northern Tribune* 30 Oct 1880
[6]Ibid 28 Jul 1883; Runge *Vessel File*

CAYUGA

[1]Feltner *Diving Times* Aug/Sep 1981; Green 1859:20
[2]Marx 1967:59
[3]Hall 1878:48
[4]Wolfe 1979
[5]Doner 1958
[6]Feltner *Diving Times* Apr/May 1981; *Detroit Free Press* 11 May 1895
[7]*Detroit News* 19 Jul 1895
[8]*Detroit Free Press* 19 Jul 1895
[9]Ibid
[10]Ibid 6 Sep 1895
[11]Ibid 20 Sep 1895
[12]Ibid 6 Jun 1896; 23 Jul 1896; *Cheboygan Tribune* 24 Jun 1897; *Detroit Free Press* 17 Aug 1899
[13]Ibid 7 Sep 1900

CEDARVILLE

[1]Ratigan 1981:16-33
[2]Feltner *Diving Times* Jun/Jul 1981; U.S. Coast Guard 1967; *Detroit News* 7 May 1965; *Milwaukee Journal* 7 May

1965; *Akron Beacon Journal* 8 May 1965; *Bay City Times* 8 May 1965; *Detroit Free Press* 8 May 1965; *Grand Rapids Press* 8 May 1965; *Bay City Times* 9 May 1965; *Cleveland Plain Dealer* 9 May 1965; *Detroit Free Press* 9 May 1965; *Cleveland Plain Dealer* 10 May 1965; *Detroit Free Press* 10 May 1965; *Milwaukee Journal* 11 May 1965; *Cleveland Plain Dealer* 13, 14, 15 May 1965; *Detroit Free Press* 15 May 1965; *Cleveland Plain Dealer* 10 June 1965; *Sault Ste. Marie News and Upper Peninsula Farm Journal* 25 Jun 1965; 1, 2, 3, 7 Jul 1965; *Cleveland Plain Dealer* 10, 16 Jul 1965; *Milwaukee Sentinel* 17 Jul 1965; *Milwaukee Journal* 24 Aug 1965; *Cleveland Plain Dealer* 25 Aug 1965; 5 Sep 1965; 12 Dec 1965; *Milwaukee Journal* 15 Feb 1966; 8 Mar 1967; 31 Dec 1970

CIRCASSIAN

[1]*Detroit Free Press* 1 Dec 1860
[2]Ibid 2, 5 Dec 1860
[3]*Detroit Free Press* 5 Dec 1860; *Milwaukee Sentinel* 12 Dec 1860
[4]*Conneaut Reporter* 11 Dec 1860; *Detroit Free Press* 18 Dec 1860
[5]Runge *Shipwreck Log*
[6]*Certificate of Enrollment* #90, Chicago Custom House, 20 Nov 1860

COLONEL ELLSWORTH

[1]Feltner *Soundings* 1981; *Marine Casualties* Dec 1867
[2]*Detroit Post* 18 Mar 1868; *Milwaukee Sentinel* 6 Apr 1868; *Detroit Post* 16 Apr 1868; *Detroit Free Press* 4 Jun 1868
[3]*Detroit Post* 26 Oct 1868
[4]*Milwaukee Sentinel* 7 May 1870
[5]*Marine Casualties* Jun 1872
[6]*Detroit Free Press* 12, 18 Jun 1872
[7]*Milwaukee Sentinel* 11 Sep 1875
[8]U.S. Weather Bureau 1898

[9]*Milwaukee Sentinel* 3 Sep 1896; *Detroit Free Press* 11 Sep 1896; 3 Feb 1897; 14 Aug 1897

EBER WARD

[1]Ship Masters' Association, *Annual Directory*, Captain Timese LeMay, Pennant No. 520, 1903:17
[2]*Detroit News* 21 Apr 1909
[3]Feltner *Diving Times* Nov/Dec 1980; *Telescope* 1982
[4]Hyde 1986:98
[5]Feltner, op.cit.
[6]*Detroit News* 4 Jun 1909; *Milwaukee Sentinel* 22 Jun 1909

FRED MCBRIER

[1]Mansfield (1) 1899:441
[2]Wright 1969:115
[3]Mason 1945
[4]McEwen & Lewis 1953:117
[5]Ibid:235
[6]Mansfield (1) 1899:520
[7]Barry 1973:148
[8]*Detroit Free Press* 5 Oct 1890; *Chicago Inter-Ocean* 5 Oct 1890; *Cheboygan Tribune* 9 Oct 1890

GENESEE CHIEF

[1]Dowling 1946:7
[2]Labadie, Pat, private communication, 1991
Runge *Vessel File*
[3]Dowling 1946:7
[4]*Detroit Advertiser & Tribune* 14 Mar 1863; 21 Apr 1863; Runge *Vessel File*; *Certificate of Enrollment #5*, Cleveland Custom House 17 Apr 1863
[5]*Milwaukee Sentinel* 15 Apr 1868; Lytle & Holdcamper 1975:83; *Certificate of Enrollment #127*, Detroit Custom House 5 Sep 1868
[6]*Merchant Vessels* 1885
[7]Mansfield (1) 1899:759; *Detroit Free Press* 26 Aug 1891; 4 Sep 1891

HENRY CLAY

[1]Woodruff 1991:33
[2]*Cleveland Herald* 9 Dec 1850

ISLANDER

[1]Olson 1971:36
[2]Davis 1947:39
[3]Olson 1971:5
[4]Ibid:38
[5]Arnold Transit Company 1978:16
[6]*St. Ignace Republican News* 9 Apr 1942

J. A. SMITH

[1]*Milwaukee Sentinel* 9 Sep 1887; *Detroit Free Press* 10 Sep 1887; *Chicago Inter-Ocean* 10, 11 Sep 1887
[2]*Chicago Inter-Ocean* 13 Sep 1887; *Cheboygan Tribune* 15 Sep 1887; *Cheboygan Democrat* 15 Sep 1887
[3]*Certificate of Enrollment*
[4]*Detroit Free Press* 18, 19 Apr 1873

J. H. OUTHWAITE

[1]*Cheboygan Tribune* 14 Apr 1898; *Detroit Free Press* 21, 22, 23, 24, 26 Apr 1898; *Cheboygan Tribune* 28 Apr 1898
[2]*Detroit Free Press* 28, 29 Apr 1898; 3, 4, 5 May 1898
[3]Ibid 6 May 1898
[4]Ibid 15, 17, 18, 23 May 1898
[5]Ibid 1, 4 Jun 1898
[6]Ibid 17 Jun 1898
[7]Barcus 1960
[8]Barry 1981:49-53
[9]U. S. Steamboat Inspection Service, *Annual Report*, 1905; *Detroit Free Press* 29, 30, Nov 1905; Ibid 2 Dec 1905
[10]*Great Lakes Register* 1904:87

J. H. TIFFANY

[1]Fincham 1843
[2]*Milwaukee Sentinel* 1 Dec 1859; *Detroit Free Press* 1 Dec 1859
[3]*Detroit Free Press* 2 Dec 1859

[4]Ibid 20 Apr 1860
[5]Ibid 5 Dec 1860
[6]*Chicago Tribune* 19 Jun 1874; 26 Aug 1874; *Buffalo Express* 27 Aug 1874
[7]*Chicago Tribune* 28 Aug 1874; *Chicago Inter-Ocean* 12 Apr 1875
[8]*Chicago Tribune* 19 Jun 1874

JAMES R. BENTLEY

[1]Kemp 1976:224; McEwen & Lewis 1953:43, 262, 397, 483
[2]McEwen & Lewis 1953:371
[3]*Chicago Inter-Ocean* 14, 15 Nov 1878; *Cleveland Herald* 15, 18 Nov 1878
[4]*Cleveland Herald* 18 Nov 1878
[5]Ibid 19 Nov 1878

L. B. COATES

[1]Letters from John Dodd to Mary Duman 1882-1898: William C. Duman Collection
[2]Ibid
[3]*Northern Tribune* 12 Aug 1882; *Detroit Free Press* 22 Aug 1882; *Cheboygan Democrat* 24 Aug 1882; *Northern Tribune* 26 Aug 1882
[4]Davis 1947:27
[5]*Northern Tribune* 28 Jul 1883; 4 Aug 1883
[6]Letters from John Dodd to Mary Duman 1882-1898: William C. Duman Collection
[7]Ibid
[8]Ibid
[9]Davis 1947:46
[10]Greenwood 1984:261
[11]Arnold Transit Company 1978:12
[12]Grover 1911:114
[13]Ibid:104
[14]Ibid:103

LANDBO

[1]Runge *Vessel File*
[2]Greenwood 1984:111
[3]Meakin 1977:38

[4]Ibid:40
[5]Turner 1987:32

LEVIATHAN

[1]*Detroit Post* 19 Sep 1867
[2]*Northern Tribune* 17 Aug 1878
[3]*Milwaukee Sentinel* 22 Sep 1879
[4]Ibid 11 Sep 1875; Van der Linden (II) 1984
[5]*Cheboygan Tribune* 3 Dec 1891

M. STALKER

[1]White 1950:220; Ryan 1928:47
[2]Ryan 1928:36
[3]White 1951:81
[4]White 1951:84; *Detroit Free Press* 29 May 1863
[5]White 1951:81
[6]*Marine Casualties* Aug 1869
[7]Board of Lake Underwriters 1876; *Inland Lloyds* 1886
[8]*Milwaukee Sentinel* 9 Nov 1886
[9]*Detroit Free Press* 6 Nov 1886; *Milwaukee Sentinel* 6 Nov 1886
[10]*Cheboygan Tribune* 11 Nov 1886

MAITLAND

[1]Feltner *Diving Times* Feb/Mar 1981; *Marine Casualties* Jun 1871; *Milwaukee Sentinel* 15 Jun 1871; *Detroit Free Press* 15 Jun 1871; *Detroit Advertiser & Tribune* 15 Jun 1871; *Detroit Post* 15 Jun 1871; *Milwaukee Sentinel* 16 Jun 1871; *Detroit Advertiser & Tribune* 17 Jun 1871; *Detroit Post* 17 Jun 1871
[2]*Detroit Advertiser & Tribune* 3 Jul 1871
[3]*Detroit Post* 1 Jul 1871

MILWAUKEE

[1]Feltner *Diving Times* Dec/Jan 1982
[2]Ibid
[3]Ibid; *Chicago Inter-Ocean* 12 Apr 1875
[4]Feltner op.cit; *Detroit Advertiser & Tribune* 10 Jul 1869; *Detroit Free Press* 8

305

Jun 1870; *Detroit Advertiser & Tribune* 18 Aug 1870
[5]Feltner op.cit; *Detroit Advertiser & Tribune* 2 Sep 1870; 8 Jun 1871; 5 Sep 1871
[6]Feltner op.cit; *Chicago Inter-Ocean* 12 Apr 1875

MINNEAPOLIS

[1]Feltner *Soundings* 1980, *Diving Times* Apr/May 1980; *Chicago Inter-Ocean* 5 Apr 1894; *Cheboygan Tribune* 5 Apr 1894
[2]Feltner op.cit; *Detroit Free Press* 5 Apr 1894; *Chicago Inter-Ocean* 5 Apr 1894; *Cheboygan Tribune* 12 Apr 1894
[3]*Cheboygan Tribune* 12 Apr 1894
[4]Ranville & Campbell 1976:44, 234

MYRTIE M. ROSS

[1]Roberts 1975
[2]Hirthe & Hirthe 1986:79
[3]Stieve 1989
[4]*South Haven Sentinel* 17 Dec 1892
[5]Ibid 13 Jul 1894
[6]Ibid 11 Aug 1894
[7]*South Haven Weekly Times* 23 Nov 1900
[8]Ibid
[9]*Certificate of Enrollment #69*, Port Huron Custom House, 23 Jun 1902
[10]Poole *Vessel Card File*

NORTHWEST

[1]Feltner *Diving Times* Feb/Mar 1981
[2]Feltner op.cit; *Detroit Free Press* 7 Apr 1898; *Buffalo Express* 7 Apr 1898
[3]*Detroit Journal* 12 Apr 1898; *Detroit Free Press* 13 Apr 1898

PESHTIGO (Propeller)

[1]*Detroit Advertiser & Tribune* 21 Apr 1869; *Certificate of Enrollment #282*, Chicago Custom House 20 May 1869
[2]*Great Lakes Register* 1908:135; *Detroit Free Press* 26 Jul 1895; 16, 23 Dec 1895

[3]U.S. Steamboat Inspection Service, *Annual Report* 1899:66
[4]*Detroit News* 25 Oct 1908; *Detroit Free Press* 25, 26, 27, 28, 29, 30 Oct 1908

RICHARD WINSLOW

[1]Feltner *Diving Times* Feb/Mar 1982; Snider 23 Jun 1934
[2]*Detroit Post* 5 May 1871
[3]Underhill 1958:38
[4]*Detroit Free Press* 11 Jun 1871
[5]*Buffalo Courier* 6 Jul 1871
[6]*Certificate of Enrollment #41*, Buffalo Custom House 5 Mar 1890
[7]*Chicago Inter-Ocean* 6 Sep 1898
[8]Mansfield (2) 1899:888
[9]*Chicago Inter-Ocean* 6 Sep 1898; *Detroit Free Press* 5 Sep 1898; *Milwaukee Sentinel* 5 Sep 1898
[10]*Detroit Free Press* 8 Sep 1898; *Detroit Journal* 8 Sep 1898; *Cheboygan Tribune* 8 Sep 1898
[11]*Detroit Journal* 15 Sep 1898; 12 Oct 1898
[12]*Detroit Free Press* 27 Sep 1898; 18 Apr 1899
[13]*Marine Review* 11 Dec 1902:24

ST. ANDREW

[1]Yeoman 1987:84
[2]*Detroit Free Press* 27 Jun 1878
[3]*Chicago Inter-Ocean* 28 Jun 1878
[4]*Cleveland Herald* 28 Jun 1878
[5]Cutler & Hirthe 1983:22

SANDUSKY

[1]*Milwaukee Sentinel* 26 Nov 1869
[2]Snider 3 Nov 1934
[3]Feltner *Diving Times* Oct/Nov 1981
[4]*Certificate of Enrollment #102*, Chicago Custom House 11 Sep 1856
[5]*Detroit Free Press* 19 Sep 1856
[6]*Chicago Tribune* 17 Sep 1856
[7]*Milwaukee Sentinel* 23 Sep 1856
[8]*Detroit Free Press* 23 Sep 1856

[9]*Detroit Advertiser & Tribune* 24 Sep 1856
[10]Ibid 30 Sep 1856
[11]*Milwaukee Sentinel* 1 Oct 1856

SEA GULL

[1]*Merchant Vessels* 1888
[2]*Cheboygan Tribune* 4 May 1893
[3]Ibid
[4]Ibid
[5]Ibid

UGANDA

[1]Mansfield (1) 1899:508
[2]*Detroit News* 21, 22 Apr 1913; *Milwaukee Sentinel* 21 Apr 1913; *Detroit Free Press* 22 Apr 1913

WILLIAM H. BARNUM

[1]Stanton 1962:27
[2]Board of Lake Underwriters 1873
[3]Ibid 1875
[4]Feltner *Telescope* 1981; *Inland Lloyds* 1893
[5]*Chicago Inter-Ocean* 4 Apr 1894
[6]*Detroit Free Press* 4 Apr 1894
[7]*Cheboygan Tribune* 5 Apr 1894
[8]Mansfield (2) 1899:699
[9]Feltner op.cit; *Detroit Tribune* 5 Apr 1894
[10]*Chicago Inter-Ocean* 5 Apr 1894
[11]*Cheboygan Tribune* 12 Apr 1894; *Mackinaw Witness* 25 May 1895
[12]*Cheboygan Tribune* 31 Aug 1963; Leete 1963; *Petosky News Review* 9 Oct 1863
[13]*Inland Seas* (2)5 1969:245

WILLIAM STONE

[1]Ranville & Campbell 1976:26
[2]*Detroit Free Press* 14 Oct 1901; *Milwaukee Sentinel* 14 Oct 1901; *Detroit Free Press* 15 Oct 1901

PART IV — UNDISCOVERED WRECKS

A. D. PATCHIN

[1]Heyl (2) 1956:1; *Detroit Free Press* 29 Mar 1850
[2]*Detroit Free Press* 10 Feb 1850; *Northern Islander* 12 Dec 1850; *Detroit Advertiser & Tribune* 10 Aug 1850
[3]*Detroit Free Press* 2 Oct 1850
[4]*Ibid* 16 Oct 1850
[5]*Milwaukee Sentinel* 4 Dec 1850
[6]Lytle & Holdcamper 1975:239
[7]Elliott 1967:16

ANNA SMITH

[1]*Cheboygan Tribune* 5 Dec 1889
[2]Ibid
[3]Ibid
[4]Ibid 12 Dec 1889

AUGUSTUS HANDY

[1]*Detroit Free Press* 4 Sep 1855
[2]Ibid 6 Sep 1855
[3]Ibid 10 May 1861

BONNIE DOON

[1]*Marine Casualties* Nov 1867; *Milwaukee Sentinel* 19 Dec 1867
[2]*Marine Casualties* Aug 1863
[3]*Milwaukee Sentinel* 6 Apr 1868; *Detroit Free Press* 17 Apr 1868
[4]*Detroit Free Press* 22 Apr 1868
[5]Board of Lake Underwriters 1870
[6]*Merchant Vessels* 1876
[7]*Detroit Free Press* 22 Apr 1868
[8]Board of Lake Underwriters 1860; Ibid 1863; Ibid 1866
[9]Hall 1878:43

CHALLENGE

[1]*Milwaukee Sentinel* 25 Jun 1853; Lytle & Holdcamper 1975:249
[2]*Detroit Free Press* 27 Jun 1853
[3]Hyde 1986:100

[4]*Milwaukee Sentinel* 27 Jun 1853; *Detroit Free Press* 29 Jun 1853; *Milwaukee Sentinel* 2 Jul 1853; Board of Lake Underwriters 1853
[5]*Detroit Free Press* 12 Apr 1853

CLARION

[1]*Detroit Free Press* 26 Jan 1852; Board of Lake Underwriters 1851; Mansfield (1) 1899:665
[2]*Detroit Free Press* 9 Sep 1857
[3]Ibid 4 May 1860
[4]Ibid 31 Oct 1860; 7 Nov 1860
[5]Ibid 9 Nov 1860

COLONIST

[1]*Detroit Free Press* 6 Sep 1854
[2]Board of Lake Underwriters 1860; 1863; 1866; Association of Canadian Lake Underwriters 1869
[3]Board of Lake Underwriters 1860; 1863
[4]*Marine Casualties* Sep 1863; May 1869; Oct 1869
[5]Mills, John M. 1979:29; *Marine Casualties* Nov 1869
[6]*Detroit Post* 24 Nov 1869
[7]Runge *Vessel File*

CONDOR

[1]White 1951:81; *Detroit Free Press* 9 Sep 1857
[2]Board of Lake Underwriters 1860
[3]*Milwaukee Sentinel* 4 Sep 1861; *Detroit Free Press* 6 Sep 1861
[4]*Detroit Advertiser & Tribune* 20, 24, 25 Nov 1862; *Detroit Free Press* 27 Dec 1862
[5]*Detroit Advertiser & Tribune* 28 Nov 1868

D. N. BARNEY

[1]Barton 1851:11
[2]Mansfield (1) 1899:182-190

[3]*Detroit Free Press* 31 May 1849; *Milwaukee Sentinel* 3 Jun 1849
[4]Woodford 1991:30

DOLPHIN

[1]*Certificate of Enrollment #215*, Chicago Custom House 13 Mar 1868
[2]*Certificate of Enrollment #58*, Detroit Custom House 19 Apr 1866
[3]*Certificate of Enrollment #108*, Milwaukee Custom House 27 Apr 1867; *Detroit Free Press* 2 Apr 1862
[4]*Marine Casualties* Jul 1869; *Detroit Free Press* 13 Jul 1869; *Detroit Advertiser & Tribune* 13 Jul 1869

ELVA

[1]Runge *Vessel File*; Truscott 1973
[2]Ranville & Campbell 1976:155
[3]Roberts 1975
[4]*Muskegon Chronicle* 6 Nov 1969; *Telescope* Sep-Oct 1973

FAVORITE

[1]Runge *Vessel File*
[2]Meakin 1974:234
[3]Ibid 1978:13
[4]Ibid 1975:15
[5]Ibid 1976:193

FLIGHT

[1]*Cleveland Herald* 27 Apr 1857
[2]*Detroit Free Press* 1 Jan 1860
[3]*Marine Casualties* May 1863
[4]Ibid Nov 1863
[5]*Detroit Advertiser & Tribune* 17 Sep 1863
[6]*Detroit Free Press* 14 Nov 1865
[7]Ibid 14 Nov 1865

FRANCIS PALMS

[1]*Detroit Free Press* 24 Jul 1868; *Buffalo Courier* 20 Sep 1868
[2]*Detroit Post* 27 Mar 1871

[3] *Detroit Free Press* 15 Nov 1872; *Milwaukee Sentinel* 18 Nov 1872
[4] *Milwaukee Sentinel* 7 Oct 1879
[5] *Detroit Free Press* 3 Nov 1889
[6] Ibid 3 Nov 1889
[7] Ibid 3 Nov 1889
[8] Ibid 4 Nov 1889
[9] *Marine Record* 12 Nov 1889
[10] *Cheboygan Tribune* 7 Nov 1889; *Detroit Free Press* 6 Nov 1889

FREE STATE

[1] Dowling 1946:7
[2] *Detroit Free Press* 24 Jun 1856; Board of Lake Underwriters 1860, 1863, 1866; *Marine Casualties* May 1870; Jun 1871
[3] *Detroit Free Press* 2 Dec 1859
[4] Lytle & Holdcamper 1975:262; *Marine Casualties* Sep 1871
[5] *Detroit Advertiser & Tribune* 2, 3 Oct 1871
[6] *Chicago Tribune* 4 Oct 1871; *Detroit Advertiser & Tribune* 5 Oct 1871
[7] *Detroit Free Press* 21 Oct 1871; 8 Nov 1871

GERTRUDE

[1] Mansfield (1) 1899:709
[2] Runge *Vessel File*
[3] *Milwaukee Sentinel* 24 Apr 1868
[4] *Marine Casualties* Apr 1868; *Milwaukee Sentinel* 24 Apr 1868; *Detroit Free Press* 27 Apr 1868

GLAD TIDINGS

[1] *Marine Casualties* Sep 1868; *Detroit Post* 12 Oct 1868
[2] *Marine Casualties* Nov 1868
[3] *Marine Casualties* Nov 1870; *Detroit Post* 7 Nov 1870
[4] *Detroit Free Press* 7 Jul 1873
[5] Hall 1878:9, 23
[6] *Milwaukee Sentinel* 13 Sep 1879
[7] Mansfield (1) 1899:767; *Detroit Free Press* 11 Apr 1895

[8] U.S. Life Saving Service 1895:153

HENRY J. JOHNSON

[1] LaFayette 1977:1; Mansfield (1) 1899:554
[2] Moore 1907; Dickinson 1967
[3] LaFayette 1977; Mansfield (1) 1899:554-570; Hatcher 1950; Michigan Department of State 1989
[4] Mansfield (1) 1899:566
[5] LaFayette 1977:26; Rankin 1963
[6] *Detroit Free Press* 25 Jul 1902
[7] Ibid

ISLAND QUEEN

[1] *Detroit Free Press* 3 Aug 1858
[2] Ibid 4 Jan 1859
[3] Ibid 22 Sep 1859
[4] Ibid 23 Sep 1859

J. C. LIKEN

[1] *Cheboygan Tribune* 8, 29 May 1890; Mansfield (1) 1899:754
[2] *Detroit Free Press* 6 May 1890
[3] Ibid 14 May 1873
[4] *Cheboygan Tribune* 8 May 1890

J. E. SHAW

[1] *Detroit Free Press* 27 Sep 1854
[2] Ibid 23, 24 Sep 1856; *Milwaukee Sentinel* 24 Sep 1856; *Cleveland Plain Dealer* 25 Sep 1856; *Milwaukee Sentinel* 26 Sep 1856; 19 Mar 1857; *Detroit Free Press* 25 Mar 1857

JOHN JEWETT

[1] Hirthe & Hirthe 1986:49
[2] *Marine Casualties* Nov 1870
[3] Hall 1872:50
[4] *Inland Lloyds* 1891
[5] Wolff 1979:59
[6] Runge *Shipwreck Log*

JULIA DEAN

[1]Hyde 1986:104
[2]Cronyn & Kenny 1958
[3]*Detroit Free Press* 25, 26 Oct 1855
[4]*Northern Islander* 13 Mar 1856
[5]Davis 1947:35

KATE HAYES

[1]*Detroit Free Press* 23 Jul 1856; *Milwaukee Sentinel* 23 Jul 1856; *Detroit Advertiser & Tribune* 25 Jul 1856; *Milwaukee Sentinel* 26 Jul 1856
[2]*Milwaukee Sentinel* 1 Aug 1856; *Detroit Advertiser & Tribune* 6 Aug 1856; *Milwaukee Sentinel* 9 Aug 1856
[3]*Detroit Advertiser & Tribune* 25 Jul 1856

LAWRENCE

[1]*Detroit Free Press* 15 Apr 1850; *Milwaukee Sentinel* 16 Apr 1850; *Detroit Daily Advertiser* 15, 18 Apr 1850
[2]*Detroit Free Press* 1 Jun 1882; *Northern Tribune* 3 Jun 1882
[3]*Cheboygan Democrat* 8, 15 Jun 1882; *Northern Tribune* 1 Jul 1882; *Cheboygan Democrat* 13 Jul 1882; *Detroit Free Press* 18, 22 Aug 1882; *Cheboygan Democrat* 24 Aug 1882; *Northern Tribune* 26 Aug 1882; 2 Sep 1882; *Cheboygan Democrat* 7, 28 Sep 1882; *Northern Tribune* 28 Jul 1883; *Cheboygan Democrat* 2 Aug 1883; 27 Sep 1883

LEANDER

[1]*Detroit Daily Advertiser* 14 Jul 1838
[2]*Detroit Free Press* 19 Nov 1857

LUCY J. CLARK

[1]*Certificate of Enrollment #88*, Chicago Custom House 23 May 1879
[2]*Cheboygan Democrat* 8 Nov 1883; *Northern Tribune* 10 Nov 1883; *Chicago Inter-Ocean* 13, 14 Nov 1883;

Cheboygan Democrat 15 Nov 1883; *Northern Tribune* 17 Nov 1883; *Cheboygan Democrat* 22 Nov 1883
[3]*Cheboygan Democrat* 6 Dec 1883

MAROLD II

[1]*Milwaukee Sentinel* 13 Nov 1936; Runge *Vessel File;* Ratigan 1981:39
[2]*Milwaukee Sentinel* 3 Jan 1937; *Chicago Tribune* 3 Jan 1937; Runge *Vessel File*
[3]*Milwaukee Sentinel* 1 Mar 1937; *Detroit Free Press* 1 Mar 1937
[4]*Milwaukee Sentinel* 1 Mar 1937; *Detroit Free Press* 1 Mar 1937
[5]Rapprich 1972:87
[6]Lacey 1986:69-80
[7]Rapprich 1972
[8]Ibid

NEWELL A. EDDY

[1]*Cheboygan Democrat* 22 Apr 1893; *Cheboygan Tribune* 27 Apr 1893
[2]*Cheboygan Tribune* 27 Apr 1893
[3]Ibid 27 Apr 1893; Mansfield (1) 1899:765

NIGHTINGALE

[1]Barnet 1867; Thompson 1859; Scott 1886
[2]Hyde 1986:98; Putnam 1917:154
[3]*Marine Casualties* Sep 1869; Runge *Shipwreck Log*
[4]Putnam 1917:155; Snow 1955:224
[5]*Detroit Advertiser & Tribune* 6 Jun 1871; *Detroit Tribune* 8 Jun 1871; *Detroit Post* 12 Jun 1871
[6]Hyde 1986:98

ODD FELLOW

[1]*Milwaukee Sentinel* 10 Oct 1851; Ibid 13 Nov 1851
[2]*Buffalo Express* 5 Dec 1854; *Milwaukee Sentinel* 8 Dec 1854; *Detroit Free Press* 9, 15 Dec 1854

OLIVER LEE

[1]*Detroit Free Press* 9, 18 Sep 1856
[2]Mills, John M. 1979:71; Lytle &
Holdcamper 1975: 130; *Detroit Free
Press* 16 Jan 1845
[3]Bugbie 1964
[4]*Detroit Advertiser & Tribune* 15 Jul
1869
[5]*Cleveland Plain Dealer* 4 Sep 1856;
Detroit Advertiser & Tribune 16 Sep
1856; *Detroit Free Press* 18 Sep 1856
[6]*Detroit Free Press* 19, 25 Nov 1857; 1
Dec 1857; *Cleveland Plain Dealer* 24 Dec
1857
[7]*Detroit Free Press* 23 Jun 1858

ORIENTAL

[1]*Detroit Free Press* 18 Apr 1854; Ibid 31
May 1854
[2]Mansfield (1) 1899:678
[3]*Detroit Free Press* 18 Oct 1859
[4]Ibid 22 Oct 1859; Lytle &
Holdcamper 1975:287
[5]*Detroit Free Press* 22 Oct 1859

PERSEVERANCE

[1]*Detroit Free Press* 8 May 1855
[2]Board of Lake Underwriters 1855
[3]Ibid 1857
[4]*Detroit Free Press* 29 Nov 1864

PESHTIGO (Schooner)

[1]*Certificate of Enrollment #66*, Chicago
Custom House 12 Apr 1876
[2]*Detroit Free Press* 27 Jun 1878; *Chicago
Inter-Ocean* 28 Jun 1878
[3]*Chicago Inter-Ocean* 29 Jun 1878

R. G. WINSLOW

[1]*Detroit Free Press* 4 Dec 1860; 15 Apr
1862
[2]*Marine Casualties* Nov 1867; Dowling
1975; *Milwaukee Sentinel* 19 Dec 1867
[3]*Cheboygan Democrat* 20 Sep 1868

REMORA

[1]U.S. Steamboat Inspection Service,
Annual Report 1886
[2]*Certificate of Enrollment #68*, Detroit
Custom House 14 Apr 1888
[3]*St. Ignace Republican News* 12 Feb 1942
[4]Ibid 6 Oct 1939

ROBERT BURNS

[1]*Marine Casualties* Nov 1869; *Mil-
waukee Sentinel* 26, 30 Nov 1869
[2]*Milwaukee Sentinel* 25 Nov 1869;
Detroit Advertiser & Tribune 15, 22 Jul
1870; Ibid 22 Jul 1872
[3]*Detroit Post* 3 Jun 1870; *Chicago
Tribune* 23 Jun 1870
[4]*Milwaukee Sentinel* 18 Aug 1849; 27
Nov 1849; 30 Nov 1850; 3 Dec 1850; 8
Apr 1854; 5 Dec 1854; 19 Mar 1861;
Marine Casualties Nov 1863, *Milwaukee
Sentinel* 13 Dec 1864; 12, 14 Nov 1867;
Marine Casualties Nov 1867; *Detroit
Post* 30 Sep 1868; 3 Oct 1868

THOMAS KINGSFORD

[1]*Marine Casualties* April 1871; Hall
1872; *Detroit Tribune* 12 Apr 1871;
Detroit Free Press 14 Apr 1871
[2]*Detroit Post* 15, 22 Apr 1871; *Detroit
Free Press* 23 Apr 1871
[3]*Detroit Tribune* 10, 15 Jun 1871; *Detroit
Free Press* 15 Jun 1871; *Detroit Advertiser & Tribune* 14 Jul 1871

W. S. LYONS

[1]*Marine Casualties* Oct 1871; Hall 1872;
Detroit Post 17, 18, 19 Oct 1871
[2]*Detroit Free Press* 21 Oct 1871; *Detroit
Post* 25 Oct 1871
[3]*Detroit Free Press* 8 Nov 1871; *Detroit
Post* 13 Nov 1871; *Detroit Advertiser* &
Tribune 9 Dec 1871; *Detroit Free Press*
22 Dec 1871

WALRUS

[1]*Detroit Daily Advertiser* 4 Jun 1857
[2]*Marine Casualties* Nov 1868
[3]*Milwaukee Sentinel* 16 Nov 1868;
Detroit Post 17 Nov 1868; *Detroit Free Press* 17 Nov 1868

WELLINGTON

[1]Mansfield (1) 1899:439
[2]Runge *Vessel List*
[3]*Marine Casualties* Sep 1867; *Detroit Post* 19 Sep 1867; *Detroit Advertiser & Tribune* 19 Sep 1867; *Milwaukee Sentinel* 19 Dec 1867

WHITE SWAN

[1]*Detroit News* 11 Jan 1957
[2]Ibid
[3]*Detroit News* 3 Apr 1949

APPENDICES

VESSEL FACTS – Appendix A

[1]Greenwood 1984
[2]*Merchant Vessels*
[3]Feltner *Estimating the Size of Vessels,* 1982
[4]McEwen & Lewis 1953:563; *Oxford English Dictionary* 1971:3346
[5]Corbett 1898; Holmes 1900:153
[6]Dorr1876:24; Corkhill 1977
[7]Mansfield (1) 1899:413; Wright 1971:4
[8]Wright 1971:5
[9]Wright 1971
[10]Schmeckebier 1924
[11]U.S. Customs Service *Certificates of Vessel Enrollments*
[12]U.S. Customs Service *Master Abstracts of Vessel Enrollments*
[13]U.S. Department of Commerce *Great Lakes Water Levels* 1971

PRESERVE – Appendix B

[1]Halsey 1990

[2]Michigan Department of Natural Resources c. 1983
[3]Quaife 1945:208
[4]Wright 1972
[5]Halsey 1990
[6]Underwater Salvage Committee *Meeting Minutes* 19 Jan 1982
[7]Ibid 13 Aug 1982
[8]Ibid 26 Oct 1982
[9]Ibid 9 Dec 1982
[10]Ibid 19 Apr 1983
[11]Halsey 1990
[12]Harrington 1990

GLOSSARY

[1]McEwen & Lewis 1953
[2]Kemp 1976

SOURCES

[1]Wright 1972
[2]Mansfield (1) 1899:787-903
[3]Lytle & Holdcamper 1975
[4]Mills, John M. 1979
[5]Poole
[6]Runge *Shipwreck Log*
[7]Jensen
[8]Feltner & Feltner 1982

BIBLIOGRAPHY

With the exception of newspapers and special notes, this *Bibliography* includes the complete bibliographic citation for each of the references listed in *Sources*. If further literature on Great Lakes maritime history is desired, the *Bibliography* by Feltner & Feltner contains over 1,000 citations.

Anderson, Melville B., trans. *Relation of the Discoveries and Voyages of Cavelier de LaSalle from 1679 to 1681: The Official Narrative.* Chicago: Caxton Club, 1901.

Arnold Transit Company and Straits Transit, Inc. *100 Years of Passenger Travel.* Booklet. Grand Marais, Michigan: Voyager Press, 1978.

Association of Canadian Lake Underwriters. *Lake Vessel Register.* Toronto: 1869.

Barcus, Frank. *Freshwater Fury.* Detroit: Wayne State University Press, 1960.

Barnet, James. *Barnet's Coast Pilot for the Lakes.* 4th ed. Chicago: By the Author, 1867. (See Thompson, Thomas S. This ed. is the first authored by Barnet alone after his split with Thompson c. 1863. Barnet published a 6th, 7th and 8th ed. independent of Thompson in 1872, 1874 and 1887.)

Barry, James P. *Ships of the Great Lakes: 300 Years of Navigation.* 2nd ed., Berkeley, California: Howell-North Books, 1973.

_____. *Wrecks and Rescues of the Great Lakes: A Photographic History.* LaJolla, California: Howell-North Books, 1981.

Barton, James L. *Commerce of the Lakes, and Erie Canal.* Buffalo: Beaver's Power Presses, 1851.

Beasley, Norman. *Freighters of Fortune: The Story of the Great Lakes.* New York: Harper & Brothers Publishers, 1930.

Beeson's Marine Directory of the Northwestern Lakes. Chicago: Harvey C. Beeson. (Annual in the period 1888-1921 and published at various times with various names in Detroit. Contains an annual list of vessels lost.)

Board of Lake Underwriters. *Lake Vessel Register.* Buffalo, c.1850-c.1880.

Bowen, Dana Thomas. *Shipwrecks of the Lakes.* Cleveland: Freshwater Press, 1952.

Branstner, Susan M. "Tionantate Huron Indians at Michilimackinac." *Michigan History* 73 (1989):24

313

Brehm, Victoria, ed. *Sweetwater, Storms, and Spirits.* Ann Arbor, Michigan: University of Michigan Press, 1991.

Bugbie, Gordon P. "Lake Erie's North Shore Line." *Telescope* 13 (1964):112.

Burgtorf, Frances D. *Chief Wawatam.* Cheboygan, Michigan: By the Author, 1976.

Burton, C. M. *LaSalle and the Griffon.* Historical paper delivered before the Society of Colonial Wars of the State of Michigan, 1902. Detroit: Winn & Hammond, 1903.

Charlevoix, P. F. X. de S. J. *History and General Description of New France.* Translation by Dr. John G. Shea, New York, 1900.

Cissel, James H. "Bridging the Straits of Mackinac," *Michigan Alumnus Quarterly Review* XLII (Spring 1937).

Coffman, Edna M. *Mackinaw City Settlers and The Savage Straits.* Grand Marais, Michigan: Voyager Press, 1976.

Corkhill, Michael. *The Tonnage Measurement of Ships: Towards a Universal System.* London: Fairplay Publications, 1977.

Corbett, Sir Julian S. *Drake and the Tudor Navy.* London: Longmans, Green & Co., 1898.

Cronyn, Margaret, and Kenny, John. *The Saga of Beaver Island.* Ann Arbor, Michigan: Braun & Brumfield, 1958.

Curwood, James Oliver. *The Great Lakes: The Vessels That Plough Them: Their Owners, Their Sailors, and Their Cargoes, Together With a Brief History of Our Inland Seas.* New York: G. P. Putnam's Sons, 1909.

Cutler, Elizabeth F., and Hirthe, Walter M. *Six Fitzgerald Brothers –Lake Captains All.* Milwaukee: Wisconsin Marine Historical Society, 1983.

Davis, Marion Morse. *Island Stories: Straits of Mackinac.* Reprinted from *Michigan History Magazine.* Lansing: Franklin DeKleine Co., 1947.

Dean, Jewell R. "Recovery of the Steamer *Humphrey.*" *Inland Seas* 1 (1945):18-30.

Dickinson, J. N. "The Canal at Sault Ste. Marie, Michigan: Inception, Construction, Operation, and the Canal Grant Lands." Ph.D. Thesis, University of Wisconsin, 1967.

Disturnell, John. *A Trip Through the Lakes of North America.* New York: Charles Scribner, 1863.

Doner, Mary F. *The Salvager, The Life of Captain Tom Reid on the Great Lakes.* Minneapolis: Ross & Haines, 1958.

Dorr, E. P. *Rules for Construction, Inspection and Characterization of Sail and Steam Vessels.* Buffalo: By the Author, 1876.

Dowling, Rev. Edward J. "The Vanishing Fleets: The Story of the Great Lakes Package Freighters." *Inland Seas* 2 (1946):7-16.

_____. "The Winslow Fleet." *Telescope* 22 (1975): 68:81.

Dunnigan, Brian Leigh. "The British Army at Mackinac: 1812-1815." Reports in *Mackinac History and Archaeology*, n7. Mackinac Island State Park Commission, 1980.

Elliott, James L. *Red Stacks Over the Horizon: The Story of the Goodrich Steamboat Line*. Grand Rapids, Michigan: Wm. B. Eerdmans Publishing Co., 1967.

Evans, Stephen H. *The U.S. Coast Guard, 1790-1915, A Definitive History*. Annapolis, Maryland: U.S. Naval Institute, 1949.

Feltner, Charles E. "The Wreck of the *Minneapolis*." *Diving Times* (April/May 1980).

_____. "The Wreck of the *Colonel Ellsworth*." *Diving Times* (June/July 1980).

_____. "The Wreck of the *William H. Barnum*." *Diving Times* (August/September 1980).

_____. "*Eber Ward* Shipwreck." *Diving Times* (November/December 1980).

_____. "The Wreck of the *Minneapolis*." *Soundings* 20 n3 (1980).

_____. "First You Need a Map — or The Wreck of the *Colonel Ellsworth*." *Soundings* 21 n1 (1981).

_____. "The Strange Tale of Two Ships" (*Maitland* and *Northwest*). *Diving Times* (February/March 1981).

_____. "The Wreck of the *William H. Barnum*." *Telescope* 30 n2 (1981).

_____. "Raise the *Cayuga*." *Diving Times* (April/May 1981).

_____. "The *Cedarville* Tragedy." *Diving Times* (June/July 1981).

_____. "Warriors of the Deep, Part I: Johnny Green the Treasure Salvor." *Diving Times* (August/September 1981).

_____. "The *Eber Ward* Shipwreck." *Diver Magazine* (September 1981).

_____. "The Wreck of the Brig *Sandusky*." *Diving Times* (October/November 1981).

_____. "Warriors of the Deep, Part II: Peter Falcon the Ship Salvor." *Diving Times* (December/January 1982).

_____. "The Wreck of the *Richard Winslow* and the Great Anchor Heist." *Diving Times* (February/March 1982).

_____. "The Wreck of the *Eber Ward*." *Telescope* 31 n2 (1982).

_____. *Estimating the Size of Nineteenth Century Great Lakes Vessels*. Dearborn: Michigan: Seajay Publications, 1982.

_____, and Jeri Baron. *Great Lakes Maritime History: Bibliography and Sources of Information*. 1st ed. Dearborn, Michigan: Seajay Publications, 1982.

Fincham, John. *A Treatise on Masting Ships and Mast Making*. London: Whittaker & Co., 1843.

Great Lakes Register. Cleveland: Bureau Veritas International Register of Shipping, 1896-1934. (Acquired and published by the American Bureau of Shipping from 1916 to 1934. Discontinued in 1935.)

Great Lakes Vessel File. Institute for Great Lakes Research, Bowling Green State University, Perrysburg, Ohio.

Green, John B. *Diving With and Without Armor*. Buffalo: Faxon's Steam Power Press Co., 1859; reprint ed., Mason, Michigan: Maritime Press, 1991.

Greenwood, John O. *Namesakes 1920-1929*. Cleveland: Freshwater Press, Inc., 1984.

Grover, Frank R. *A Brief History of Les Cheneaux Islands*. Evanston, Illinois: Bowman Publishing Company, 1911.

Hall, J. W. *Marine Disasters of the Western Lakes During the Navigation of 1871*. Detroit: Free Press Book & Job Printing Establishment, 1872.

_____. *Hall's Record of Lake Marine Embracing the Marine Casualties of 1877*. Detroit: Wm. Graham's Steam Presses, 1878.

Halsey, John R. *Beneath the Inland Seas: Michigan's Underwater Archaeological Heritage*. Lansing: Bureau of History, Michigan Department of State, 1990.

_____. "The Reeck of a Small Vessel." *Michigan History* 75 n2 (1991):31.

Harrington, Steve, ed. *Diving Into St. Ignace Past: An Underwater Investigation* of *East Moran Bay*. Mason, Michigan: Maritime Press, 1990.

Hatcher, Harlan. *The Great Lakes*. New York: Oxford University Press, 1944.

_____. *A Century of Iron and Men*. Indianapolis: Bobbs-Merrill, 1950. (Cleveland Cliffs History.)

_____, and Walter, Erich A. *A Pictorial History of the Great Lakes*. New York: Crown Publishers, 1963.

Havighurst, Walter. *The Long Ships Passing*. New York: Macmillan Co., 1944.

_____. *Three Flags at the Straits: The Forts of Mackinac*. Englewood Cliffs, New Jersey: Prentiss-Hall, 1966.

Hemming, Robert J. *Gales of November: The Sinking of the Edmund Fitzgerald*. Chicago: Contemporary Books, 1981.

Hennepin, Father Louis. *A New Discovery of a Vast Country in America*. 2 vols. London: M. Bentley, J. Tonson, H. Bontwick, T. Goodwin and S. Manship, 1698; reprint ed. by Reuben Gold Thwaites, ed., Chicago: A. C. McClug & Co., 1903.

Henry, Alexander. *Travels and Adventures in Canada and the Indian Territories Between 1760 and 1776*. New York, 1809.

Heyl, Erik. *Early American Steamers*. 6 vols. Buffalo: n.p., 1953-1969.

Hilton, George W. *The Great Lakes Car Ferries*. Berkeley, California: Howell-North, 1962

Hirthe, Walter M. and Mary K. *Schooner Days in Door County*. Minneapolis: Voyageur Press, Inc., 1986.

Holmes, Sir George C. V. *Ancient and Modern Ships: Part I, Wooden Sailing Ships*. London: Chapman & Hall, 1900:153.

Holt, W. Stull. *The Office of the Chief of Engineers of the Army, Its Non-Military History, Activities and Organizations*. Service Monographs of the United States Government. No. 27. Baltimore: Johns Hopkins Press, 1923.

Hyde, Charles K. *The Northern Lights: Lighthouses of The Upper Great Lakes*. v. VI of the Michigan Heritage Series, Michigan Natural Resources Magazine, Department of Natural Resources, State of Michigan. Lansing: TwoPeninsula Press, 1986.

Inland Lloyds Vessel Register. Buffalo: Art-Printing Works of Matthews, Northrup & Co. (c. 1882-?). Originally published as *Lake Vessel Register, System of Classification*. Buffalo: Board of Lake Underwriters (c. 1850 - c. 1880).

Jenks, William Lee. *History of St. Clair County*. 2 vols. Chicago: Lewis Publishing Co., 1912.

Jensen, J. Norman. *J. Norman Jensen Shipwreck Card Collection*. (8,500). Chicago Historical Society Library, Clark St. at North Ave., Chicago IL 60614.

Kemp, Peter, ed. *The Oxford Companion to Ships and the Sea*. London: Oxford University Press, 1976.

Kloster, Joan. "The Mackinac Transportation Company." *Anchor News* (November/December 1989):104.

Lacey, Robert. *Ford: The Men and the Machine*. Boston: Little, Brown & Co., 1986.

Landon, Fred. *Lake Huron*. New York: Bobbs-Merrill Co., 1944.

LaFayette, Kenneth D. *Flaming Brands: Fifty Years of Iron Making in the Upper Peninsula of Michigan, 1848-1898*. Marquette: Northern Michigan University Press, 1977.

Larsen, Curtis E. "Geological History of Glacial Lake Algonquin and the Upper Great Lakes." *U.S. Geological Survey Bulletin 1801*. Washington: U.S. Government Printing Office, 1987.

Leete, Fred, III. "Electronic History-Finders." *Inland Seas* 19 (1963):292.

Lytle, William M., and Holdcamper, Forrest R., comp. *Merchant Steam Vessels of the United States 1790-1868*. "The Lytle-Holdcamper List." Staten Island, New York: Steamship Historical Society of America, 1952; rev. and ed. by C. Bradford Mitchell and Kenneth R. Hall, 1975. (Includes Supplement No. 1, 1978.)

MacDonald, William A. "Journal of Shipwrecks in the Vicinity of the Lighthouse at Waugoshance." (July 1872 to October 1906.) *Inland Seas* 3 (1947):21-24.

MacLean, Harrison John. *The Fate of the Griffon*. Chicago: Swallow Press, 1974.

Mansfield, J. B., ed. *History of the Great Lakes*. v. 1. Chicago: J. H. Beers & Co., 1899; reprint ed., Cleveland: Freshwater Press, 1972.

_____. *History of the Great Lakes*. v. 2. Chicago: J. H. Beers & Co., 1899; reprint ed., Cleveland: Freshwater Press, 1972.

Marine Casualties of the Great Lakes 1863-1873. Microfilm Publication No. T729. Washington: National Archives, n.d.

Marine Record (Weekly). Cleveland: Smith & Swainson, 1878-1902. (The official newspaper of the Lake Carriers' Association and the Cleveland Vessel Owners' Association.)

Marine Review. v. 1-65, March 6, 1890-October 1935. Cleveland: Penton Publishing Co. (Weekly March 6, 1890-March 25, 1909; Monthly April 1909-October 1935.) Absorbed the *Marine Record* in 1902. *Marine Review* merged into *Marine Engineering and Shipping Age* in 1935, which merged into the *Marine Engineering/Log*.

Marshall, O. H. *The Building and Voyage of the Griffon In 1679.* Buffalo: Bigelow Brothers, n.d.; reprint ed., Publications of the Buffalo Historical Society 1 (August 1870); 253-288.

Mason, George C. "A List of Hulls Built by F. W. Wheeler & Co., Bay City, Michigan." *Inland Seas* 1 (1945):54-55.

Marx, Robert F. *They Dared the Deep: A History of Diving.* Cleveland: World Publishing Co., 1967.

McEwen, W. A., and Lewis, A. H. *Encyclopedia of Nautical Knowledge.* Cambridge: Cornell Maritime Press, 1953.

McKee, Russell. *Great Lakes Country.* New York: Crowell, 1966.

_____. *Mackinac, The Gathering Place.* Lansing: Michigan Natural Resources Magazine, 1981.

McPhedran, Marie. *Cargoes on the Great Lakes.* Toronto: Macmillan Co. of Canada, 1952.

Meade, George G. *Report of the Survey of the North and Northwest Lakes.* Part of the Report of the Chief Topographical Engineer, Accompanying Annual Report of the Secretary of War, 1860. Detroit: Daily Free Press Steam Printing House, 1861.

Meakin, Alexander C. "Four Long and One Short: A History of the Great Lakes Towing Company, Part I." *Inland Seas* 30 (1974):231-241.

_____. "Four Long and One Short: A History of the Great Lakes Towing Company, Part II." *Inland Seas* 31 (1975):14-27.

_____. "Four Long and One Short: A History of the Great Lakes Towing Company, Part VI." *Inland Seas* 32 (1976):192-199.

_____. "Four Long and One Short: A History of the Great Lakes Towing Company, Part VII." *Inland Seas* 33 (1977):113-120

_____. "Four Long and One Short: A History of the Great Lakes Towing Company, Part VII." *Inland Seas* 34 (1978):13-20.

Merchant Vessels (see U.S. Treasury Department, Bureau of Navigation).

Michigan Department of Natural Resources. *Michigan Great Lakes Bottomland Resources* (Booklet), n.d.

Michigan Department of State. *Fayette: A Visitor's Guide.* Lansing: Michigan Department of State, 1989.

Mills, John M. *Canadian Coastal and Inland Steam Vessels, 1809-1930.* Providence, Rhode Island: Steamship Historical Society of America, 1979. (Includes Supplement No. 1, 1981.)

Moore, Charles, ed. *The St. Mary's Falls Ship Canal.* Detroit: Semi-Centennial Commission, 1907.

Noble, Dennis L. and O'Brien, T. Michael. *Sentinels of the Rocks.* Marquette: Northern Michigan University Press, 1979.

O'Brien, T. Michael. *Guardians of the Eighth Sea: A History of the U.S. Coast Guard on the Great Lakes.* Washington: U.S. Coast Guard, 1976.

Olson, Ellis. *Wood Butchers of the North.* Cheboygan, Michigan:Cheboygan Tribune, 1971.

_____. *Cheboygan Historical Sketches.* Cheboygan, Michigan: Cheboygan Tribune, July 4, 1978.

Parkman, Francis. *The Jesuits in North America.* Boston: Little, Brown & Co., 1895.

Plumb, Ralph G. *History of Navigation of the Great Lakes.* 61st Congress, 3rd Session, House Committee on Railways and Canals. Washington: 1887.

Poole, John E. *John E. Poole Vessel Card File Collection* (10,000). Institute for Great Lakes Research, Bowling Green State University, 12764 Levis Parkway, Perrysburg, Ohio 43551.

Porter, Phil. *The Eagle at Mackinac: The Establishment of United States Military and Civil Authority on Mackinac Island, 1796-1802.* Mackinac Island: Mackinac State Historic Parks, 1991.

Public Archives of Canada. *Board of Trade, Ships Registry Papers, Trade and Communications Records.* Ottowa.

Putnam, George R. *Lighthouses and Lightships of the United States.* Boston: Houghton Mifflin Co., 1917.

Quaife, Milo M. *Lake Michigan.* New York: Bobbs-Merrill Co., 1945.

R. L. Polk and Company's Marine Directory of the Great Lakes. Detroit: R. L. Polk & Co., 1884, 1888, 1891.

Rankin, Ernest H. "Fayette." *Inland Seas* 19 (1963):204-208.

Ranville, Judy, and Campbell, Nancy. *Memories of Mackinaw.* Mackinaw City, Michigan: Mackinaw City Public Library, 1976.

Rapprich, William F. "A Memorable Yacht: From Halcyon Days to Holocaust." *Inland Seas* 28 (1972):87-95.

Ratigan, William. *Straits of Mackinac: Crossroads of the Great Lakes.* Grand Rapids, Michigan: Wm. B. Eerdmans Publishing Co., 1957.

_____. *Great Lakes Shipwrecks and Survivals.* 3rd ed. Grand Rapids, Michigan: Wm. B. Eerdmans Publishing Co., 1981.

Roberts, Ralph. "Ships That Never Die - No. 197." *Detroit Marine Historian* (May 1975).

Rogers, Frank F. *History of the Michigan State Highway Department: 1905-1933.* Lansing: Michigan Historical Society, 1933.

Rogers, Robert. *Concise Account of North America.* London: J. Millan, 1765.

Rubin, Lawrence A. *Mighty Mac: The Official Picture History of the Mackinac Bridge.* Detroit: Wayne State University Press, 1958.

Runge, Herman G. "Runge Shipwreck Log 1679-1943." From the *Herman G. Runge Collection* acquired by the Milwaukee Public Library in 1958.

_____. *Herman G. Runge Great Lakes Vessel File* (85,000). Local History and Marine Room, Milwaukee Public Library.

Ryan, James A. *The Town of Milan.* Sandusky, Ohio: By the Author, 1928.

Schmeckebier, Laurence F. *The Customs Service, Its History, Activities and Organization.* Monographs of the United States Government, No. 33. Baltimore: Johns Hopkins Press, 1924.

Schoolcraft, Henry R. *Narrative Journals of Travels From Detroit Northwest Through the Great Chain of American Lakes to the Sources of the Mississippi River in the Year 1820.* Albany, New York: E. & E. Hosford, 1821; reprint ed., n.p.: Arno Press, Inc., 1970.

Scott, George. *Scott's New Coast Pilot for the Lakes.* 1st ed. Detroit: Detroit Free Press Book and Job Printing House, 1886. (2nd, 3rd, 4th, 5th, 6th, 7th and 8th eds. published in 1888, 1890, 1892, 1899, 1901, 1906, 1914, respectively, with five supplements issued in various intervening years.)

Ship Masters' Association of the Great Lakes. *Annual Directory of Names, Pennant Numbers and Address of All Members.* Cleveland: Marine Review Print and various other printers or publishers for different editions. Name later changed to International Shipmasters' Association. 1893-1967.

Shurtleff, Mary Belle. *Old Arbre Croche: A Factual and Comprehensive History of Cross Village, Michigan.* Cross Village, Michigan: By the Author, 1963; reprint ed. Richard A. Pohrt, 1975.

Snow, Edward Rowe. *Famous Lighthouses of America.* New York: Dodd, Mead & Co., 1955.

Snider, C. H. J. "Big Boys." *Schooner Days, CXLIV. Toronto Evening Telegram,* June 23, 1934.

_____. "Tarry Breeks and Tartan Topsails." *Schooner Days, CLX. Toronto Evening Telegram,* November 3, 1934.

Stanton, Samuel Ward. *Great Lakes Steam Vessels.* No. 1: American Steam Vessels Series. Meriden, Connecticut: Meriden Gravure Co., 1962.

Steinman, David B. *Miracle Bridge at Mackinac.* Grand Rapids, Michigan: Wm. B. Erdmans Publishing Co., 1957.

Stieve, Jeanette. *Wooden Shipbuilding: South Haven, Michigan, Merchant Vessels Built Between 1866 and 1902.* South Haven: Michigan Maritime Museum, 1989.

Strickland, William Peter. *Old Mackinac or, the Fortress of the Lakes and Its Surroundings.* Philadelphia: James Challen & Son, 1860.

Tappenden, Richard P. "A Possible Solution to the Mystery of the *Griffin*," *Inland Seas* 2 (1946):3-6.

The Compact Edition of the Oxford English Dictionary. Oxford, England: Oxford University Press, 1971.

Thompson, Thomas S. *Thompson's Coast Pilot for the Upper Lakes*. 1st ed. Chicago: James Barnet, 1859. (2nd and 3rd eds. also published by Barnet in 1861 and 1863. 4th, 5th, 6th eds. authored by Thompson and published in Detroit by Detroit Free Press Books and Job Printing House in 1865, 1869 and 1878, respectively.)

Thwaites, Reuben Gold, ed. *The Jesuit Relations and Allied Documents: Travels and Explorations of the Jesuit Missionaries in New France 1610-1791*. 73 vols. Cleveland: Burrows Brothers Co., 1896-1901.

Truscott, Charles H. "The Lakes Unique Gospel Ship." *Telescope* (September-October 1973):132-138.

Turner, Gordon. *Pioneering North: Historical Highlights of the Cheboygan Area*. Cheboygan, Michigan: Cheboygan Daily Tribune, 1987.

Underhill, Harold A. *Plank-On-Frame Models and Scale Masting and Rigging*. 2 vols. Glasgow: Brownson & Ferguson, 1958.

U.S. Coast Guard. "*Cedarville—Topdalsfjord* Collision." *Proceedings of the Merchant Marine Council*. Washington: 1967.

_____. *Marine Board of Investigation: Sinking of the Edmund Fitzgerald 10 November 1975*. Report No. USCG 16732/64216. Washington: July 26, 1977.

U.S. Customs Service. *Certificates of Vessel Enrollments From Various Great Lakes Customs House Districts*. Washington: National Archives.

_____. *Master Abstracts of Vessel Enrollments From Various Great Lakes Customs House Districts*. Washington: National Archives.

_____. *Collectors of Customs Reports of Casualty from the Customs House Districts*. Record Group 36, Washington: National Archives.

U.S. Department of Commerce. *United States Great Lakes Pilot*. Washington: National Oceanic and Atmospheric Administration, 1964 to present.

_____. National Oceanic and Atmospheric Admistration, National Ocean Survey. *Great Lakes Water Levels, 1869-1970*. Detroit: Lake Survey Center, 1971.

U.S. Life Saving Service. *Annual of the U.S. Life Saving Service*. Washington: 1895. (See U.S. Treasury Department.)

U.S. Steamboat Inspection Service. *Annual Report of the Supervising Inspector General*. Washington, 1872-1914.

U.S. Treasury Department. *U.S. Life-Saving Service. Annual Report For Fiscal Year July 1-June 30*. Washington, 1876-1914.

_____. Bureau of Navigation. *List of Merchant Vessels of the United States*. Washington. (Current annual since 1868.) (Government departments producing this series has varied over the years, e.g., Department of

Commerce, Bureau of Navigation, 1916; and Treasury Department, Bureau of Customs, 1957, etc. Commonly referred to as simply *"Merchant Vessels."*)

U.S. Weather Bureau. *Wrecks and Casualties of the Great Lakes During 1895, 1896 and 1897*. Washington: 1898.

Van der Linden, Rev. Peter J., ed., and the Marine Historical Society of Detroit. *Great Lakes Ships We Remember*. Cleveland: Freshwater Press, 1979; rev. ed., 1984.

Van der Linden, Rev. Peter J., ed, and the Marine Historical Society of Detroit. *Great Lakes Ships We Remember II*. Cleveland: Freshwater Press, 1984.

War Department, Corps of Engineers. *Survey of Northern and Northwestern Lakes*. Bulletin No. 1. Detroit: U.S. Lake Survey Office, 1891. (Numbers 1 to 70 published periodically from 1891 to 1963. Renamed *Great Lakes Pilot* in 1964.)

Weber, Gustavus A. *The Weather Bureau, Its History, Activities and Organization*. Service Monographs of the United States. No. 9. New York: D. Appleton & Co., 1922.

Whitcomb, D. C. *A Lake Tour to Picturesque Mackinac*. Detroit: Detroit & Cleveland Steam Navigation Co., 1923.

White, Wallace B. "The Ghost Port of Milan and A Druid Moon." *Inland Seas* 6&7 (1950-1951).

Williams, Meade C. *Early Mackinac: A Sketch Historical and Descriptive*. 1st published in 1897, rev. 1901 and 1912. 1st ed. AuTrain, Michigan: Avery Color Studios, 1987.

Wolfe, Tom. *The Right Stuff*. New York: Farrar, Straus & Giroux, Inc., 1979.

Wolff, Julius F. *The Shipwrecks of Lake Superior*. Duluth: Lake Superior Marine Museum Association, 1979.

Wood, Edwin O. *Historic Mackinac*. 2 vols. New York: Macmillan Co., 1918.

Woodford, Arthur M. *Charting the Inland Seas: A History of the U.S. Lake Survey*. Detroit: U.S. Army, Corps of Engineers, Detroit District, 1991.

Wright, Richard J. *Freshwater Whales: A History of the American Ship Building Company and Its Predecessors*. Kent, Ohio: Kent State University, 1969; reprint ed., 1971.

_____, comp. "Inventory of Shipwrecks Within Michigan Coastal Waters." Bowling Green, Ohio: Northwest Ohio Great Lakes Research Center, and the Michigan Department of Natural Resources in Lansing, (c. 1972).

Yeoman, R. S. *A Guide Book of United States Coins*. 40th rev.ed. Racine: Western Publishing Co., 1987.

INDEX

D

D&C Line, 27
D. M. Norton, sloop, 271
D. N. Barney, sch, 48, 212
Dagwell, Charles T., 46
Davidson's Shipyard, James, 121
Davis, Marion Morse, 21
Davis Co., S. H., 267
Dearborn, Michigan, 70
Deliyanides, Dean, 108
DePeyster, sch, 18
Derby, William, 131
Detour, Michigan, 191, 255
Detroit, 12, 17-18, 37, 71, 97, 101, 110, 121, 128, 166, 172, 179, 188, 202-203, 218, 221-222, 227-228, 234, 237, 241, 246, 261, 263, 267-268
Detroit Advertiser & Tribune, the, 186
Detroit Daily Advertiser, the, 273
Detroit Dry Dock Co., 36, 68, 70
Detroit Free Press, the, 31, 113, 126, 178, 236, 246
Detroit River, 240
Detroit Springwells shipyards, 176
Detroit, sloop, 19
Dickerson, Ray, 178
Diver support services, 59
Diving Times, the, 170
Dobbins, A. P., 113
Dodd, John, 80, 98, 134-137, 250
Dodd, Samuel, 134
Dolphin, sch, 228-229
Dossin Great Lakes Museum, 101, 172
Duluth, 12, 171, 237
Duluth Harbor, 122
Duluth, Daniel Greysolon, 12, 14
Duman, Lawrence, 134, 136-138
Duman, Mary, 134-136
Duman, Nathalie, 138
Duman, Thursa (Werner), 137-138
Duman, William C., 133-134, 138-139, 167
Duncan Bay, 110, 114-115, 145-146
Duncan City, 115, 117
   establishment of, 114
Duncan, Jeremiah W., 114
Dunkelberg, George, 170, 207
Dunkirk, New York, 266
Dunn, Thomas P., 22
Durocher Dock & Dredge Co., 208

E

E. M. Peck, prop, 160, 199
E. M. Peck, sch, 239
East Moran Bay, 12, 289
Eber Ward, prop, 5, 46, 57, **100-104**, 106, 195-196, 220, 290-291
Edison, Thomas Alva, 147
Edmund Fitzgerald, prop, 46, 182
Edward Buckley, prop, 137
Elva, barge, 165, **230-232**
Embury-Martin Lumber Co., 140
Emily B. Maxwell, sch, 98
England, 8, 14, 82
English, 14-15
Enos, Roy, 180
Enrollment, Certificate of, 283-284
Enterprise, sch, 251
Erastus Corning, bark, 131
Escanaba, 122, 177, 237, 242-243, 272
Estereicher, Franz, 189
Euclid, Ohio, 99
Everett, Captain, 273
Exile, sch, 148

F

F. A. Georger, sch, 107
F. W. Backus, prop, 226
Fairport, Ohio, 132
Falcon Marine Co., 158
Falcon, Guilford Ward, 158
Falcon, Joseph Guilford, 158
Falcon, Peter, 127-128, 133, 153, 155, 157-158, 269
False Presque Isle, 121
Farwell, William J., 97
Faust, Oscar, 162
Favorite, prop, 233-235
Ferry service in Straits, first scheduled, 68
Fitzgerald, Captain, 237
Fitzgerald, Edmond, 182
Fitzgerald, Edward L., 182
Flight, sch, 21, 26, **236**
Ford, Henry, 70, 255
Forester, sch, 48
Fort de Buade, 14
Fort Detroit, 17
Fort Howard, Wisconsin, 235
Fort Mackinac, 18-19, 26, 204, 217
   ceded to the United States, 19
Fort Michilimackinac, 15, 17, 48
   attacked by Indians, 15
Fort Niagara, 31

SHIPS HAVING COMPOUND PEOPLE NAMES

Arranged alphabetically by their last names.
They are indexed under the full name.

335

INFORMATION

STRAITS OF MACKINAC

BOTTOMLAND PRESERVE

- Great Lakes Submerged Lands Management Unit — 517-373-1950
  Land & Water Management Division
  Department of Natural Resources
  P. O. Box 30028, Lansing MI 48909

- Bureau of History — 517-373-6358
  Department of State, Lansing MI 48918

DIVING SERVICES

- Straits Diving Center — 800-999-0303
  589 S. State, St. Ignace MI 49781

- Divers Alert Network (DAN)
  24-hour emergency number — 919-684-8111

BOOK PRODUCTION

This book was created by the authors using Xerox Ventura Publisher software running on a Dell 310 personal computer equipped with a DP-Tek Truepoint intelligent printer controller and LaserTrax PostScript Interpreter software. Camera-ready copy was produced on an Hewlett-Packard LaserJet II printer equipped with a DP-Tek video adapter card. The typeface is PostScript Palatino at 600 x 600 dpi. Book manufacture was done by McNaughton & Gunn in Saline, Michigan.

TO ORDER THIS BOOK

To order *Shipwrecks of the Straits of Mackinac*, please request from:
SEAJAY PUBLICATIONS, P. O. Box 2176, Dearborn MI 48123-2176 (313-561-4914).

Also available is *Great Lakes Maritime History: Bibliography and Sources of Information* — a book for those interested in doing Great Lakes maritime research.

ABOUT THE AUTHORS

CHUCK FELTNER was born in North Carolina and earned a PhD degree in Engineering from the University of Illinois. As a boy, Chuck lived on the Outer Banks, a strand of islands off the coast of North Carolina that is strewn with shipwrecks. A PADI Divemaster, he has searched for, found, and documented numerous wrecks around the Great Lakes. He served as the first Public Member-at-Large on Michigan's Underwater Salvage Committee.

Chuck and Jeri with Seajay and boat *Gemini*[3] at St. Helena Island
(Photo by Anne O'Connell, 1991)

Dr. Feltner is widely known in the midwest marine historical and scuba diving communities for his published articles and presentations on shipwrecks, and courses on *How to Research Great Lakes Shipwrecks*. He is cofounder, and was chairman for the first five years, of the Great Lakes Shipwreck Festival, an annual event sponsored by the Ford Seahorses Scuba Diving Club of Dearborn, Michigan. For the past 28 years, he has worked for Ford Motor Company and presently is Director of Manufacturing Planning and Information Systems for the Ford Automotive Components Group.

JERI BARON FELTNER was born and raised in Michigan. An enthusiastic diver with over 20 years of experience, she is a PADI Divemaster. Her underwater films of the wrecks of the propeller *Eber Ward* and brig *Sandusky* received acclaim at underwater shows in Chicago, Detroit and Toronto.

Jeri is co-author with her husband of *Great Lakes Maritime History: Bibliography and Sources of Information*. She was Editor from 1980 to 1982 of *Diving Times*, a midwest newspaper on scuba diving. Ms. Feltner worked for Ford Motor Company for ten years followed by a three-year stint in the ski travel business. Presently, she is President of Seajay Publications, a firm dedicated to the publication of high-quality material on maritime history and scuba diving.

337

WHAT THE REVIEWERS SAID

"*Shipwrecks of the Straits of Mackinac* successfully distills years of the Feltners' painstaking research. It combines an authoritative and entertaining shipwreck guide with the historical context necessary to understand the place of these shipwrecks in Great Lakes history."

C. Patrick Labadie
Director, Canal Park Marine Museum

◆

"The best shipwreck book blending history with the dive experience. Sets a new standard of excellence."

Mike Kohut
President, Recreational Diving Systems

◆

"*Shipwrecks of the Straits of Mackinac* represents an enormous amount of work above and below the water. I especially liked the weaving of different aspects of Great Lakes history into the shipwreck stories."

Dr. John R. Halsey
State Archaeologist, Bureau of History, Michigan Department of State

◆

"An excellent book. The authors have collected a tremendous amount of information and have presented it in an organized and interesting fashion. It will be of interest to both divers and the general public."

Dr. David A. Armour
Deputy Director, Mackinac State Historic Parks

◆

"A well-written and very informative book. The data on the vessels is clear and accurate. The enthusiasm of the authors is effectively conveyed to the reader."

Rev. Edward J. Dowling, S.J.
Professor Emeritus, University of Detroit